W9-BRF-624

Breathe
Cry
Breathe

Breathe Cry Breathe

From Sorrow to Strength in the
Aftermath of Sudden, Tragic Loss

Catherine Gourdier

HarperCollins*Publishers*Ltd

Breathe Cry Breathe
Copyright © 2021 by Catherine Gourdier
All rights reserved.

Published by HarperCollins Publishers Ltd

First edition

No part of this book may be used or reproduced in any manner whatsoever
without the prior written permission of the publisher, except in the case
of brief quotations embodied in reviews.

Some names and identifying details have been changed to protect the privacy of individuals.

HarperCollins books may be purchased for educational, business
or sales promotional use through our Special Markets Department.

HarperCollins Publishers Ltd
Bay Adelaide Centre, East Tower
22 Adelaide Street West, 41st Floor
Toronto, Ontario, Canada
M5H 4E3

www.harpercollins.ca

Library and Archives Canada Cataloguing in Publication

Title: Breathe cry breathe : from sorrow to strength in the aftermath
of sudden, tragic loss / Catherine Gourdier. Names: Gourdier, Catherine, author.
Identifiers: Canadiana (print) 20210117842 | Canadiana (ebook) 20210119330 |
ISBN 9781443461191 (softcover) | ISBN 9781443461177 (ebook)
Subjects: LCSH: Gourdier, Catherine—Family. | LCSH: Grief. | LCSH: Bereavement—
Psychological aspects. | LCSH: Parents—Death—Psychological aspects. |
LCSH: Sisters—Death—Psychological aspects. | LCSH: Traffic accident victims—
Family relationships. | LCGFT: Autobiographies.
Classification: LCC BF575.G7 G68 2021 | DDC 155.9/37092—dc23

Printed and bound in the United States of America
LSC/C 9 8 7 6 5 4 3 2 1

Trigger warning: This book mentions suicidal ideation, which some people may find disturbing.

In loving memory of my parents, Bill and Neta,
and my youngest sister, Julie

My siblings and I will "love you forever, remember you always"

Prologue

In Grade Four, my best friends were boys. Jimmy, shy with horn-rimmed glasses, and freckle-faced David, who had brush-cut platinum blond hair and delightful dimples when he smiled, which was often. We'd ride our bikes home together from Our Lady of Lourdes School. In the winter, we would walk the slushy streets to their homes, about a kilometre from our school, then I'd trudge the last few blocks on my own.

On their way home the evening of December 8, 1965, after attending the Feast of the Immaculate Conception mass at our school, David and Jimmy were struck by an eighteen-year-old drunk driver. December 8 is my mother's birthday, so I've never forgotten the date. I heard that the young driver sat in the ditch crying, cradling the dead boys in his arms.

"Killed instantly," the papers said. Journalists and coroners blurt that out much too quickly. They don't know for certain that a death was instant. They don't know if the victims writhed in pain or cried for help—only that they were dead by the time paramedics arrived.

For a week or more, I walked by the dark smears on the brown grass. Why hadn't anyone cleaned it up? Seeing their blood upset me, yet I couldn't keep myself from stopping to look at it.

At only eight years old, my first funeral was a double funeral. As I watched the cloaked caskets being rolled up the aisle, I envisioned my friends' bloodied bodies inside and fainted. I vaguely remember being pulled up from the kneeler I'd landed on.

Their empty desks at school disturbed me, but as much as I missed them, my sadness waned in a few weeks.

Years later, after attending the double funeral of my own family members, I realized grief doesn't vanish so quickly. Grief packs a suitcase and moves into your heart and head.

Chapter 1

NOVEMBER 7, 2009

With a dead body and a severed head in the trunk of my husband Don's grey sedan, we drove from Toronto to Kingston to attend my youngest sister Julie's surprise birthday party. Julie loved scary movies, so we'd decided to throw a horror-themed costume party at my brother Dave's house, a mere ten-minute drive from my parents'. Don is a film producer and was in the midst of shooting a *Resident Evil* sequel, so we'd packed some movie props to use as decor for the party.

It was an unusually summer-like day for November, so I wasn't surprised when we pulled into the driveway and found my sister-in-law Barb on her knees in the front yard, tending to the golden mums. The slanting sun highlighted the red in her short auburn hair. She smiled and waved a dirty-gloved hand at me. My husky, almost-six-foot-tall, fifty-year-old brother, Dave—"Moose" to his

3

friends—strolled toward us. His hands were like baseball mitts toughened by thirty years of installing hardwood floors and carpets. Don held out his smooth executive palm and gave Dave's a shake. Perched on tiptoes, I put my arms around Dave's neck and nuzzled my cheek into his beard. His bear hug almost lifted me off the ground.

After our greeting, Dave lugged the dead body downstairs and dumped it on the floor of the family room. Don carried in crows and a bloodied head and plunked them in front of the fireplace. My decorating maven sister Teresa, whom we call Treas, had erected a cemetery of grey plastic tombstones, stretching cotton cobwebs across the top of them, as well as around picture frames hung around the room.

Treas's eleven-year-old daughter, Abbey, grabbed the black crows and shrieked as she arranged them, positioning them as if they were pecking at the wide-open eyes of the realistic-looking severed head.

Next, Don and I drove around the corner to my brother Mike's house. Nobody (but me) called him "Mike," not even his wife, Sharon. His nickname is "Cork." He has a stouter build than Dave, and the cutest, dimpled grin I've ever seen. We were starving, so we dumped our bags downstairs and scooped up his daughters—my teenaged nieces—and headed to the Loyal Oarsman pub to grab something to eat. Haley is the quiet one with long, pale blond hair. Samantha, who prefers to be called "Sam" or "Sammy," is the spunky one. I have fun annoying her, so I call her Samantha.

The pub on Bath Road, two blocks around the corner from my

childhood home in Kingston, Ontario, had quickly become my family's favourite hangout after it opened in 1999, which happened to be the year Don and I married. Don took the girls inside to get a table, while I lingered in the parking lot to call my mother.

Julie answered on the first ring. "Well, hi, Cath" was followed by her signature giggle.

"Whatcha doin', Jule?"

She told me she'd just taken a "hot, steamy bath."

Then she said what she said every week. "When ya comin' down, Cath?" which tugged at my heart, making me wish I lived closer.

"I'll be home for Christmas," I fibbed, "so pretty soon. I'll bring your birthday present and your Christmas presents."

Julie squealed, "Mimosas!"

Even my father, a beer or rye drinker, drank mimosas on Christmas morning while we sat around the tree opening gifts and eating Mom's banana bread.

"Bring your new baby!"

My "baby" was a kitten I'd adopted that week. "You can help me name him. Can I speak to Mom, Jule pie?"

"I knew it was you," said Mom a moment later. "Her eyes always light up when it's you."

That comment would warm my heart forever.

"We're at the Oarsman. I wanted you to know so you don't come over with Julie."

"Okay, dear. I've ordered ten pizzas to be delivered at about seven thirty. Do you think that'll be enough?" With the surprise party only a few hours away, I heard the excitement that animated my mother's voice.

"Should be—if we need more, we'll order more. I wish Julie was getting dressed up too."

"Then she'd know, honey."

I leaned against the car and adjusted my straw-coloured fedora to shield my light-sensitive eyes from the afternoon sun. "I can put some makeup on her when she arrives," I said.

"She'd love that."

I could tell Mom was smiling by the sound of her voice.

As I was about to say goodbye, she said, "Oh, Cath, can you and Don drive us home afterwards? We don't like driving in the dark."

Mom was not a fan of driving—day or night. She would basically only drive to the shopping mall and to the hair salon, both within three kilometres of our home. And tonight we would all be drinking.

"Sure, we'll all take a cab and pick up the cars tomorrow."

We'd planned to stay at their house, as we always did. We had only gone to Mike's so Julie wouldn't see us.

"I can't wait to see Jule's face when she sees us all dressed up."

"Me too, honey. Bye, dear."

"See ya in a few hours."

With a spring in my step, I joined Don and my nieces inside for fish and chips.

A little later, back at Mike's, we put on our costumes. I changed with my nieces in Haley's room, a typical teenager's room, with photos of her and her friends splashed all over the walls and clothes splayed on the bed and the floor. While I helped the girls apply their *Walking Dead* makeup, they laughed at my attempts to speak in a Count Dracula voice.

I dressed as a funky vampire in a black '80s, Madonna-style lace skirt, tights, boots with studded straps, a V-necked top that revealed my "bloodstained" décolletage and a high-collared black cape with a bright red lining. I used cheap drugstore hair-colouring to spray my blond hair black, making it stiff and coarse. I drew thick eyeliner around my eyes, extending out to my temples, and smudged the hollows of my cheeks. I painted my lips black too and added a bit of blood dripping from the corners of my mouth.

When I was done, I peeked into Sam's room to see how Don was doing. He had dressed as a zombie, wearing a pair of tattered, blood-stained denim overalls and a bloody plaid shirt.

While we were preparing for the party, Mom, Dad and Julie attended 5:15 p.m. mass at Our Lady of Lourdes Church, as they did every Saturday. The church was across the street from our family home on Days Road. They were to arrive for the party by six thirty.

It was not even six but already dark when Don and I headed to Dave and Barb's house, just around the block. We drove because we were bringing Julie's gift bag, as well as some bottles of booze.

As I climbed the stairs to the main floor of their split-level house, to my right I could see Barb in the kitchen, preparing a snack tray. To my left, open bathroom and bedroom doors revealed more family members getting zombified. My gorgeous sister Deb was dressed as a French maid zombie in a black miniskirt, white bibbed blouse, fishnets and four-inch-heeled black pumps. I stepped into the bathroom and backcombed her fine blond hair, generously spraying it so it would stick up, as if in fright. She looked sexy and ridiculous.

We were laughing when the phone rang. I heard Barb answer the call in the kitchen.

I glanced at my watch: 6:23 p.m. I assumed it was Mom saying they were on their way.

I finished dabbing drops of blood on Deb's décolletage, then poked my head out of the bathroom. "They'll be here soon. Everyone downstairs!" *Julie's going to laugh her head off when she sees us,* I thought.

I could see Barb where she stood in the kitchen.

She hung up, hesitated for a second, then with a sombre look said, "Your mom was hit by a car."

I was in such a good mood, family all around, laughing and anxious for Julie's arrival, that I didn't at first absorb the news. I was heading to the kitchen when the phone rang again.

Barb answered, listened, hung up, then said quietly, "She was thrown, Cath."

I screamed. Barb had spoken softly so as not to alarm the others, but I couldn't help myself. As the eldest, I should have reacted in a more mature fashion. I should have thought about the children waiting to holler "Surprise!" to their aunt. But all I could picture was Mom's petite body bouncing off the hood of a car.

I dashed for the front door. "Don! We have to go! We have to go *now*!"

Don, smudged circles under his eyes and fake blood dripping down his cheek, followed me outside. I was shaking so much I could barely stand, let alone drive. My husband had missed so many of our family events due to his insane work schedule. I was thankful he was with me then.

Outside I released another scream, this one so loud I didn't even recognize the voice as my own. I saw a masked couple crossing the lawn toward the house and thought it was one of my other sisters and a brother-in-law.

"Mom's been hit by a car! Mom's been hit by a car!"

I was saying everything twice, as if I couldn't believe the words that came out of my mouth the first time.

The masks came off, revealing the wide-eyed shock of my eldest niece, Shannon, and her fiancé, Mark. I ran toward the car, yelling, "Hurry, Don, hurry!"

While Don drove, I couldn't stop rambling. "I can't believe this is happening. I can't believe it, not today."

Chapter 2

The short drive to 491 Days Road, our family home, was a blur. Flashing lights of police cruisers and yellow tape blocked the commotion, which seemed to be unfolding at the end of our driveway. Shedding my vampire cape, I stepped up to the taped boundary and searched the darkness for my father. I saw cops and bystanders but not family. Inside the blockade, I recognized Tina Carey, a nurse in her late sixties who sang in the church choir.

Tina approached me at the barricade. "Which one are you?"

Even without Halloween makeup, people often couldn't tell us Gourdier sisters apart.

"Catherine."

I realized the ambulance had come and gone. "How bad is my mom?"

Tina hesitated. "It's serious." She clutched my arm, fear in her eyes. "Catherine . . . Julie was struck too."

I locked eyes with her. I could barely speak. "How . . . how serious?"

Tina's grasp on my forearm tightened. "Very serious."

I ran back to the car and crumpled into the front seat.

On the way to the hospital, Don attempted to comfort me. "I have a feeling they'll be okay."

"Mom's fragile, she's almost eighty," I said, looking straight ahead. "And my sweetie pie. How could this happen? They were walking home from church for Christ's sake! Why today? We're having a surprise party!" I couldn't stop blabbering. I turned to Don. "Tina said it was serious. This is not good."

Ten minutes later, we pulled into the last parking space at the emergency entrance to Kingston General Hospital. Two ambulances sat outside. I leapt out of the car before Don had time to shift into park. Together we stormed into the reception area looking like characters from *Night of the Living Dead* and headed for the emergency ward, but locked double doors prevented our entrance. We stopped, at a loss. The patients in the waiting room stared at us.

A nurse, realizing who we were there to see, took out a pass key and opened the doors. She guided us down the hallway to a dimly lit room furnished with a burgundy sofa, two blue wing-backed chairs, a coffee table and landscape prints in plastic gold frames on the walls. It was meant to feel cozy, like a living room, but it didn't. Dad, my sister Nancy and her husband Pete were already there. I don't recall who else. All I remember is my father's forlorn face.

He sat in a wing-back chair in the corner. When he saw me, he leaned forward and, using the arms of the chair for support, stood up. His bushy brows framed sad, frightened eyes.

"She's not gonna make it, Cath."

My father showed no sign of noticing that I was dressed like a vampire, fake blood dripping from the corners of my mouth. He only saw *me*. Ordinarily he would have joked, saying something sarcastic like *I thought this was a costume party. When are you gonna get made up?* followed by a jovial laugh.

He looked me straight in the eyes. "I saw her rolling down the road. She's not gonna make it."

He saw Mom get hit! All I could do was hug him tight.

I was praying when a nurse entered the family lounge. *Please, tell us they're alive.*

"The doctor will be here shortly. We're waiting for all your family to arrive."

During the next few minutes more siblings, their spouses and some of my older nieces filled up the room. We waited, sitting, standing, pacing, leaning against the walls. No one said a word. I don't know why this popped into my head, but I looked at Barb and said, "The pizza."

Barb stared at me quizzically.

"The pizzas are going to be delivered any minute, right?" I later found out that my brawny nephew Scott had paid for the pizzas and then, after hearing the heartbreaking news, punched a hole in the wall of his garage.

I thought back to thirty years earlier, when Mom had been hit crossing Days Road, injuring her right hip and thigh. During surgery, the doctor had removed a chunk of fat, resulting in a slimmer physique on that side. She'd joked, "Now can you do the same to my other hip?"

I drifted into the quiet hallway and pressed my face against the wall, feeling its coolness on my cheek. The silence made sense. This was where people waited to hear if their loved one was going to live or die. I leaned in, my lips almost touching the wall that separated us from the emergency ward. I whispered, "Mom, you have to live, okay? Hail Mary full of grace, the Lord is with thee, you're strong, Mom, blessed art thou amongst women and blessed is the fruit of thy womb, Jesus. Holy Mary Mother of God, don't die, Mom, please don't die. I love you so much. Please, don't die."

Just as I took a deep breath to prepare myself to see the sad faces of my family, an orderly walked by and gave me the once-over. I'd forgotten I was a vampire.

Back in the lounge, I felt queasy as I watched my family slowly pacing back and forth across the room, just like the zombies some were still dressed as. My poor father sat there not knowing what to do or where to look. My second youngest sister, Nancy, a wreck herself, sat close, her hand resting on his forearm.

The whole scenario felt so unreal that without thinking, I blurted, "I feel like I'm in a *Grey's Anatomy* episode."

My family just stared at me with confused, sad eyes.

AFTER AN INTERMINABLE five more minutes, a middle-aged doctor wearing blue scrubs stepped into the centre of the room.

Not knowing who to address, his eyes darted from one stricken face to the next.

With no pleasantries or introduction that I recall, he said, "I'm sorry. I don't know their names."

I waited a beat. No one answered, so I did. "The older one is our mother, Wanita."

Why had I used her given name? To sound "official," perhaps? The only people who called Mom "Wanita" were her two brothers and cousins on her side of the family. Everyone else called her "Neta" (pronounced *Neeta*), the nickname Dad had given her.

"The younger one is our sister Julie."

"Well, Wanita is dead."

There it was. The news we'd feared.

My family crumbled around me. They shrieked and cried and hugged each other. Some collapsed onto the floor. Some days, I still hear their cries.

I just stood there, frozen, watching, clenching my jaw, wailing inside my head.

Why did the doctor just blurt out the dead word? He could have prepared us to hear it or not used the word *dead* at all. He could have said, *I'm so sorry, despite all of our efforts to save your mother . . .* We could have filled in the rest.

I was too stunned to move. My husband was there, but I don't remember him holding me.

I do remember that in that moment, he witnessed me morphing into someone he didn't know. He'd seen me disappointed. He'd seen me upset. But he'd never seen the look that was on my face after the doctor said my mother was dead. He must have sensed an invisible wall around me that said, *Leave me alone. I have to figure out what to do.*

Don is the most intelligent person I've ever met. He watches everything from PBS to *Game of Thrones* and sports; he reads news all day and at least one book a month. I refer to him as a walking encyclopedia. And as a producer, it's his job to fix things. But he couldn't fix things that night. He couldn't bring my mother back to life.

I had been with Don when his mom died of congestive heart failure in 2007. She was eighty-three and ready to die. Don, his children, his five sisters and I stood around her bed. Because of all the morphine, she wasn't in pain, and even though she was dying, there were moments of laughter. That's the way it should be when you have to say goodbye to a loved one.

But my mom had already passed, and Don had no idea what to do to console me.

I didn't know what shock felt like, but I was pretty sure it had taken over my body. Should I speak up or not? While my family wept uncontrollably, I cautiously asked the doctor:

"And . . . Julie?"

The doctor looked around at my distraught family and said, "Let's wait another minute."

Oh no, I'd spoken too soon.

When the sobbing subsided, he said, "Julie has severe head trauma. She may last a couple of hours or a couple of days, but she's going to die."

My family's cries became louder. Although my sister Carol is a strong, confident mother of five, she curled up on the sofa and wept. I wanted to hug her, but I couldn't move.

Why hadn't the doctor been more compassionate? Why hadn't he said, *We're doing all we can to keep her comfortable, she's not in any pain.* Anything except the blunt declaration "She's going to die."

Several weeks later, as we sat quietly on the sofa in our family home, out of the blue my sister Deb turned to me and said, "I can still hear him."

I was pretty certain I knew what she meant. "You mean the doctor saying, 'Well, Wanita is dead'?"

"Yep."

"Me too, Deb—me too."

Like a skipping CD, his voice would play over and over in my head for months. *Well, Wanita is dead, well, Wanita is dead, well, Wanita is dead.*

Mom was dead, and Julie was going to die no matter what.

HELPLESS, I looked around the hospital lounge at what used to be my happy-go-lucky family. A nurse guided us to Mom's bedside in the brightly lit emergency ward.

One look at her, and, oh, how I wished I'd thought of asking to see her before my family did. Mom's naked body, bare shoulders exposed, lay under a white sheet. Her mouth was open on a slant, eerily like Edvard Munch's painting *The Scream.* Her dentures had been removed, exposing pink gums. Her red lipstick was smudged above her lip, her fine silver hair askew, a bloody impact mark on the right side of her forehead.

How could they have shown her to us like this?

I'd *never* seen Mom without teeth. She was private about that. Not like Dad, who'd take his front teeth out to make us laugh. I'd never even seen Mom with her hair wet. She taught me how to swim the way she swam, doing the breaststroke with her head above water so she wouldn't ruin her weekly salon-coiffed hairdo. She'd put herself "together" every day, with colour-coordinated jewellery and shoes, even to go grocery shopping. What a frightful vision of our beautiful mother to have forever in our minds.

Fifteen of us surrounded her bed. Everyone sobbed. Everyone except me.

I was in my own dead zone. I raised the sheet, gently lifted out Mom's arm and held her limp fingers in my palm. I looked at her rings—her wedding ring, her twenty-fifth anniversary gold and diamond ring, and her fiftieth anniversary ring, a row of teeny diamonds on a gold band. All worn on her wedding finger.

I gazed at her face and surprised myself by smiling while everyone else was crying. At fifty-two, I knew I was fortunate to have had my mother for as long as I had. That previous April, we'd spent ten days together, just the two of us.

I'd taken her to California to celebrate her eightieth birthday, even though her birthday was in December. I was between film gigs, so we decided not to wait until November, the month we'd initially planned to take our trip. At least fate had dealt me that precious card. I couldn't imagine saying goodbye to her had we not had that holiday together.

Mom was excited to be touring around the narrow streets of the Hollywood Hills that she'd only seen in the movies. We drove uphill in my red PT Cruiser rental until we found the parking lot of the corner store that apparently had one of the best views of the "Hollywood" sign. Mom, sunglasses on, stepped out of the car and smiled as I directed "A little to your left," until the famous sign was in a good position behind her for a souvenir photo.

Mom was especially curious to tour the Kodak Theatre, where the Academy Awards were held. She'd seen me on TV when I attended the Oscars for *Chicago* with my friend David Lee, who won for Best Sound. When we stepped inside the theatre with a tour group, I whispered and showed her where David and I had sat. She got excited, grabbed my hand, pointed to the seats, and exclaimed proudly to the guide and group, "My daughter sat right there at the Oscars!" We strolled along Hollywood Boulevard to the legendary Grauman's Chinese Theatre, where Mom placed her hand, fingers spread, in Marilyn Monroe's concrete handprint. We had lunch at a celebrity favourite, the Polo Lounge in the Beverly Hills Hotel. Sharon Stone was sitting in a booth behind us. Of course, Mom wanted to meet her. I'd worked with Sharon on *The Mighty*, so I found the nerve to go over and say, "My mom would be thrilled to meet you." Sharon came over and shook Mom's hand, and they exchanged a few pleasantries. We visited the gravesites of Marilyn, Natalie Wood and Dean Martin. Marilyn's and Natalie's graves had flowers; Dean's had cigar and cigarette butts. Mom loved everything to do with movie stars.

We shared a king-sized bed in a suite at Le Montrose in West Hollywood. As Mom lay on her side reading her paperback mystery novel, the bedside lamp highlighted how sparse her silver hair had become. It made me wonder what my hair would be like in my seventies. Only two weeks earlier, we'd gone to New York and taken a walk in Central Park.

In that emergency room, I couldn't look at my mom's face too long. I didn't want that unsettling vision of her locked in my head. The staff had taken the time to remove her clothes, earrings and necklace, so I didn't understand why they didn't also attempt to make her more presentable to her family. If I'd seen her first, I would have put her dentures back in and pulled the sheet over her bare shoulders. I would have touched up her red lipstick, combed her hair and wiped the blood off her forehead. I don't know if you can close the mouth of a dead person, but I would have tried.

Between sobs, Teresa yelled, "Why aren't they doing anything?" It was heartbreaking to hear her cry out that way. Mom was obviously gone from her body.

Tears soaked Dave's face and beard. Dad's and Mike's faces, too, were wet.

My sister Carol, fifty-one, gripped Mom's exposed bare feet at the end of the bed and cried out, "You were supposed to be at Shannon's wedding!" Shannon, twenty-six, was the eldest grandchild. Her wedding date was set for the following summer.

A nurse handed us a baggie of Mom's personal items. Dangly chandelier-style earrings with red stones, a coordinating bracelet with two stones noticeably missing, and her watch.

My insides went crazy digesting the horror, but despite my anxiety, I had to think what needed to be done next.

And where was Julie?

Everyone was sobbing. Then there was me, observing them, not shedding a tear.

Father Brennan, our priest, surprised us by showing up in the emergency room. He said to me, "I can sure tell you have eldest sibling syndrome." He put his hand lightly on my shoulder. "It's okay to cry, Catherine."

"Thank you, Father, but I have to figure out . . . what to do . . ."

Despite being racked with an inconsolable pain, I forced myself to remain composed. As the eldest, wasn't that my responsibility?

I wandered away from Mom's bed, looking for my sister. Hearing nurses talking, I glanced to my right. There she was. Lying on a bed, hooked up to machines.

Julie.

She had been only ten steps from our mother's bed the whole time.

Her eyes were closed. There was a tube down her throat. She wore a blue hospital gown. There was a patch of deep red blood in the hair on the side of her head.

The nurses were facing the opposite direction, reading Julie's medical chart, and hadn't noticed that I'd stepped up to her bedside. Ever so lightly, I stroked her pert little nose with my index finger.

"Did you know she's wearing dentures?" asked one nurse.

"Really? She is?" replied the other.

Julie wasn't able to clean her teeth properly, so by the time she was thirty, she had to have all but a couple of her bottom teeth extracted. Dr. Chan, her dental surgeon, had made the dentures look exactly like her real teeth, slightly discoloured with a bit of a crossover on her two front teeth. No one could tell she wore them. Julie knew how to take them out at night, put them in the cleaning tray and insert them back into her mouth in the morning, and was quite confident doing so. I didn't want them removed, as they had been for my mother. I didn't want her cute face distorted.

Placing my hand gently on Julie's bare arm, I turned to the nurses. "Leave them in, please."

Their wide-eyed reaction showed I'd caught them off guard.

"She's my sister. Please. Leave them in."

"We're waiting on the doctor. You'll have to step out."

I wanted to keep gazing at Julie's sweet face, but the nurse grabbed the pale pink drape and motioned for me to move out of the way.

Powerless, I stepped back as the drape was drawn, blocking my view of my comatose sister.

A FEW DAYS EARLIER, I was busy shopping for tiles, tubs and cabinets, because we were renovating the bathrooms in our Toronto house. During the renos, we had rented a furnished suite downtown. When I got back to the room at four thirty, it hit me: today, November 2, was Julie's birthday. Though the party was on Saturday, I called her immediately.

Julie kept the cordless phone with her all the time, carrying it around the house or putting it on her lap while she leaned back on her pink fuzzy oversized pillow watching television from her bed.

Speeding up the melody, I sang "Happy Birthday to You," ending dramatically with "*Happy fortieth birthday, Sista Juuulllee Piiiiee, happy birthday to you!*"

She giggled mischievously. "I'm drinking champagne, Cath!"

"Really, Jule?" I glanced over at Julie's yellow gift bag on the floor beside my suitcase. A bottle of champagne, too tall, was peeking out the top of the bag.

"Yep, I am." She giggled again.

She got excited when I told her I had a new kitten, then proceeded to tell me what Victor and Nikki were up to on her favourite soap opera, *The Young and the Restless*.

"Can I speak to Mom now please, Jule?"

"I thought it was you," Mom said. "She always giggles the whole time she talks to you."

"Is she really drinking bubbly?"

Laughing, she said, "Yes! The little monkey wanted to have a glass while watching the *Y & R*, so we're both having some."

Sometime in the early '90s, Julie came by bus to visit me in my downtown Toronto apartment. We went to Yorkville to have lunch at an outdoor café. The next week a business colleague said, "It's so nice of you to do volunteer work." I didn't have a clue what he was talking about. "I saw you walking down Yonge Street holding hands with that girl."

I wasn't doing volunteer work. Julie had Down syndrome. We did the same things all sisters did together: shopping, going to the movies, playing games, swimming, dining out. Julie also had a knack for humour. She understood when something was funny, and she knew how to make a joke. My parents allowed Julie one glass of wine a week, on Saturday nights when they went out to dinner after mass. Julie may have had Down syndrome, but she wasn't a child. At restaurants, if they put a straw in her soft drink, she'd take it out and say, "I'm not a baby." And at forty she was certainly old enough to drink bubbly.

I had called home again Friday, the night before the party.

"Hey, Mom, do you need us to pick up the cake or anything tomorrow?"

"No, honey, I think everything is taken care of."

"Okay, good. Jule's gonna love her party!"

Suddenly Mom tittered like a schoolgirl.

"What's so funny?"

"Your father," she said. "Last Saturday we went to the Halloween party at the Oarsman. When I was coming back from the ladies' room, he grabbed me by the arm and pulled me onto the dance floor. I tossed my purse to the side and we jived. I didn't even notice till the song was over that the floor had cleared, and everyone was watching us."

I'd never heard my mother say so much in one breath.

My parents had a smooth style of jiving, effortlessly in sync, even though Mom was five foot one and my father six feet tall. They always seemed to be on their own planet when they danced together.

Dad had tried to teach me once, but I couldn't get it. I'd take one step too many or turn the wrong way. Dad had been diagnosed with Parkinson's disease about five years earlier and was upset he couldn't golf or curl the way he used to. It was now a special occurrence for him to get up and dance in the crowded bar.

Mom continued proudly. "People came up to us and said, forget about Best Costume, you should win a prize for Best Dancers!"

To find out that after fifty-four years together Dad could still make Mom feel like a girl at a school dance made my heart sing.

"Where are you staying during the renovations?"

"Yorkville. At the Minto."

"That's where all the movie stars go during the film festival!"

Mom and her celebrity fascination. She was in such a delightful mood, I didn't want to end the call.

"Sorry, Ma, I've gotta shower and change. Don's working late, so I'm meeting a friend for a bite."

Mom jumped in. "Where?"

"The bar at the Four Seasons."

"You took me there once. We drank fancy champagne."

We did. Veuve Clicquot.

"See you tomorrow. Love you, Mom."

"I know you do, dear."

After hanging up, I thought how peculiar it was for her to respond that way. She never ever said "I know." She'd always reciprocated with "I love you too, honey."

No one wanted to leave Mom's body, but a nurse told us we had to step out so they could move her to another area. After one last loving squeeze, I released Mom's cool hand from my warm one. I glanced again at her contorted face, her wide-opened mouth gasping for her last breath.

Mom, I'm so sorry you had to die this way.

As my family made their way back to the gloomy sitting room, I asked Don for the car keys, then went outside.

Was I supposed to call my uncles, aunts, Mom and Dad's best friends? I didn't know. Sudden family death was new to me.

I opened the passenger door of Don's car and sank into the leather seat. I looked to my right. Two ambulances were still parked there. *Their ambulances.* My head felt heavy, and I wanted to lie down— but I had to make the calls, didn't I?

Aunt Joan, my dad's sister, and I had always been close, so she was the first.

She saw my name on her call display. Without uttering a word, she cried out, "Neta's not with us anymore, is she, Cath? Is she?"

I didn't know how she knew, but I was relieved I didn't have to tell her.

As Aunt Joan cried, I took a shallow breath and spoke robotically. "No, AJ, she's not."

Crying louder, she asked, "And Julie?"

"She could live a couple of hours or a couple of days, but she's going to die."

I'd repeated the doctor's exact words. It *was* hard to share sad news. My bedside manner needed attention too. I hadn't yet processed what the words coming out of my mouth meant for me. For my family.

Next I called Mom's younger brother, Uncle Mike. He's a retired elementary school teacher, now a model aircraft hobbyist. He plays guitar too and, like me, enjoys singing.

Seeing my number on call display, he answered pleasantly, "Well, hello there!"

Only two weeks earlier, he and Mom had been on a mini-holiday together. Don and I had arranged for them to fly with us to New York City to attend the premiere of the film *Amelia*, about Amelia Earhart. They'd visited the film sets in Toronto: Mom to meet the movie stars, Uncle Mike to see the 1930s Lockheed Model 10 Electra planes. Hotels near Central Park were quite expensive, so I'd asked my seventy-nine-year-old mom and sixty-seven-year-old uncle if they would consider sharing a room. Without any hesitation, they both responded, "Absolutely, I wouldn't mind at all!"

For the premiere, Mom and I had dressed elegantly in sparkly black knit jackets, long black skirts and two-inch pumps, not too high to walk the few blocks from the hotel to the theatre. The men wore dark suits and shiny black shoes.

As celebrities arrived, we were hurried along the red carpet. Just before stepping into the theatre, I snapped a photo of Uncle Mike with Harry Connick Jr. in the background.

In the crowded theatre lobby, Mom vanished for a few minutes. When she reappeared, she grabbed my arm. "I just introduced myself to Mariska Hargitay!" Hargitay was the lead actress from *Law and Order: SVU.*

At the after-party, held on the Ladies Wear floor of Bloomingdale's, Mom and I lost our dates in the sea of guests, servers and clothing displays.

"Oh! There's Ewan McGregor!" she cried. "I haven't met him yet."

Mom had spotted him in the VIP section. The entrance was patrolled by a security guard. I couldn't find Don, so had to quickly figure out how I was going to get us into the actors' circle. A passing waiter offered up a tray of champagne flutes. I grabbed us each a glass.

"Follow me, Mom. Walk with purpose!"

In our classy attire, we walked right past the security guard.

My mother wound her way through the crowd straight to Ewan McGregor. Not shy at all, the polar opposite of my father, she chatted away as if she were talking to a friend of my brother's instead of to a movie star. Mom also saw Richard Gere, and though she'd already met him twice, she wanted to say hello. Richard was talking with a man unknown to me, so I approached his wife, former Bond girl Carrie Lowell. I introduced myself as the rehearsal manager on *Chicago.*

"My mom would love to say hello to your husband."

Carrie nonchalantly tapped Richard on the shoulder. "Honey, someone wants to say hello."

He remembered us and, behaving like the charming lead from *Pretty Woman*, held Mom's hand as he conversed with her.

When we left the VIP section, a man wearing a sweater and jeans, an investor in the film whom I'd met previously, stood on the other side of the rope, hoping to be let in.

"Catherine, how did you get in there?" he asked. The bubbles having made me carefree, I said, "My mom got us in."

We giggled and grabbed two more flutes from a passing tray, then strolled around admiring the fall fashions.

That night was the last time Mom and I drank champagne and laughed together. But what an enchanting and memorable evening it had been.

Uncle Mike, Mom and me at the *Amelia* premiere in New York City, October 2009, two weeks before the accident. Photo courtesy of Don Carmody

"Uncle Mike, it's not good," I said. "Mom was hit by a car . . ." It was so hard to get the words out. "She's gone."

Silence.

I continued. "Julie was hit too." *Breathe.* "The doctor said she's not going to make it either. Could you call Uncle Don, please?" Don is their older brother.

He began to sob. "I can't call him. I can't. I'll have to get Dale to tell him." Dale is Uncle Don's son, my eldest cousin on Mom's side.

"I'll call you later," I said. "When we know more. Love you."

I couldn't make any more calls. I couldn't listen to anyone else cry. I had to check on Julie.

BACK IN THE LOUNGE, as each of us sat or paced in silence, a different doctor came in. He was a short, dark-haired, baby-faced man.

"Could I please have your attention for a moment? We want to try something with Julie. We want to try to take the pressure off her brain. We'd like to insert a tube to drain the blood out."

He was the brain surgeon? He looked too young.

We'd been told that Julie was going to die. Did this mean the other doctor had made a mistake and she might live?

I was the only one who'd seen Julie in the emergency ward. I don't even think I told anyone I saw her, except my husband, who hovered over me.

"We'll keep you updated," the doctor said. Then he exited the room, leaving us all in a numbed state, staring into nothingness.

But the news of the operation had given me a thread of hope that our sister might survive. I left the family room to use the washroom and startled myself when I looked in the mirror. Staring back at me was a melancholy vampire. I whispered, "My scary face was for you, Jule. For you, cutie pie angel face." Tears washed away the thick eyeliner rimming my eyes, forming charcoal streaks down my cheeks.

After Julie had gone into surgery, I asked Don to take me back to Dave's to change and shower the black out of my hair. The route took us along Days Road, where we were stopped by the police blockade. An officer waved us to detour left. My jaws clenched as I turned my head to look back at the police officers, the flashing lights and orange cones. The scene looked like the movie sets I'd worked on. But this was not a film. The flashing lights blocked the street to my childhood home because my mother was dead and my sister was probably going to die too.

At my brother's, I opened the front door to a dangling skeleton. Only a few hours earlier, the home had been filled with exuberant laughter as we'd turned Dave's basement into a haunted house. I glanced at the cobwebbed graveyard downstairs, the plastic headstones carefully placed, the strewn bloodied body and severed head with the crows pecking at it.

Carrying my overnight bag, I went to a guest bedroom to change. As I pulled down my lace skirt, my phone rang. Frantically I reached in my purse and pulled it out.

"Aunt Cath." It was Shannon, my niece. Why had *she* made the call? Probably because Shannon is the eldest of five and has the same ingrained feeling of responsibility to take care of things that I have. Tenderly, she said, "We need you to come back now."

I wondered what the urgency was. My fear was that Julie had died, and they didn't want to tell me over the phone. I hadn't even washed my face yet. My hair was still black. I changed into my jeans and pulled a top over my head.

Don emerged from the bathroom. He wasn't a zombie anymore.

I repeated the words I'd screamed to him a couple of hours earlier, but this time my voice was barely audible. "We have to go *now*."

In the emergency ward, we were greeted by my brother Mike (I think), who escorted us to what looked like a conference room in the critical care unit. Dad and my siblings were seated around a long oblong table. Several booklets were laid out in the middle of it. I picked one up: *Guidelines for the Bereaved*. As I leafed through, a woman appeared at the doorway and offered to speak to my father.

Dad asked, "Who's that, Cath?"

"A grief counsellor," I told him.

Without a beat, he said, "I don't want to talk to her."

Nancy did, though, and wandered down the hall with the woman.

I think it was about 11 p.m. when the surgeon gave us an update. He reiterated that there was compression on Julie's brain. They'd been successful with inserting the tube to let out blood to release some of the pressure. It sounded like good news, but he didn't say she was going to live. He said only, "You can see her now."

We were escorted to a room in the intensive care unit, similar to the emergency room but with white drapes separating the beds. About twenty of us surrounded Julie's bed. I was surprised they had allowed us all to come in. Someone must have let them know our mother had passed away, so they let the rules slide. The others hadn't yet seen Julie unconscious, hooked up to machines, and they stared in disbelief. I stepped closer. I took her child-sized, limp, warm hand, raised it to my lips and kissed it. And kissed it again.

No one said a word. I spoke for all of us.

"We love you, Julie."

Dad, looking sorrowful, stood on the opposite side of the bed, surprised me by saying, "Doesn't even look like her."

Since her fair-skinned face was unscathed, I thought she did look like our Julie. Her hair was dishevelled, though, with a blob of blood on the right side of her head, an oxygen tube down her throat, another tube draining blood from the back of her head, and a breathing machine pumping her lungs. Perhaps Dad was right.

Attempting to soothe him, I looked into his lost eyes and said, "You can hold her hand, Dad."

He glanced at my hand holding her right hand, then slowly reached for Julie's left hand.

I had to be strong for Dad. I could only imagine how devastating it was for him to know his baby girl was dying too.

I turned to my sobbing nieces, Samantha and Haley. I held up Julie's wee hand and struggled to maintain my composure. "She's still alive. You can hold her hand."

They stared back at me and didn't move. I coaxed them gently, "It's okay. Come and say . . ." I choked up. I was about to say what I was terrified to admit. "Come and say goodbye to Aunt Julie."

They moved up beside me. I guided their hands onto Julie's, mine on top of theirs. Together we held her warm hand. I looked at her innocent face and prayed. *Please, wake up.*

I asked the nurse if Julie could hear us, but she didn't know.

MOM WAS THIRTY-NINE YEARS OLD when she gave birth to Julie Christine on November 2, 1969.

When our baby sister was three days old, she had to have major surgery. She had a life-threatening condition called duodenal atresia, common in infants with Down syndrome. The first portion of the small intestine, the duodenum, becomes blocked, and no food or fluid can pass through the stomach. Surgery was crucial but risky on a newborn. The doctor told us she had a 20 percent chance of survival.

I was scared she was going to die before I even had a chance to meet her.

The day of Julie's surgery, the principal at Our Lady of Lourdes, who was a nun, led the school in a prayer for Julie over the PA system. A few days later, Mom came home with our baby sister cradled in her arms. The seven of us—from three-year-old Nancy to me, three months shy of thirteen—gathered round. We all said "aw" when we saw her cute little face, and "ew" at the four-inch scar down her tiny belly.

Into the late 1960s, children with Down syndrome were still being institutionalized. My parents didn't want anything to do with that cruelty. My dad's longtime friend Paul Rea vividly remembered Dad saying, "There's no way she's going anywhere. She's going to be raised at home with all of us, and that's that."

Julie was our sister. And we adored her.

As I now stood by her bedside, a nurse said, "Excuse me," and squeezed past to attend to the IV drip inserted into Julie's hand. She put more fluid into the bag.

"What are you doing?" I asked.

"Giving her morphine."

"Why? I thought she couldn't feel anything."

The nurse hesitated. "This is in case she can."

In case she can? What did that mean? She was either brain dead or not. I stared at Julie's sweet face and prayed she wasn't suffering.

I'm always aware of the time, sometimes too much. But I had no sense of time that night. I had no idea how long we'd been at the hospital. Was it 11 p.m. or 2 a.m.? I glanced over at my devastated father, his mouth turned down, his eyes blank and glassy. I had to take him home.

Don took the wheel, with Dad in the front seat and Nancy and me in the back. No one spoke during the ten-minute drive. Though sick with grief, I suddenly thought of a way to help Dad: I'd move in with him. Don could drive me back to Toronto first thing in the morning to grab my funeral wardrobe, other clothes and my cats, then drive us both back to Kingston in my car. Don could then take the train back to Toronto. The job I was doing, rewriting a bad horror script, I could do anywhere. If I could manage to work at all.

Police cruisers and yellow tape still surrounded the accident site blocking Days Road at the corner of Castell Road, two houses from our home. I got out of the car and informed the young police officer that it was our mom and sister who'd been hit. I needed to take my father home.

In an authoritative voice, the young officer said, "Sorry, you can't go in yet."

Another officer approached and asked what was going on. I don't raise my voice often, but I couldn't help myself. "It was our mother and sister who were hit, and *he* said we can't take my dad into our own house!" I pointed. "It's right there!"

The officers relented, pulled back the tape and let us pass. My sister Nancy reprimanded me for yelling. But I wasn't myself. I'd never felt so much pain until that night. I'd yelled to defend our father.

When we opened the front door, we were greeted by a hollow silence. I looked at the beige push-button phone on the wall by the kitchen, the same place our black dial phone had hung almost fifty years ago. The realization that I couldn't call Mom anymore hit me hard.

I'd called her every weekend since I'd left home to go to Seneca College in Toronto in 1975. I would speak to Julie for a few minutes as well, especially since she usually answered the phone. Dad thought long-distance calls cost too much, so he didn't talk long, if at all. I remember sometimes hearing him shout from the background, "Neet, are you still talking to Cathy?"

For thirty-four years I never missed a call, no matter where I was in the world. I'd even called home while I watched a dragon boat sail by on a canal in Bangkok. We'd chat about the actors I'd met, local gossip or the new shoes we'd purchased. The last couple of years we'd talked about whose funeral she'd attended that week. With my parents in their seventies, it had gotten to the point where their weekly outing was likely to be to a wake or a funeral.

That week my outing would be her funeral.

Nancy stayed with my dad so I could finally shower. The spray of water sent black paint cascading down my pale body, pooling around my feet in the white bathtub.

Julie and I had often showered together. I'd sing a silly upbeat song, like Bobby Sherman's "Julie, Do Ya Love Me?" It was written in 1969, the year she was born. We'd stand close together under the shower head while I washed her hair, massaging the shampoo until I had enough extra lather to put a foamy beard on my face, then plop some on her nose and chin. She got a kick out of that. I'd squeeze gobs of conditioner into her thick, dry hair, and let it absorb while I carefully shaved her underarms.

"You look mahvellous," I'd tease.

She'd giggle the whole time. "Caaaathhh . . ."

During our phone chat the day before the accident, Mom had said, "When you come home, can you do Julie's eyebrows?"

Her brows joined in the middle, but because Julie found tweezing painful, I would use a little Nair cream. She would sit on the toilet lid while I carefully dabbed the depilatory between her brows, making sure it didn't drip into her eyes. So she wouldn't touch it, I'd sit beside her on the bathtub rim for the few minutes needed for the cream to dissolve the hairs.

After my shower, I slipped on a terry robe, wrapped a towel around my wet hair and then looked into Dad's room. Nancy was lying beside him on the double bed. I thought I should be the one comforting him. But Nancy, forty-three and a mother of two, probably knew better than I did what to do or say.

My husband had been my protector that evening, but I didn't sleep in my old queen bed with him that night. Julie was still alive. I wanted to feel closer to her, so I slept in her room on her twin mattress. Lying on my side, I held her fleece nightgown, blue and white with a large snowflake, tightly to my chest. I thought of the photo I'd taken of her wearing it, holding her mug of "hot steamy tea," as she called it. I prayed, *Please God, let her live. Please live, Julie.*

I know I eventually fell asleep, because I dreamed of her. I was standing beside her hospital bed wearing my ghoulish makeup, staring at her. She opened her eyes and said, *You don't scare me. I know it's you, Cath.* Then she giggled. As I turned to walk away, she said, *Don't go. Where is everybody? Where's Mom?*

Then I woke up.

I wanted to get up, to join Don, but I couldn't move. I could not believe what had happened. There I was, lying in Julie's bed, while she was alone in the intensive care unit being kept alive by machines. I wished that I had stayed with her.

And I prayed she wasn't scared.

Chapter 3

As I made up Julie's bed early the next morning, I glanced at the framed eighteenth-century bedtime prayer that hung on the pink wall above her bed: *Now I lay me down to sleep, I pray the Lord my soul to keep, If I should die before I wake, I pray the Lord my soul to take.* In the corner of the frame, tucked behind the glass, was a photo of a sleeping, two-year-old Julie.

I took the prayer down off the wall.

I had to see Julie again before we left for Toronto.

Don and I arrived at her bedside at 7:40 a.m. I placed the framed prayer on a shelf above her bed. I held her hand. "Hi, Jule. I love you . . . so much." I stared at her, the tubes coming out of her mouth and head, the dried blood in her hair. I studied the monitors and was disappointed in myself that, after decades of watching medical shows, I still didn't know what the lines and numerical readouts meant. I let my tears flow.

Don stood close but didn't hold me. I guess my sorrow scared him. I'm sure he wanted to be my hero, but he didn't know how. He knew losing Julie was the worst thing that could ever happen to me.

Why had that first doctor said she had no chance of surviving? She was breathing, and they'd released the pressure from her brain, hadn't they? What lines on the monitor determined that she was brain dead? There wasn't anyone around to ask. If she was kept on life support, I could hold her hand and kiss her cute little nose for months. It was incredibly hard to leave her, but I had to execute my plan of driving to Toronto to get my belongings so I could live with Dad. At the time, I wasn't thinking how long I'd stay, only that I needed to be there.

During the two-hour-plus drive home, I sat in the back seat and began calling my close friends, one by one. "Accident . . . Mom is dead . . . Julie's probably going to die . . ." After only three calls, I couldn't do it anymore. I was blubbering too much.

When we arrived home, I ran upstairs to my bedroom closet and chose some funerary clothes: black pencil skirt, black dress, black patent pumps, black jacket. Maybe that was why I rarely wore black. It's death wardrobe. I grabbed jeans, yoga pants, running shoes—and my cats, Callie and Freddy. I would discover later that I'd forgotten to pack blouses to wear with my skirt. I forgot to pack pantyhose and underwear too.

Like a rag doll, I slumped silently in the passenger seat of my car while Don drove back to Kingston. Callie and Freddy slept in their crates on the back seat.

Back in Kingston, we dropped off the cats at my parents' house, then rushed to the hospital.

We were directed to the fourth floor, to an airy room outside the intensive care unit. Dad was hunched in a chair. My siblings sat or paced, each lost in their own grief world.

A man and woman in business attire were talking with Nancy. They approached Dad with a document. Nancy introduced them as representatives of Trillium Gift of Life. They were asking for permission for the donation of Julie's organs. Dad, as her legal guardian, had to sign a consent form.

Dad looked up at me, bewildered. "What do you think, Cath?"

Me? I'd been gone for six hours. No one had confirmed to me there was no hope for Julie.

Hadn't the pressure on her brain been relieved? I didn't remember a discussion about taking her off life support. Had my family agreed to let Julie go while Don and I were gone? I wasn't the least bit prepared to answer my father.

Dad's haunted eyes looked deep into mine, imploring for help with the decision. I crouched in front of him and placed my hands on his knees. I struggled to find words to help him feel comfortable choosing to have his baby girl's organs extracted to save others.

"It's a good thing to do, Dad. I'm going to, should anything happen to me. I've got a signed release for my organs in my wallet."

I stood over him, watching his quivering hand sign the document.

I don't remember how long we stayed at the hospital after Dad signed that form. I don't remember if we were given the opportunity to be with Julie when she died. We did not stand around her bed and watch her being "unplugged" from the machines. We did not watch her die. As far as I know, none of us were there to hold Julie's hand as she took her last breath. But Dad had given the doctors permission to let her go. We had to let our special angel's spirit fly so the earth angels could take her organs and transplant them into the bodies of strangers we would not be allowed to meet.

There are moments of that weekend I recall so clearly, but it still bothers me that I don't remember if we were offered the chance to say goodbye to Julie, or if I even said my last goodbye. Or if I said goodbye but it was so painful I pushed the memory away.

Chapter 4

Dad had been getting the *Kingston Whig-Standard* delivered for almost fifty years. At seven on Monday morning, I found the paper on the kitchen table. I hoped Dave had dropped in early and snatched it off the front porch. I prayed Dad hadn't seen the front-page headline: "Accident Kills Two Women."

A sick feeling washed over me as I read on. "What was to have been a weekend family celebration turned tragic when two women were run down by a car . . ."

They spelled my mother's name wrong: as Juanita, not Wanita. They called Julie *handicapped*.

"Several congregants confirmed, 'It's a dangerous area for pedestrians to cross, a poorly lit stretch of road along which cars travel at high speeds, and there are no traffic signals or crosswalks for pedestrians.'"

I could not believe I was reading an article in my hometown newspaper about the tragic deaths of my own mother and youngest sister. I had to hide the paper from Dad. I folded it and placed it in the outside pocket of my suitcase.

Dad didn't ask about the paper, so perhaps he had seen it but was too disturbed to speak about it.

Before my sisters arrived to choose viewing clothes for Mom and Julie, I decided to go to the grocery to store to pick up a tub of Greek yogurt. I had no appetite, but yogurt was something healthy I could eat a spoonful of here and there throughout the day. When I got back, I found my sisters had already laid out Mom's fuchsia pantsuit on her bed. Her wardrobe was a rainbow, and so was her shoe rack on the wall behind her door. Pumps, sandals and slippers, in colours ranging from black to hot pink and canary yellow. Her sparkling personality shone in the vibrant clothing she left behind. Glancing at a photo of Mom a week later, Dad said, "She was always smiling, Cath." Even her clothes seemed happy.

A necklace with a rhinestone *N* dangling from its chain was also laid out on a black tank top. The year before, for Mother's Day, I'd given Mom a woven necklace of chunky stones, in various shades of pinks and purples. The necklace was designed by Sharon Friendly, my former singing teacher. Mom and I had met up with Sharon during our spring holiday in San Diego, where she gifted Mom the matching earrings. Mom had worn them several times with her fuchsia suit on our vacation, so I think Mom would've chosen the matching set for her viewing. She had such an array of costume jewellery that Deb had bought her a four-foot-tall jewellery armoire to house her massive collection. I searched the drawers until I found that set. Not knowing if the *N* necklace was a gift from one of my sisters, or if they'd object to my decision, I needed to consult them first. So I took the stone necklace to show them.

The sadness in Julie's room was almost suffocating. My four sisters were standing around her bed, speaking quietly, almost whispering. I noticed Julie's brown Tim Hortons uniform laid out on her bed. The whole outfit, including the coordinating headband and visor. All they were missing was her hairnet!

Julie had worked at Tim Hortons for seventeen years. A couple of times I'd snuck into the café and sat where she couldn't see me, so I could watch her in action. Carefully she would push the small trolley around, filling up the glass sugar jars, cleaning tables, and giggling when friendly customers chatted with her. Her managers had even created an award plaque especially for Julie: The Giggle Award. It read, *For always being sweet and happy.* She enjoyed her job, but being a Tim Hortons employee was not who she was. I worried that my sisters were seriously planning for Julie to wear her work uniform as her viewing outfit.

My heart beat faster as I prepared myself to intervene. Then I noticed that Julie's blue fleece nightgown with the big snowflake was also laid out on the bed. I know Julie often wore it, but I felt that it was too childish, especially since she had just turned forty. Choosing clothes for the funeral of our youngest sister was an unthinkable task, but though Julie was the size of a young girl, I always thought that she should dress her age. I would take her shopping in the petite sections at women's-wear stores.

I was distressed, believing that they were thinking of burying Julie in either a Tim Hortons uniform or a child's nightie. They looked so sad that I didn't know how to confront them. I needed my mother. But I went to my father.

Dad was in the living room reading the paper.

Clutching Mom's necklace, I trembled as I said, "Dad, they want Julie to wear her Tim Hortons uniform."

Dad lifted his gaze and stared at me.

"They have her nightgown with the snowflake out too." More calmly, but still shaking, I added, "She's not a child. She should be dressed like a woman—right, Dad?"

He seemed a bit flustered, but he understood. "I think so too, Cath."

I shouldn't have disturbed my distraught father at all.

Julie was a sister to all of us, so I knew my sisters should have their own opinions, and I knew they meant well, that they believed they were making a respectable decision. I was nervous, but I needed to stop them. I imagined our relatives and friends seeing Julie in her coffin with a Tim's visor on her head and felt like yelling, *Please, no!* I could not let that be everyone's last vision of her. My mother would have simply suggested in her quiet, calm way that they might want to choose something else. *Mom, please help me state my case.*

I took a breath as I re-entered Julie's room. My sisters watched as I set Mom's necklace on the white dresser and opened a drawer. I pulled out a sleeveless, light green top accented with bronze sequins, along with the coordinating cardigan—an ensemble Julie and I had purchased on one of our shopping escapades in Toronto. I held it up to show them. They listened to my explanation.

"Please, I know she loved her job, but she should be dressed like a woman."

Teresa searched the dresser and found a headband to match the outfit I had picked out. To finish, we added a dainty necklace with pale peach-coloured stones.

Mom and Julie, spring 2008, in our backyard in Toronto. Julie is wearing the clothes she wore for her viewing. This photo was used for their obituary.
PHOTO COURTESY OF THE AUTHOR

After I explained why Mom's stone necklace was special, they also accepted my desire to exchange the *N* necklace for the stone one.

My sisters looked at me with mournful eyes as I made these

decisions and did what eldest siblings sometimes do: took charge. I didn't know if they were upset with me or not, and that worried me. I needed their love now more than ever.

Emotionally drained, I went to the basement, curled up on the sofa and sobbed.

THERE ARE MANY DECISIONS that need to be made quickly when someone dies, and that's difficult to do when you're in a state of shock. I soon realized why being a funeral director was an honourable career path.

I vaguely remember looking at caskets that afternoon in the basement of the funeral home with my siblings and father. It was a nightmare experience to be choosing not one but two coffins. While the funeral director, Mr. Moore, toured us around the room, I watched my dazed family wandering in the sea of caskets. Opened satin-lined coffins in mahogany, walnut, cherry, maple, oak, pine and veneer were displayed. There was also a small white coffin for children. Caskets are expensive, so we chose ones in reasonably priced pine.

Dad whispered to me, "Get me the same one, okay, Cath?"

Useful information, but I was not ready to even think about losing our father as well.

Because our family was large and well known in the community, Mr. Moore warned us the lineups for the visitation would be long. He suggested we make several photo boards to give the mourners something to peruse as they waited to offer condolences.

By coincidence, that weekend I'd brought four photo albums from our childhood years to Kingston. Nancy had called the night before asking me to bring some, because she was looking for baby pictures of herself for a display they were creating at the school where she worked.

I'd always taken tons of pictures. I'd received my first camera for my twelfth birthday, a Kodak Instamatic. I loved photography so much that, when I was fifteen, I bought myself a used 35mm Minolta. In my teens, I worked after school and Saturdays at a variety store and got a 25 percent discount on photofinishing. I have an array of floral sticky-plastic-paged albums filled with photos from the 1970s.

When we returned from the funeral home, we gathered in my parents' living room. My sisters and I sat on the carpet, the guys on the sofas. Family memories were scattered all over the floor: photos of our birthday parties, First Communions, graduations, Christmas mornings, swimming at the cottage and random snapshots of us at home. We found photos of me and my sisters with permed, poofy '80s hair and blouses with padded shoulders. My brothers had '70s moustaches, and Dad had sideburns.

We opened the sheers on the front window facing Days Road to let more sunlight in. There we were, looking at photos of Mom and Julie, sitting roughly fifty feet from where their bodies had lain three days earlier.

On the top bunk bed in the downstairs bedroom, I found the collages I'd made for Mom and Dad's fiftieth anniversary, Mom's seventy-fifth birthday and Dad's seventy-fifth. Julie was the star of my early photo albums, and by 2000, Mom and Dad had started using their own camera more regularly, so we had lots of recent pictures of her too. The photo board process helped us relive some happy times.

But when I glanced at the boards my sisters were making, I saw they weren't just gluing on photos of Mom; they also had photos of "Nanny" with her grandchildren. Since I didn't have children, I chose to make a photo board of my trips with her. I included a picture of Mom standing beside a limo in front of our house in Hidden Hills, California; Mom behind bars in the cellblock set of *Chicago*; and one with Richard Gere's arm around her. Another photo I'd taken of her in front of Wolfgang Puck's Spago restaurant in Beverly Hills, Mom walking on the beach in Venice, one from the *Amelia* film set with Hilary Swank, and other photos of our recent adventures together.

As I pasted a photo of Mom in front of the "Hollywood" sign on the pink Bristol board, reliving happy moments in my mind, Carol spoke sharply. "What are you doing?"

Huh?

"You're not seriously going to put that up, are you?"

Why not? Why is she so mad?

"Yes," I said.

Carol yanked the picture of Richard Gere and Mom off the board, tearing it, then yelled, "He is not a friend!"

I grabbed the photo out of her hands and shouted back. "She loved celebrities! If you don't know that about her, you don't know her at all! I don't have fuckin' children. This is what *we* did together, and she *loved* it!"

My whole body shook. I couldn't believe I'd yelled so loud. That I'd said "fuckin'" to my sister. She snapped something back that hit another nerve. I don't remember what it was. All I know is she had no right to tell me how to do my tribute to my own mother.

"You're just jealous you didn't get to go away with her!"

This time Carol didn't respond. She went into the kitchen and sobbed. I could see her through the '60s-style room divider, the open shelving filled with knickknacks between the dining room and kitchen. I don't think I'd ever seen Carol cry, not even when we were kids. To me she always seemed tougher than the rest of us.

I was sorry I'd raised my voice, but I did not understand why displaying pictures of our beautiful mother was a bad thing to do. Why was it wrong? I couldn't retract what I'd said. The damage was done. She'd really hurt me by telling me I couldn't share my photos. I was so shaken I hadn't considered that perhaps our father had heard us as he lay in bed upstairs. I could only hope his lorazepam had taken effect and he'd been asleep.

Carol had given my parents five grandchildren and was happily married to her college sweetheart. From my perspective, she had a perfect, traditional family life. Marrying at age forty-two and not having children hadn't been my ideal game plan, but that's how my life had turned out. The only reason I could think of for her anger was envy at the time I'd had with our mother. Carol was busy being a supermom, while I was treating our mother to fancy dinners and flying business class to California.

We both hurt like hell, and then we'd hurt each other. I felt awful.

My other sisters shared Carol's view and said I shouldn't put up a board with Mom on our trips. "They aren't family photos," they said. But their reasoning made no sense to me. Mom was in the photos. Why wouldn't they want glamorous photos of her on display? Dad didn't like to go out, except to a pub or to play golf or curl, but Mom enjoyed getting away from her routine of cooking and cleaning and found it exciting to dress up for the theatre or an elegant dinner. She got tremendous pleasure from sharing photos with her friends. And she loved to meet actors.

In 2002, when I was the rehearsal manager for *Chicago,* I took her on a tour of the prison set, where we found Richard Gere on a break, sitting in a jail cell, reading a newspaper.

"Excuse me, Richard, my mother would love to meet you."

Richard stood and asked in a friendly tone, "Where are you from?"

"Kingston," Mom said.

"I went to school across the lake from you, in Syracuse," he said.

An assistant director called him for rehearsal, so that was the end of our short chat, but Mom was thrilled.

As she and I made our way out of the studio, arm in arm, the leading ladies in 1920s garb walked in.

Catherine Zeta-Jones said to me, "Is that your mom?"

I nodded, smiling proudly.

"Well, hello, Catherine's mom!" Catherine shook Mom's hand.

Ecstatic, Mom squeezed my arm. Renée Zellweger and Queen Latifah said hello too.

In 2001, Mom flew to Los Angeles to attend the premiere of *Three*

Thousand Miles to Graceland, starring Kurt Russell and Kevin Costner. At the party afterwards, I seated my fashionably dressed mother at a round banquet table in the large crowded room, while Don and I went to the buffet. When we came back, plates in hand, a man was leaning over talking to my mother. It was Kevin Costner.

"Mom! How did you get him to come to you?" I asked after he'd left.

Giddily she answered, "He was standing behind me, so I just patted him on the bum." My mother had patted Kevin Costner's bum. Brazen. A trait I came by honestly. "He told me it was probably not one of his best movies for me to see." The film had vulgar language and was rather violent, but it was entertaining. "I told him, I don't care, I liked it!"

In 2003, I produced a low-budget film and wrote the screenplay based on Sarah Willis's coming-of-age novel *Some Things That Stay*, set in 1954. I cast Mom and several family members in a church scene as parishioners. Mom and I wore white lace gloves, pastel summer dresses and shell-shaped hats. She laughed, "I haven't worn a hat to church in thirty years!"

Nancy, her husband Pete, and my nieces Cedar and Marley sat in the front row with Mom and me. Deb and my niece Brittany sat a couple of rows back beside the attractive young actor Kevin Zegers. Mom glanced back at Kevin and said to me, "Can I get a picture with him?"

I wanted to be in the movie with them, so I gave myself a line in a scene during mass when parishioners offered up their intentions.

Holding Mom's hand, I said, "I'd like to pray for my father, who had a heart attack." I reminded Mom not to smile as I was saying my line. When the film came out, she alerted her friends: "I wasn't supposed to smile, because my husband had a heart attack. That's why I look so sober." Unfortunately, you can't really see Mom's face, because she took my direction too seriously and held her gaze downwards for the short scene. But at least I had Mom forever on celluloid, holding my hand.

Mom was paid eighty bucks cash that day, but she refused to keep it. Instead she handed it to me. "Here, put this back into your movie." That gesture was both thoughtful and comical, as if eighty dollars would make a huge difference to our $80,000-a-day production cost. When the DVD was released, I tried to give her a free copy, but she refused, declaring adamantly, "I want to buy my own. To support your film."

The night before the accident, she'd said excitedly, "Don't forget to bring the pictures from New York. I want to take them to the next luncheon." Mom belonged to a group of senior friends called the Lunchabouts, who met once a month.

"Oh, and that picture with Harry Connick? Can you tell it's him?"

I smiled to myself. "Yes, Mom, you can tell."

"Oh goody," she said.

The following spring, I would dine with the Lunchabout ladies at Swiss Chalet. I shared Mom's California and New York photos with them. They were delighted to view the adventures of their beloved friend.

Mom had loved to show off her photos to her friends. And I loved to show off my mother.

MY FIRST TIME seeing a dead body was at my second funeral, for my grandpa, Bert Scullion. He died October 9, 1967, at sixty-two years of age. I was ten.

My mother's birth father, Bernard Tuepah, died of pneumonia also on October 9, but in 1929, at the age of twenty-three, when Grandma was seven months pregnant with Mom. Grandma supported Mom and Uncle Don by working as a midwife. While going through Mom's belongings, I found a small booklet in which Grandma listed the names of all the babies she had helped bring into the world. Grandma didn't marry Grandpa Scullion until my mom was twelve years old. I could only imagine how difficult it would've been for Mom not to have a father until she was almost a teenager. I couldn't imagine life without my dad at all. It must have been hard on Grandma as October 9 approached each year. She died at sixty-seven years old on October 6, 1976.

The visitation for Grandpa Scullion was in their house in the small community of Tamworth, Ontario. The big old house had once been a train station. The railway sign announcing "Tamworth" still hung on the exterior brick wall. There was a water pump on the front lawn, and I have a picture of Mom in her late teens posing flirtatiously in a two-piece swimsuit, one hand on the pump, one foot resting on the tap. The interior ceiling was high, but other than that, any signs that it had been a train station were long gone. A red shade over a black jaguar lamp cast an eerie glow in the living room. People were smoking, drinking, laughing, as if it were a party, even though Grandpa's deceased body was right there in the open casket.

From a couple of feet away, I peered at Grandpa lying in the ivory-satin-lined coffin. His hands were folded across his chest, a burgundy bead rosary threaded through his thick fingers, his skin greyish, lips and eyes closed tight. Mom, wearing a dark bouclé suit and black pumps, took my hand and guided me onto the kneeler in front of the coffin. She blessed herself, then prayed, quietly mumbling a Hail Mary, her rosary dangling from her fingers. She did not cry.

After saying goodbye to Grandpa, Carol and I, and I think my brother Dave, were sent to play with our cousins, the Lymans. We walked about a kilometre on the moonlit country road to their house. There we laughed and engaged in silly shenanigans, as only cousins do. We did not cry either.

When I was little, Grandpa would bounce me on his knee, slowly at first. "This is the way a lady rides," he would say. Then his knee would bounce a bit faster. "This is the way a gentleman rides." Then I would grab his forearms to steady myself, and he'd bounce me higher. "And this is the way a farmer rides!" When I visited Grandma the next summer, I missed my Grandpa, but I don't remember being too sad. Though I loved Grandpa very much, he wasn't *my* dad.

THE FUNERAL DIRECTOR greeted my sombre family, thirty-six of us, in the lobby of Tompkins Funeral Home, then led us into the room to view Mom's and Julie's bodies. As if in a trance, my siblings and I shuffled toward the open caskets. The coffins were placed end to end, with Mom's feet at Julie's head. Holding my husband's hand tighter than I ever had, I remained strong, not allowing my sadness to reveal itself.

The first casket was my mother's. Her eyes were sunken and shut so tightly that only a hint of her eyelashes was visible. I found out later that she no longer had eyes. They'd been donated for research. Mom wore the coordinating pink stone necklace and earrings I'd given her.

I stepped aside and whispered to the funeral director, "Please, Ian, I would like Mom's necklace after the wake."

The mortician had removed the red nail polish Mom had been wearing for Julie's party and painted her nails pink to match her burial outfit. The pink was too pale, though. Her suit was a deep pink, not baby girl pink. Mom would have continued to shop until she'd found the perfect matching shade. Her suit jacket was buttoned all the way up. She never buttoned up her suit jackets. Mom wouldn't have been happy about that. Her hands were already set with her rosary draped through her fingers, so I didn't say anything.

We moved on to Julie's coffin. To hide the gash on her head, I'd asked Ian to have her hair swept to that side, different from how she usually wore it. Her face was perfect. Peaceful. She looked like she was sleeping, until my gaze travelled down her body.

When I chose the green ensemble, I'd completely forgotten about the organ donation surgeries. Her scoop-neck top exposed the stitched incision where they'd taken out her heart and lungs. Her kidneys and liver now also gone, her pelvic bones protruded, and her torso was sunken like the Scarecrow without his straw stuffing. Julie had weighed a mere eighty-seven pounds. With so many organs missing, there was not much left of her.

Nancy voiced her displeasure at the poorly masked scar. We stepped away while the staff applied more makeup.

I'd always thought touching a dead person would be creepy and that I wouldn't be able to do it. I was wrong. I wasn't the least bit hesitant to caress their faces or place my hand on their hands. It's not creepy at all when the dead are your loved ones. As if bidding them good-night, I leaned in and kissed their foreheads.

My family was huddled quietly, staring at the coffins, when the funeral director said, "Excuse me, I'm sorry, we have to open the doors now."

I realized Uncle Mike wasn't with us, so I left the viewing room to look for him. The lineup of mourners funnelled through the adjoining chapel. At the head of the aisle, between the chapel pews, they paused to sign the guest book for Mom. The guest book for Julie was presented at the front of the chapel, and six photo boards on easels lined the aisle between them. I spotted Uncle Mike deep in the lineup.

As I approached, a woman behind him pointed to my "Mom" board and said, "Is that Hilary Swank?"

Uncle Mike turned to her. "Yes, that's who it is."

"Mom met Hilary on the *Amelia* movie set," I said.

The woman's eyes widened, as Uncle Mike and I smiled at the treasured memory.

Hundreds came to offer their sympathies. People told me that they stood in line for an hour. That the lineup wound outside and halfway around the building. It included my nieces' basketball teams, neighbours, classmates, teachers, business colleagues, waitresses and bartenders from local pubs, our friends, old boyfriends and girlfriends, my parents' friends, Julie's friends. One of my mom's best friends, Joan, flew in from Regina. My cousin Bonnie came from Nova Scotia.

If they had died natural deaths, would so many have come? I wondered.

THOUGH I HADN'T SLEPT, I wasn't tired when I rose at seven the next day, the morning of the funeral. My mind was busy figuring out how to get through the day. Letting my husband sleep some more, I grabbed a terry robe from the hook behind the door and tiptoed down the hall. I peeked into Dad's room. He was still sleeping, Callie curled at his feet. Good. Julie's bedroom door was open. Solemnly I stood there barefoot for a few minutes just staring at her empty bed.

In the living room, I parted the white sheers on the front window. The eastern sky looked ominous, more like dusk than dawn. The sun hadn't yet risen above the roofline of the church across the street. Some of my family had been baptized or had had their First Communions and Confirmations at that church. When we were young, before any special ceremonies, Mom would line us up on the front porch, the morning sun glaring in our eyes, and Dad would take our photo: my sisters and me wearing identical dresses (made by Mom), white socks and T-strap shoes, and my brothers wearing identical shirts and grey flannel pants. Maybe the sun didn't want to shine on our house on this particular day.

I looked past the road where their bodies had lain, past the empty church parking lot, and fixed my gaze on the oak doors through which their caskets would pass in a few hours. Four years earlier, on their fiftieth anniversary, my whole family had watched as Mom and Dad renewed their wedding vows in that church. Whenever I came home to visit, I'd attend the Saturday 5:15 p.m. mass with my parents and Julie. We always sat in the second-last pew on the right. Dad was an usher, helping people find seats and passing the collection basket between the pews, so it was more convenient for him to sit near the back. I would hold their hands during the Lord's Prayer. During the rite of the sign of peace, we hugged and kissed each other instead of shaking hands like most of the congregation.

The night before, I had answered the phone when Father Brennan called to ask if anyone would like to come and place the floral arrangements on the altar. Before answering him, I looked around the kitchen and living room. Every chair and sofa had a grief-stricken family member on it, a beer or wine glass in hand. Deadened eyes stared off into space or down at the floor. I couldn't bring myself to ask any of them. I didn't want to do it by myself either, so I asked a couple of my nieces to help.

The bulk of the flowers from Tompkins Funeral Home sat in a clump at the base of the altar, but our personal arrangements, *Mom, Sister, Wife* and *Daughter*, were reserved for their gravesite.

Father Brennan excused himself, leaving us to complete the task. I directed the girls to move the flowers from one spot to another and back again, several times, trying to get them to laugh. I couldn't believe I was arranging flowers for the funeral of my own mother and sister. It was as if a funeral planner had temporarily inhabited my body.

Before the service, we went to the funeral home for our last look at their bodies. Each member of our families got a moment alone to say goodbye.

I stepped up to Mom's casket first. Don and his children stood behind me. I didn't hold my gaze too long on Mom's face, because I didn't want to remember her like that, with a sallow skin tone and her eyelids glued shut. I placed the photo of Uncle Mike, Mom and me from our recent trip to New York in her casket, then leaned in and kissed her forehead. I rested my hand on hers, caressed her cold fingers. Tears rimmed my eyes as I struggled to speak.

"Thank you for being my mom. I love you. Bye, Mom." There was so much more I wanted to say, but I felt uncomfortable with everyone listening and waiting on their turn. Besides, I would have the rest of my life to talk to her.

We moved on to Julie's casket. I laid a bottle of bubbly on the satin lining, the very bottle that had been in her birthday gift bag. I kissed her cool cheek and ran my finger down the tip of her little nose, like I used to do. I rested my hand on her rubbery, doll-like hands and squeezed lightly.

"I love you so, so much." I couldn't say any more without bursting into tears. I didn't want to leave her either, but I had to. The rest of my family had to say their goodbyes too.

As each of us took our turn, the others stood hushed in the viewing room. There were thirty-six immediate family members plus Aunt Joan, Uncle Mike, Uncle Don and Aunt Wilda. Forty of us standing, lining the room, silently staring at the coffins.

Before we left and made our way to the black stretch limousines, I asked the funeral director to please bring my mother's rings to me. Mom had told me that she wanted me to have the unique ring I had chosen from a diamond wholesaler friend of mine on behalf of Dad for their twenty-fifth wedding anniversary. Once seated in the limo, I noticed Debbie was wearing that ring. While I was in the ladies' room, the funeral director had given the rings to one of my other sisters to distribute. I wanted to say, *Sorry, I'm supposed to get that ring*, but I didn't. Instead I said, "It looks good with all your gold rings." I would be given Mom's fiftieth wedding anniversary ring instead, one she'd worn for only four years.

My sisters and I sat facing each other in the back of the limo, following the hearses. Our cousin Dave Burke worked at the funeral home, so we were blessed to have a beloved family member as our driver. It was the saddest of occasions, yet looking down at our feet, I couldn't help smiling. We weren't wearing traditional black pumps. Our shoes were all different colours.

My niece Brittany had come up with the idea of all of us wearing a pair of "Nanny's" shoes to the funeral. A fitting tribute, as Mom was a bona fide shoe-aholic. We added a line in the program that read: "There is no way we can ever fill Nanny's shoes, but for today . . . *we* are walking in them." Each of us—me, my four sisters, my sisters-in-law, my ten nieces, as well as my stepdaughters—walked up the aisle wearing a pair of Mom's shoes: pink, yellow, black, brown, silver, gold, turquoise, zebra print, red, and sparkly gold and silver ballet slippers. Not everyone wore Mom's size eight like Deb and I did, but the kids had stuffed the toes and plodded up the aisle in them as best they could. I wish I'd been mindful enough to have someone take a photo or video of our procession of rainbow feet. It would have been a cheerful memory from a devastatingly sad day.

The parking lot was packed, and the overflow of cars lined Days Road in front of our house. In the foyer of the church, Carol and I stood on either side of Dad, our arms around his. I remained composed until I saw Marguerite, a colleague, standing along the back wall. When our eyes met, she started to cry. The tears I'd been suppressing suddenly overflowed. Then, ever so slowly, we walked behind the two caskets that were being wheeled up the centre aisle.

I sat between Dad and Don in the front row beside the coffins. The rest of my family sat beside us or behind us. Every pew was filled. Mourners also stood, lining the back and side walls. Someone estimated about seven hundred people in attendance. My husband said to friends a couple of weeks later, "You'd think her family was royalty, there were so many people at the funeral."

The service started with the eulogies. Because my brother-in-law David knew of our mom's love of fashion, he stepped up to the altar to say his words of remembrance carrying one of her purses and with her pretty pink scarf slung around his neck.

My sister-in-law Barb gave a touching tribute to Julie in which she mentioned Julie's love of country music, especially Randy Travis. She referred to her singing as "joyful noise." I smiled recalling singing karaoke with Julie, and sitting beside her at mass listening to her proudly sing the hymns off key. Barb ended by saying, "Julie was the heart of the family." She most certainly was.

I held Dad's arm tighter and leaned into his trembling body as I listened to Shannon, who delivered her reading beautifully. My goddaughter Abbey sang "Here I Am, Lord." Clutching my husband's arm, I listened to her angelic rendition and cried.

I don't remember walking down the aisle and out of the church, but I do remember suddenly being outside and seeing throngs on the steps. As I approached the limo, I overheard a woman commenting on our multicoloured shoes. I looked up and saw my friend Georgina. I felt a spurt of pride. I balanced myself on the open door of the vehicle, lifted my right leg and pointed to my foot adorned with a grey-and-white plaid pump, a sparkly flower on the toe.

"Georgina, look! We're all wearing a pair of Mom's shoes!"

Georgina's eyes glistened. She was the costume designer who had fitted my mom in a '50s dress for the film *Some Things That Stay*, which I had produced.

Another woman overheard us. "That's why the shoes were so many different colours!"

EVEN THOUGH I was travelling behind the hearse that was carrying my mother's and sister's bodies to their final resting place, seeing so many in attendance at the funeral and the reaction to our Mom's shoes put my mind in a happy place for a short while.

St. Mary's Cemetery was a twenty-five-minute drive from the church. I didn't think many people would follow us, knowing they'd have to turn around and drive back to the church for the reception. But when I emerged from the limo, I saw that many had. Our cousins—the Tuepahs, Burkes and Gourdiers—and a few friends walked slowly toward the coffins and two mounds of dirt.

My arm linked in Dad's, with Don close behind, we stood in a semicircle around the open graves. Wooden crucifixes lay on top of the closed coffins.

A dilemma my siblings and I had faced was how to lay out the bodies in the ground. We'd asked Dad if he wanted Mom in the middle, and Julie on one side of her, with space for him on the other side. Or did he prefer Julie in the middle? Or did he want to be in the middle? Dad was too distressed to choose, so we decided for him. Mom would lie in the middle with Dad and Julie on either side.

Dad and Julie were dependent on Mom. She cooked their meals, bought their clothes, booked their doctors' appointments, helped Julie get dressed, reminded Dad to take his pills, even taught Dad how to use the TV remote. Or *tried* to teach Dad to use the remote. When he couldn't figure it out, he'd holler, "Neet!" Downstairs she'd go. She would touch a button, and his sporting event would appear.

Mom was their core, so it seemed fitting to have her in the middle. I envisioned Mom someday spreading her arms out wide and touching each of them as they lay there underground.

Father Brennan gave his last blessings and took the crosses off the coffins.

At the conclusion of the burial service, my siblings and I stood in a receiving line to greet the priest. Carrying the crosses in one hand, Father Brennan shook each of our hands as he said something. A short blessing? I don't remember. After shaking my hand, he turned to my dad, who was at the end of the line. He placed Mom's and Julie's crucifixes in Dad's hands.

By the time we returned to the crowded banquet hall, the plates of party sandwiches and desserts were half empty. I couldn't eat anyway. What I really needed was to drink something stronger than a cup of tea.

For a time, I was taken out of my grief, as relatives and friends I hadn't seen in years hugged me and shared happy anecdotes about Mom or Julie. But maintaining a cheery facade was draining. I couldn't wait to walk across the street to our home and kill some brain cells.

I DON'T REMEMBER if I drank wine or vodka. I only know I got drunk.

Three hours after burying Mom and Julie, a next-door neighbour, Randy, and my brother-in-law David sat in the living room playing guitars and singing soft rock tunes. If a stranger had stepped into our living room, he would have thought it was a birthday party or another event befitting a celebration. There were kids running around, women in black dresses and high heels drinking wine, men in suits drinking beer, reminiscing and releasing occasional bursts of restless laughter.

My gaunt dad sat in the corner, beer in hand. I asked Randy if he knew "Hey, Good Lookin'," the song my parents had danced to at the Halloween party two weeks earlier. As Randy began singing, I reached my hand out to Dad, and we jived on the carpeted floor. Awkwardly I tried to follow his lead as he twirled me around, but I was nowhere near as good a dancer as Mom. Dad stopped suddenly, then looked at me, tears welling, and sat back down. I'd meant well, but requesting that song and asking Dad to dance hadn't been a good idea at all.

Doria, a friend who had travelled by train from about four hours away, asked if there was room for her to stay at the house. We certainly were not expecting houseguests, but Julie's bed was available, so I offered it to her, then headed upstairs to the bathroom. Unbeknownst to me, Teresa had overheard and followed me.

When I came out of the bathroom, she lashed out. "You're not going to let *her* stay in Julie's room!"

I was stunned by her outburst. In that moment, I didn't think it was wrong to share Julie's bed with a friend I'd known for twenty years and who'd travelled so far to attend the funeral. Doria had met Mom and Julie and had also become a good friend of Deb's.

"Why not?"

My mind was moving in a different direction than hers. There was a poster of Ryan Malcolm, the first *Canadian Idol* winner, taped on the outside of Julie's bedroom door. I ripped it off.

"Julie is dead! I bought Julie that mattress last year, and my friend should be allowed to sleep on it!"

Teresa yelled, "You don't have kids, you wouldn't understand!"

Why had she said that? Didn't she know how cruel it was to throw that at me?

From the bottom of the staircase, Don had overheard everything. He came up and spoke calmly to Treas. "Julie's your sister, not your child. No one loves Julie more than Catherine."

Don was my hero in that moment, but despite his trying to make me feel better, Treas's words wounded me so much that I ran downstairs to the living room. Dad was sitting in the corner, my mom's best friend, Joan, on a dining room chair close beside him—both so stricken they weren't even talking to each other, just staring straight ahead. I thought, *How is he ever going to survive this?* I marched out the front door into the darkness and stood in the middle of the road where my mother and sister had been struck. Oblivious to my young nieces and nephews on the front lawn, I hollered up to the black sky, to God, "Why the fuck didn't you take them all?" Up the street I could see a car approaching, but I didn't move. My breathing became shallow and fast. Huffing, I yelled, "Can you see me?" The headlights loomed closer. *"Can you?"* My brother-in-law Pete yanked me out of the path of the oncoming car and hugged me. I was a drunken, weeping mess.

Teresa and her husband scolded me because I'd put on my hysterical wailing show in front of their kids. Yes, it was stupid to stand in front of an oncoming car. The alcohol and grief cocktail had caused my erratic behaviour.

In retrospect, I'm sure Treas was thinking of how it would affect our father. And maybe if I *were* a mother, I wouldn't have suggested our friend sleep in Julie's bed. I don't know. All I had wanted to do was help out a friend who'd come to mourn with us. My grieving heart and inebriated brain weren't thinking about whether or not my gesture would upset anyone.

To keep the peace and be the big sis to a grieving younger sis, I asked Doria to sleep on a forty-year-old bunk bed mattress in the dusty bedroom downstairs.

Nobody slept in Julie's bed that night.

Chapter 5

Don didn't want me to leave Toronto, but he understood why, for at least a couple of months, my cats and I had to move in with my father.

Once settled, I tried to put some normalcy back into my life. I'd set my alarm for 6:30 a.m., so I could get some work done before the phone started ringing, usually by nine every day. Dad would come downstairs a few minutes later in plaid flannel pyjama bottoms and undershirt. He'd make coffee, grab the paper off the front porch and read for a while. Sometimes he'd share local news stories. He usually went back to bed around seven thirty to nap for another hour or so. I'd try to get him to stay awake until eight o'clock, when he had to take his first pill of the day, but that rarely happened. I wasn't a very strict nurse.

In August that year, when I'd come to pick up Julie for her summer vacation, Mom had taught me Dad's pill regime. Standing at the sink in front of the kitchen window that was topped with a blue and white valance, she pointed to a yellow plastic pillbox on the laminate countertop. The kind with days-of-the-week compartments. She vented in a friendly manner. "I bought him this pillbox and put this note right up here." She pointed to the side of the cupboard where she'd posted a note showing the prescribed quantity and the times: 8 a.m., 12 p.m., 4 p.m. and 8 p.m. "And he *still* forgets to take them!" He was supposed to take the first pill an hour before breakfast, and the calcium tablet was to be taken four times a day. There was a daily pill for his Parkinson's. I can't remember what the yellow pill was for. Lorazepam was added to the 8 p.m. pills after Mom and Julie died.

One day during that visit, Mom and I were sitting at the kitchen table, drinking a cup of tea and chatting, when Dad sauntered in nonchalantly.

"The wills are up there, Cath," he said, pointing to the cupboard over the fridge.

I raised my eyebrows quizzically.

"Um. Okay, Dad."

He grabbed a handful of Chips Ahoy! cookies out of the cupboard and went downstairs.

Sounding as if I'd won a prize, Mom announced, "Oh! We wanted to have our eldest child and eldest son as executors, but since Dave's as sensitive as your father, we made you and Barb executors."

The wills had been there for years, yet Dad had chosen to tell me where they were hidden only two months before the accident.

THE INVESTIGATING OFFICER called a couple of days after the funeral. "We found red plastic pieces on the driver's car, one an elongated piece and another one that seems to be broken. I'm wondering if these were from the accident or something else."

I said, "They could be from Mom's earrings. She was wearing red dangly earrings."

"Okay. Thank you."

I had to ask. "Officer, who hit them?"

Without reluctance, he gave me her name.

The driver was an elderly woman, almost eighty-five years old. Though she lived less than two kilometres from our house, I didn't know her. I hoped my parents didn't know her either. As difficult as it already was for everyone, I couldn't imagine accidentally killing a friend or acquaintance.

"When can I have their clothes?"

His pause told me he hadn't seen that question coming. "As soon as we've finished our investigation."

I wanted to see what Julie was going to wear to her fortieth birthday party. I wanted to hug their clothes.

After the call, I went upstairs to check the plastic bag of Mom's items given to us at the hospital. The red pieces weren't from her earrings, but two pieces were missing from her bracelet. I'd forgotten about that. Mom's arm must have smacked the car or the pavement, sending the plastic gems from her bracelet flying through the air.

Analyzing and talking about the accident was a bizarre part of my healing process. Little did I know how long and difficult that process would be.

ONLY FOUR DAYS had passed since we'd buried Mom and Julie, yet my niece Samantha found the strength to help coach Julie's Special Olympics basketball team. I wanted to meet Julie's friends and watch them play.

I'd seen Julie play basketball twice. Once I arrived in the middle of a practice. She saw me on the sidelines and stopped at centre court to wave to me. Once my brother Dave showed up late to a game, and Julie, during a play, ran to the sidelines and hugged him, announcing proudly, "This is my big brudder, Dave." The rest of the athletes stopped playing and waved, saying, "Hi, Dave, hi."

At the community gym downtown, I sat on the sidelines on a wooden bench with Mike, Sharon and my nieces Haley and Leslie. The athletes surrounded fifteen-year-old Samantha as she introduced herself. "I'm Julie's niece, Sammy." At the mention of Julie's name, a slender girl with big brown eyes and short brown hair started crying. Her name was Coreena. She had a learning disability but did not have Down syndrome.

We watched as the athletes warmed up, dribbling the ball and running around the court. After their pre-game warm-up, I walked over to Coreena. "Hi, I'm Julie's big sister, Catherine."

She extended her hand to shake mine. "Julie was my best friend. I miss Julie." She cried some more.

I clutched her hand in both of mine. Tears flowed down her cheeks into her mouth.

"She was supposed to go to my twenty-first birthday party next week."

At a loss for words, I was thankful the whistle blew to assemble the players.

Fighting to stay composed, I watched the athletes play for a while, proud of Samantha's strength, coaching her aunt's team so soon after the funeral of her aunt and grandmother.

A cute, blond girl named Anna dribbled the ball down the sideline in front of me. She reminded me of Julie. Too much. I couldn't handle it, so I kissed my family goodbye and left the gym. Night had fallen. I climbed into my truck and bawled most of the way home.

The next week I brought a gift bag for Coreena's birthday. The community centre lobby was bustling with excited athletes, but I spotted her easily.

"Hi, do you remember me, Coreena?"

She smiled. "You're Julie's sister."

"Happy birthday." I handed her my gift bag from Julie's surprise party. I'd put in a couple of Julie's tops, one of her necklaces, two of her country CDs, chocolate and an angel figurine from her bedroom.

Hesitantly she held up the necklace. "This was Julie's?"

"Yes, honey, but I know she'd like you to have it."

The tears came, and she hugged me.

I wanted to keep in touch with her, but I wasn't ready. At that early stage of grief, spending time with her would only have made me miss my sister more.

THE PREVIOUS SUMMER, Julie had spent five days with me at Woodhaven, our lakehouse two hours northwest of Kingston. That was the longest she'd ever been away from Mom and Dad. One of those days, I was standing at the kitchen counter putting together a small tray of dill havarti cheese and whole-grain crackers. She walked in, put her arms around my waist and gave me a tender hug.

I held her tiny body snugly against mine and kissed the top of her head. She patted my back ever so lightly. The kind of patting one does as if to say, *Everything's going to be okay*. Her random act of affection overwhelmed me so much. I remember thinking, *I've never felt this much love. This must be what it feels like to be a mom.*

Just as I'd been magically blessed with twelve days of adventures with Mom in 2009, I'd been equally blessed to have five days alone with my youngest sister in the last year of her life.

A FEW DAYS after the funeral, I was going out for a walk and noticed that the blood had finally disappeared from the road. Randy, our neighbour, dressed in faded jeans and a sweatshirt, was hauling trash to the end of his driveway. I hadn't seen him since he sang at our house the night of the funeral.

Greeting him, I said, "Thank you for bringing your guitar, Randy. It made our gathering feel more like a celebration of their lives, with the music and singing."

"You're welcome," he said, securing the lid on the garbage bin. He looked out at the road. "Lorraine and I were watching TV. I heard a loud whack and dashed out of the house."

I followed his gaze to the pavement.

"I didn't know it was your mom lying on the road until I got down on my knees beside her." *He was there?* "I took her hand." *What?* He turned toward me. "She squeezed my hand really hard . . . then she looked up at me with 'help me' eyes . . ."

My fingers splayed across my open mouth. I couldn't speak. We looked into each other's eyes, his brimming with tears.

"She was fighting really strong, Catherine. Then after a few seconds, her eyes rolled back into her head."

Mom had squeezed Randy's hand and fought to stay alive while lying on the pavement in front of her own home. Envisioning Mom's frightening last moments, I began to quiver. I took his hand and held it tightly with both of mine.

"Thank you" was all I could say.

A COUPLE OF WEEKS after the double funeral, I was in Julie's nursery-sized bedroom, sitting on her bed, a white plastic laundry basket at my feet.

Looking up at the darkened television screen, I remembered when Julie had a twelve-inch RCA. In 2004, I'd swapped it out for my old twenty-five-inch Sony. She'd proudly told everyone she had her own "big-screen TV." She'd spend five hours a day watching soap operas, sitcoms, horror films or reruns of *Dallas*. My heart ached as I folded my dad's white briefs.

Seeking a distraction, I turned the television on to the local news channel, the volume barely audible. As the community announcements scrolled across the screen, I pulled Dad's navy golf shirt out of the basket and thought of my mother. She used to watch this channel while she folded laundry, checking the weather five times a day, even if she wasn't planning to go outside.

The television wasn't helping me feel better. I was in my parents' home on a Tuesday, folding my father's laundry because my mother and sister were dead. I placed the folded clothes on the mint green comforter and looked around the room.

A poster of the character Paul from *The Young and the Restless* made me smile as I recalled how excited Julie was to get his autograph. A collage on a corkboard revealed more Julie memories: swimming in my pool, in the hot tub with my husband, petting my cat, Julie as a bridesmaid at my wedding. A slew of country CDs and horror movie DVDs and VHSs filled her bookcase.

There was a white plastic headband on her dresser. She wore headbands to keep her thick brown hair out of her eyes. I picked it up, squeezed the ends together. While I was reminiscing about the many times I'd washed her hair, I heard a faint voice.

"Hello?"

Was that Dad? I heard it again, a timid, stuttering "He-hello?"

Anxiety enveloped my body. The open bedroom door was visible from the bottom of the four-step carpeted staircase, but I was not. I had to reveal myself. I finished rolling up a pair of black socks, then braced myself and stepped into the hall. There he was, my six-foot-tall dad, standing at the bottom of the stairs, his hands in the pockets of his baggy blue jeans. His sorrow-filled eyes told me what I already knew.

It was not me he was hoping to see.

I told my tears to build a dam.

"Hi, Dad." That was all I could muster. I couldn't find healing words or witty words either. Words wouldn't change anything.

Julie was not in her bedroom watching soap operas, and she never would be again. Instead, his eldest child was in his youngest child's room, doing housework his wife would normally be doing. His new reality was literally staring him in the face.

Dad simply said, "Hi, Cath," and went back downstairs to attempt to watch *Matlock*.

I went back into Julie's room, lay down in a fetal position, hugged her pillow and let the dam break.

FOR WEEKS after the funeral, friends and relatives dropped by the house every day and early evening. They meant well, but Dad didn't want constant attention. He wanted to be left alone. I tried not to bother him unless I had to remind him to take his pills. I'd sit on the sofa in the living room working, while Dad, in his jeans, sweater and slippers, sat in Mom's chair in the corner reading the paper. We could be quiet together.

One evening Dad said, "Do you think we'll ever hear from her?"

I knew he meant the driver who had struck them down like bowling pins. I had wondered, too, if the driver would ever reach out to us.

"She never even apologized, Cath."

I didn't believe it to be true, but trying to make an excuse for the driver, I said, "She's probably not allowed to contact us, Dad, until the investigation is over. The lawyers probably won't let her."

He stood up and looked out the window to the street, the street-lights lighting up the area where his beloved wife and daughter had been killed.

"She should apologize, Cath."

Though she never attempted to contact us, I had an uncontrollable urge to let her know that we knew it was an accident.

DAD WAS THE BENEFICIARY of my mother's and Julie's estates, so he had to accompany me to close their bank accounts. We sat across the desk from a young man in a suit. I placed the two death certificates in front of him.

Before we had a chance to speak, the man expressed his condolences.

Dad said, "My wife died."

The banker and I exchanged awkward glances. Dad often talked about Mom, saying he missed her, that he couldn't live without her. But he could not acknowledge Julie's death.

I bent over to put my large handbag on the floor and noticed that Dad was wearing his slippers. Driving back home, he suggested we go to the Oarsman. It was 11 a.m.

"Let's go home for a bit, then go over for lunch," I suggested. I didn't want Dad to feel embarrassed if he caught someone looking at his feet and then noticed he hadn't put his shoes on. I was here to take care of him, so I wasn't going to let that happen.

DAD NEEDED SOMEONE to live with him, but the more time I spent in Kingston, the less support I received from my husband. I knew Don missed me, but I was the only one of my siblings with neither young children nor an office job. Living with Dad was where I wanted to be. I also craved the comfort of my mother's and Julie's presence in my childhood home.

Don was still in production on his movie in Toronto, working thirteen to fourteen hours a day. Those hours weren't new to me; I was a second assistant director and often worked fifteen-hour days. On rare occasions, more. I'd been living with Dad barely two weeks when Don called and said he needed me to come back and finish choosing the decor for our bathroom renovations. I asked if we could postpone it.

He answered briskly, as if I were staff. "No. The workers have been booked for the month. I can't cancel. We have to finish it now."

No sugarcoating. No *Sorry, honey.*

I was upset but too sad to argue. I don't like being mad. It makes me uneasy. Why didn't he understand that my brain was so foggy I didn't know if I could even do it? Carol was able to come and stay with Dad, so two days later I drove back to the big city.

I'd designed most of the master bath already, but everything needed to be chosen for the guest bath: floor tiles, backsplash tile, a tub, hardware. I set off to do the task.

A stunning display of jade green marble greeted me as I entered the tile store. Natural stones, ceramic and glass tiles in far too many colours to choose from. A twenty-something salesgirl in heels and a little black dress approached.

"Can I help you?"

She could not. "I'm good, thanks."

Circling back to the green display, I made it simple. Green and white, clean and bright. A white cabinet with glass knobs, a backsplash of one-inch tiles with shells in them, a white tub and green marble tiles on the floor with green accents in the white-tiled shower. Done.

I had made a career change from sales to filmmaking at thirty-seven years old, and Don knew I enjoyed my work. I loved the rush, creativity and comradeship of the film industry so much, I didn't even mind getting up at 4:30 a.m. At least Don's pushing me to finish designing our bathrooms forced me to do something besides grieve and worry about my father and siblings.

Early the next morning, I propped myself up on the big pillows on my side of the bed. Don sat on the other side, putting on his shoes, getting ready to head off to the set.

"I need to go back," I said softly. I'd been in Toronto for two days.

He stood up, turned around and yelled, "What are you going to do? Move in with him?"

His outburst startled me. It hadn't even been three weeks since the funeral. Don adores me, but he was so blinded by the thought of my leaving him to live with my dad that anger was his only recourse. There was no way my big, tough husband could admit that he was scared too.

DON AND I MET when I did a "daily" as Helen Mirren's stand-in on the set of the Sidney Lumet film *Critical Care* in November 1996. I was called in for one day, because her regular stand-in wasn't available. A stand-in is used to help the director of photography light the actor in a flattering way—for example, to help eliminate dark circles under the eyes of women of a certain age.

Don and I were the first ones back to the set after lunch. Standing five feet eleven, with fine chocolate brown hair long enough to graze the collar of his black suit jacket, he was a ruggedly handsome man. While I sat on the set chair reading the call sheet, he approached me, and we engaged in small talk. I haven't a clue what he said, because despite his obvious success, I wasn't interested in a hot-shot producer, especially one who lived in California. I was more attracted to clever jeans-and-T-shirt guys. Two minutes later, the crew sauntered in to set up the next shot. That was it for me on set that day. But not for Don.

The next day he asked the first assistant director, "Where's the blonde who was here yesterday?"

A couple of months later, he came back to Toronto to shoot *The Mighty*. I sent in my resumé, which included my assistant-director experience. I was hired for several days to help wrangle extras. Don asked me out twice, but I said no both times because I had other plans. I was glad I was busy. I did not want to start a relationship with someone who lived in Los Angeles.

On one of my set days, we were shooting outside the Eaton Centre in Toronto in minus-20-degree weather. The first assistant director posted me at the producer's monitor. Wearing my walkie-talkie head-set, I knew when the cameras were rolling, so it was my job to let the producers know when we rolled and cut. It was so cold that I wore a red one-piece ski suit and toque. One of the producers from Mira-max wore an Elmer Fudd–style hat, with the flaps over her ears. Don, in his Michelin Man poofy down coat and navy wool toque, teased her: "Where is that wascally wabbit?" I laughed along with them. I was so surprised to hear this big shot say "wabbit" that the third time he asked me out, February 10, 1997, I said yes.

I'm a sucker for intelligent men with a sense of humour.

HAVING LOST my appetite completely, within a month my five-foot, five-and-a-half–inch frame dropped to ninety-nine pounds. My father, somehow, retained an appetite. He had even eaten a vending-machine sandwich at the hospital the night of the acci-dent. Friends delivered food to the house: three hams, a cas-serole, pies. Mom's cousin Rita dropped off a cooked eigh-teen-pound turkey with all the fixings. We made Dad ham or turkey sandwiches for days. He'd meekly utter the sweetest "thank you" as if it were one word: "kew." Then he ate every bite.

To help manage my grief anxiety, I began drinking a couple of alcoholic drinks at the end of my day. I didn't drink until I passed out or anything like that. I drank enough to help release the constant tension in my body. A lot of people have a drink to reduce their stress at the end of their workday. My "work" at the time was being executor and trying to rewrite a bad horror script, while also grieving. Having a few drinks made me feel better, and thus began my daily healing ritual. My increase in alcohol consumption helped me get to 102 pounds, where I hovered for about a year. When people commented on how thin I'd become, I'd joke, "Yeah, as it turns out, alcohol doesn't have as many calories as everyone thinks."

ONE CLOUDY AFTERNOON at the end of November, Dad and I were sitting in the living room when we heard voices outside.

I peered out the window. A man and a woman, both wearing trench coats, were squatting at the end of the driveway taking measurements. I went out to see who they were.

They introduced themselves as investigators from the insurance company for the civil suit. I hazily remembered Don and my brother-in-law David having a conversation about suing the driver. The female insurance investigator asked if she could talk to Dad. I asked her to wait while I asked him.

"Dad, they're the investigators for the civil suit. You know, David and Don got it going to try to get you some money?"

He looked confused.

"The loss of care and companionship lawsuit. Remember? They want to know if they can ask you a couple of questions."

Dad had a vacant look on his face. We'd discussed it, but he'd forgotten. We were suing because if we eventually had to move Dad to assisted living, it could cost more than he could afford. He had been given a home evaluation test, doing ordinary activities—for example, cooking. He forgot to turn the element off. With his Parkinson's symptoms advancing, we were advised to install a hand-rail for the bathtub. In the end, it was recommended that my father should not live alone.

"Okay, I guess so," he responded.

I opened the screen door and beckoned them to come inside. Dad stood up to shake their hands, then sat back down in the corner chair. The investigators sat on the sofa, and I sat on the loveseat across from them. The woman was careful in her tone and choice of words when she questioned my father. I felt as if I were a bystander watching from behind two-way glass.

Dad had been walking home from church with Mom and Julie when they were struck. I have no idea how he was spared. He couldn't answer even one question that day. I guess his post-traumatic stress prevented him from remembering any details. I'm sure he didn't want to remember. I must have been stressed as well, because later I couldn't remember anything they asked him.

A WEEK LATER, December 8, would have been Mom's eightieth birthday. My relatives in Kingston and I went to the gravesite. There was no headstone yet, so we laid our gifts on the mound of dead flow-ers and dirt: fresh flowers, a stone angel, ornament-sized high-heeled shoes and purse. I placed a wineglass with *I love you* painted on it. No one spoke. I looked around at my family's sorrowful faces, their eyes on the ground. Attempting to bring some joy to the moment, I sang, "*Happy birthday to you, happy birthday to you . . .*" No one joined me, but I finished the song anyway. "*. . . dear Mom, happy birthday to you.*" I don't remember my dad's reaction, but I remember the disoriented faces of my nieces looking at me, probably thinking, *How the heck can she sing at a time like this?* I have no idea either, but I'd always sung "Happy Birthday to You" to my mother, and I would continue to celebrate her future birthdays by singing to her. Singing brightens one's spirit. And mine needed brightening.

The next day, Dad noticed his wedding band wasn't on his finger. We looked everywhere in the house: the pipes under the bathroom and kitchen sinks, the garbage, his La-Z-Boy chair, under his bed. Nancy even borrowed a metal detector and searched the cemetery. No luck.

Though I liked the comfort of Mom's fiftieth anniversary ring, I slipped it off my middle finger. "Dad, would you like to have this? I could put it on your chain."

He took off the gold chain around his neck, the one Mom had given him for their twenty-fifth anniversary. I threaded it through the ring and put it back around his neck.

Later that evening, after everyone had left, Dad and I were sitting in the living room, in our usual spots. I heard his newspaper crinkle. I looked up from my computer to see the paper on the carpet and Dad making his way to the front window. He gazed out to the road.

How could he possibly continue to live at home with the constant reminder of the accident that killed his wife and daughter twenty steps from his front door? He turned to me, looking scared and angry.

"How good does a person have to be for bad things to stop happening to him?"

I gazed into his sad eyes and wondered the same damn thing.

DAD USED TO GOLF and was also a competitive curler until Parkinson's disease hit him shortly after he retired. Once the disease advanced, he spent most of his days in his La-Z-Boy watching sporting events, *Matlock* reruns or *Wheel of Fortune*. That December, I kept him company watching curling tournaments, for as long as I could take it. It wasn't that I didn't enjoy watching curling. I did. But Dad's hearing wasn't what it used to be. He turned the volume up extra loud to hear the players whispering to their teammates. The curlers wear microphones so the audience can listen to them discussing their strategies. Sometimes the participants forget they're on national television.

"Did he say what I think he said?" Dad once said.

"*Fuck?* Yep, he did," I said, smirking. My dad didn't use profane language except for the occasional *shit* and *damn*. I'd never heard him use the *f*-word.

We laughed. It was good to hear him laugh. There hadn't been much, if any, laughter in the house for five weeks. He seemed to be enjoying the game, and I'd had enough of the players chanting loudly "hard, hard," so I went to bed to read.

I'd only read a few pages when I heard Dad's slippers shuffling down the hallway toward my room. I thought he was going to say good-night from the doorway, but he surprised me by walking into the dimly lit bedroom. Only my reading light was on, so he didn't notice my suitcase jutting out at the foot of the bed. I opened my mouth too late to warn him. I winced as he tripped, his knees hitting the hardwood floor, his head narrowly missing the pointed corner of the bedframe.

In true fashion, Dad didn't get angry; he didn't say *shit* or *damnit* or *What the hell is that doing there?* He looked into my eyes and said, "I'm still falling for you, Cath."

And we laughed once more.

Chapter 6

Six weeks after the accident, Dave and Barb hosted Christmas dinner at their house—the house where we were to have celebrated Julie's birthday. Barb has collected snowmen figurines for decades, so this time instead of ghosts and plastic headstones, snowmen of all shapes and sizes decorated their home. Shiny bulbs and lights adorned the seven-foot spruce Christmas tree in the corner of the living room.

My married siblings who had moved out of Kingston usually didn't come home for Christmas. Twice after my marriage, Don's parents joined us in California, but other than that I always went to my parents' house for Christmas. For their anniversary in 2000, we had replaced their 1970s harvest gold stove with a more modern white one. Ever since then, Don had given Mom a welcome break by cooking the turkey himself. While Don prepped the bird, Mom and

I would sit at the kitchen table, peeling potatoes and tearing loaves of white bread into tiny pieces for the stuffing. Other siblings would bring a vegetable dish or a pie.

That first Christmas "after," my whole family was present, including Dad's sister, Aunt Joan. Thirty-two of us sat at three tables, flowing from the dining room into the living room. It warmed my heart to see us all together. It was sad, though, that Mom and Julie had to die in order for everyone to have Christmas dinner together.

Once we were seated and helping ourselves to mashed potatoes and turkey, Nancy pushed her chair back and stood up. There was a piece of paper in her hand, and her lips trembled as she spoke.

"I don't think it was coincidental that this letter from the Gift of Life arrived on our doorstep on Christmas Eve." Nancy shared the news of the gifts our special angel, Julie, had delivered to six people. A woman received Julie's heart, a man her liver, another a kidney and yet another her lungs. Two other recipients each received a cornea from her eyes.

I wondered who the recipients were. I wanted to meet the lucky ones who had a part of Julie inside them. I wanted to meet these people who were having a Merry Christmas.

ON BOXING DAY, sharp pains in my chest woke me about two in the morning. I lay there nervously, stream-of-consciousness rationalizations running through my head: *It's the middle of the night. I can't go to the hospital, because my sister's car is behind our car in the driveway. I'd have to wake her to get the keys. Dad's bedroom door's open because he's claustrophobic, and I don't want to risk waking him and then having him worry that his eldest child is possibly having a friggin' heart attack.*

I didn't want to worry anyone. Not even my husband. I took slow, deep breaths and lay awake the rest of the night, praying it was not my heart.

At six, I still had the dagger-like pains. I got up and dressed as silently as I could. I woke Don at seven and told him my chest pains were scaring me and that I wanted to go to the hospital. I didn't wait for his reaction. I went to Mom's room and woke up Deb to get her car keys. I wanted to leave before Dad woke up, but we didn't make it. That morning, Dad saw me as I passed by his room, wearing my coat.

"Where ya goin', Cath?"

I didn't look at him while spewing my lie. "Don wants to find a Starbucks."

As I was slipping my boots on by the front door, Dad, wearing only his white briefs, appeared at the bottom of the stairs. "You should check the phone book first, to see where it is."

That's my dad. Always wanting to help.

Hiding my eagerness to leave, I assured him that indeed it was a good idea. Then he went back to bed. I grabbed the phone book from our vintage '60s phone table, flipped to the page with the Starbucks listing. Then I purposely left it open near his reading chair. I hated lying to him.

As we got closer to the hospital, I felt worse. But it wasn't because of my chest pains. We were driving to the same hospital emergency department where Mom and Julie had been treated.

Mom had had her first heart attack in bed with me when she was fifty-two, the same age I was when Don took me to the hospital. Mom, Deb and Julie had come to Toronto to look for a wedding gown for Deb and bridesmaid dresses for Julie and me. I took them out to a classic steakhouse for dinner. Mom struggled to finish her filet mignon. She'd take a bite, put her fork down, chew, breathe, then eat some more. I told her she didn't have to finish. She smiled. "I don't want to waste it, honey. I don't get this kind of steak at home."

About five o'clock in the morning, I awoke to find her in her mauve sleeveless nightgown sitting on the edge of my queen-sized bed, massaging her chest. "I think it's indigestion," she said.

Teasing, I said, "I told you not to eat the rest of your steak." I tossed back the covers and went to pee.

When I returned, she was still sitting up, her hands on either side of her hips, bracing herself, taking quick shallow breaths. "Mom, if you can't sleep, then I can't sleep. I'm taking you to Emergency."

When my mother, who normally wouldn't leave the house unless her shoes matched her purse, grabbed my robe from behind the door and stepped into my terry slippers, I knew this was more than indigestion. We tiptoed past my sisters, asleep on the pullout sofa. As I was closing the apartment door, Deb's fingers suddenly appeared, holding it open. She peeked out. I could tell she was scared.

I whispered, "I'll call you."

The staff whisked Mom away in a wheelchair and asked me to wait in the lounge. It was empty, very odd for an emergency waiting room, but it was five thirty on a Sunday morning. I was only twenty-four and terrified. I couldn't call anyone yet. It was too early. I didn't want to worry my family, at least not until I found out what was wrong. I sat on the beige-vinyl–covered bench and prayed, repeating the Hail Mary over and over.

After about thirty minutes, a stocky middle-aged doctor came to me. "Your mother had a heart attack. We'll let you know when you can see her."

Do doctors take a Just Be Blunt course for speaking to families? Why hadn't she said *She's going to be okay* first?

It was time to call Dad. In 1981 there were no cellphones, so I used a phone booth by the entrance. I dug for coins in my purse. My parents didn't have a phone in their bedroom, so it took six rings for Dad to answer the one at the bottom of the stairs.

"Dad, hi. Um . . . She's okay, but Mom had a heart attack."

I told him not to worry, that she was stable. I called Debbie next, and then plunked in more coins to call Carol, who had married and moved to Ottawa. The rest of my siblings still lived at home.

A half hour later, Deb and Julie joined me in the waiting area. The rest of my family drove from Kingston (three hours) and Ottawa (five hours) and arrived before noon. The staff had been running tests for several hours and still hadn't let us see her.

Finally a nurse came out and said, "Immediate family only can visit Mrs. Gourdier."

Dad and my seven siblings filed in and stood around her bed. Mom's face glowed as she looked at us. The nurse saw the crowd and said, "I'm sorry, only immediate family members are allowed."

Mom laughed. "This *is* my immediate family." Then, "Cath, can you get me my lipstick out of my purse, please?"

Mom was going to be just fine.

She had been a smoker for thirty years, but the doctor advised her that if she wanted to live to see her grandchildren, she'd have to quit immediately. She quit that day and lived to see sixteen grandchildren and meet my three stepchildren. I remember Mom saying to me after that experience, "No one told us back then that smoking was bad for you. If they had, I never would've started."

Now, twenty-seven years later at the same age, I, too, thought I was having a heart attack. After I described my symptoms, the nurse at the reception desk asked my name.

"Catherine Gourdier," I said.

She looked up from her paperwork. "How's your father doing?" She must have known who I was because Mike and my sister-in-law Sharon both worked at Kingston General Hospital. Or because the accident had been front-page news.

Because of the threat of a heart attack, I was admitted promptly. I grasped Don's arm as we walked through the emergency ward to a bed surrounded by pale pink privacy drapes. I lay down and leaned back on the propped-up pillows. Directly across from me were the beds where Mom's dead body and Julie's comatose body had lain. I had a flashback of my family weeping uncontrollably.

I said to Don, "That's where Julie was, where those nurses were talking about her dentures." A shiver crept up the back of my neck.

A young nurse taped sensor pads on my chest, then left me lying there for about an hour. Don waited with me. By then he really needed that phantom Starbucks coffee. And a painkiller. He'd bruised his hip quite badly slipping on a patch of ice Christmas night while walking Dad out to his car. In the hospital bed, I was quite comfortable; Don, on the leanly padded visitor chair with his sore hip and no caffeine, was not.

Two hours later, the nurse peeled off the patches monitoring my heart and helped me onto a gurney. I gazed up at the ceiling and listened to the chatter of the nurses and doctors while being wheeled down the halls into the elevator and eventually to the X-ray room. My anxiety lessened. It felt good to have someone taking care of me.

I was back in the emergency bed shortly thereafter. It had now been three hours since we'd arrived, and Don was getting more restless by the minute. His distaste for the vending-machine coffee did not help his mood.

At the five-hour mark, a handsome middle-aged doctor in a white coat approached and grasped the chrome rail at the end of my bed. "Hi, I'm Dr. O'Brien, a friend of Sharon's. I'm sorry for your losses." *Everyone knew.* "You've had a major anxiety attack. They often feel like a heart attack."

He gave me one lorazepam to take immediately and four to take home. "If you feel it coming on again, take one or half of one."

I felt like saying, *Didn't you mean to give me forty? Surely, not just four?*

We had left my parents' house around 7:30 a.m. and didn't get back until 1:30 p.m. Don went straight upstairs to pack his things. Dad said the gang had gone to Jack Tuesday's pub for brunch. I wondered why they'd left Dad alone. Hadn't Deb told them we'd gone to the hospital? Had Dad waited at home for Don and me? Was that why he hadn't gone to the pub? Even while grieving, he rarely said no to a trip to the pub.

My out-of-town siblings were leaving Kingston within the hour. Teresa's family was off to their cottage, Carol's family to oversee kitchen renovations, and Deb and Dave had New Year's plans.

Don came downstairs carrying our suitcases.

Dad turned to me, his eyes wide. I'll *never* forget the fearful tone in his voice.

"You're not leaving today too, are you, Cath?"

Oh no. My plan was to move back in with Dad on January 2, when the children had to go back to school and my siblings to work. I'd had no idea everyone was leaving.

I didn't know what to say. I didn't want to leave him. I shot a pleading look at my husband. Standing behind Dad so he couldn't see, Don mouthed the words, "We're leaving."

Three days with the grieving in-laws was enough. Don worked hard and deserved some downtime. He didn't have the yearning to stay that I did, because Dad was *my* father, not his.

WE'D INVITED FRIENDS well ahead to our annual New Year's celebration at Woodhaven, our lakehouse. I hadn't called it off, because I needed the camaraderie and distraction of hosting our friends. I would have cancelled our plans and stayed with my father had I known earlier that everyone would be going back home. I was reassured, however, because Nancy, Dave and Mike lived close to Dad and would certainly be checking on him.

We arrived at the lake to find a phone message from Dad. My cell number is in my parents' phone book, but Dad had dialled the lakehouse number instead. He'd wanted to let us know we'd forgotten to close the tailgate on the truck. He had no way of knowing that a passing car had informed us at the first traffic light. He wasn't used to leaving messages on answering machines. I grinned when I heard his message. He sounded like he was paging someone over a department store intercom:

"Cath, call your dad. Cath, call your dad."

It had been less than three hours since I'd left him, but I was so happy to hear his voice.

Chapter 7

The next morning, while I draped silver garland over the fireplace mantel, my thoughts drifted back to Dad. I took a break and sat in my cottage chair. How did I ever think I could throw a New Year's Eve party only seven weeks after the accident? Life must go on. My head got that. My heart didn't.

I called him at eleven thirty a.m. on December 30. I know the precise time, because it was a Wednesday. For fifty years, Dad and his best friend Ron McCormick had gone to the Portsmouth House for a beer on Wednesdays. Since their retirement, Ron would pick him up at about eleven thirty. They'd have two beers, then come home. The phone must have been on Dad's lap, because he answered on the first ring.

"Is Ron coming today?" I asked.

"I think so. I'm waiting for him to call."

"Good. That's good. I just wanted to say . . ." I couldn't get the words out. I started crying, but did my best to hide it. "I'm thinking of you all the time, Dad." I didn't want him to hear me cry, so I used the line he always used with me. "I better let you go, so Ron can call you."

The home phone didn't have call waiting, call display or voice mail. Dad was not a phone talker either. He always had short, to-the-point conversations, but that day he surprised me by prolonging the call.

"How's Don's hip?"

"It's still black and blue. The massage therapist who was here this morning said it would be about a week before he felt better." I was surprised Dad remembered that Don fell.

"Well, you be sure to tell him I asked after him."

I was glad he couldn't see the tears in my eyes. I wanted to sound chipper but couldn't, and I stumbled through my words. "I'll see you Sunday. Bye, Dad. I . . . I love you so much." I had said "love you" to him many times but had never before added "so much."

"Same here, Cath. Same here."

He usually said "Love you too," but that day maybe saying those three words would have made him cry too.

OUR FILM INDUSTRY FRIENDS arrived at the lake that afternoon just in time for cocktail hour. Louise, with her cropped blond hair, is a special effects makeup artist (blood, scars, zombies). Her husband Ray, who sports an English moustache, long and full with the ends twisted tight, is a sculptor. Ken, of slight build with a full head of bleached blond hair, is a composer, and his slender, brunette wife Michele is a writer.

After dumping their overnight bags in the guest rooms, we put on our boots and walked the snow-covered driveway to Tequilaville, our Mexican-themed games room, about a hundred steps from the main house.

Green, blue and yellow margarita, martini, wine and highball glasses brightened the lit glass cabinet shelves behind the pine bar. A pool table sat centred on the cork floor, with a shuffleboard and foosball hockey game on either side. Teal walls splashed with multi-coloured ceramic geckos, our keepsakes from several trips to Mexico, gave the room an island feel. When Mom last visited the lake, I'd shown her a large, weather-resistant gecko I'd bought at HomeSense. I told her I was hoping to find another one to hang alongside it on the exterior wall of the building. After she died, I was so touched by the surprise she'd left me. Wrapped in tissue paper under her bed was the exact gecko I'd wanted.

My friends were enjoying their cocktails, I was inserting a classic rock CD into the player and Don was taking the cover off the pool table when the phone rang. Call display showed it was my sister-in-law Barb. I'd had a couple of sips of my martini. Dopamine and serotonin had kicked in and was making me feel happy.

"Well, hello there!"

In her sweet, soft voice she said, "Hi, Cath. Are you alone? Is Don with you?"

Why is she asking me this?

"Cath . . . your dad died."

I screamed, fell to my knees, dropping the handset onto the floor. Don picked it up, but the line had been disconnected. I started sobbing while my friends and Don stood there watching me, wondering what was wrong. Before Don could ask, the phone rang again. Don answered. Barb had called back to give more details. My reaction had petrified my husband and friends. They didn't know what to do or say.

Returning to the house, I slumped down into my favourite chair. I took a big gulp of my martini to help me become the stoic sister once again. Then I called Carol.

While she cried, I couldn't stop talking. "Carol, you got to spend so much time with him. That was good, right? He was so sad. We can't do anything. You should stay home. I have friends here, I'm staying, and I'll go on New Year's Day, okay?"

I said that and meant it, because I was trying to convince myself there really was nothing we could do.

An HOUR LATER, Louise served her homemade chicken pot-pie dinner. Apparently it was delicious, but I barely touched it. My friends and even my husband didn't know how to act around this sad, upset person, so they all went to their rooms. I sat on a bar stool at the granite counter by the kitchen and opened my laptop. In my shattered state, I sent an email blast to my entire address book.

"My mom and sister were killed seven weeks ago, and my dad died today. Happy Fuckin' New Year!"

I hadn't meant to sound harsh. I was stunned. Sick. I felt robbed. The night Mom and Julie were hit, I don't think I drank any alcohol. I was too saddened. In my family, alcohol was usually associated with celebrations. But with the shocking news of Dad's death, I couldn't take it. I stayed up and got drunk, just as I had after my Mom's and Julie's funeral.

I'd planned to move back in with Dad in three days. Learning of his sudden death, my body and mind went deeper into shock. I wanted to hear him laugh one more time. I wanted to see him look in the mirror, comb what little hair he had, and say, "Damn, you look good!" I wanted to watch the women's finals curling bonspiel with him, with the volume so loud it hurt my ears. I wanted to join him for another beer at the Oarsman. I wanted to make him eggs the way he taught me, flipping them over easy without breaking the yolk. I wanted him to keep trying to teach me how to jive. I wanted more time with him.

I thought back to our telephone chat. How he'd told me to make sure to let Don know he'd asked about him. It almost seemed as if he knew he was going to die. I popped a lorazepam with my vodka soda. I knew I shouldn't mix booze with sleep aids, but there was no way I could sleep without drugs.

The next morning, I called Deb at her home in Burlington.

Reassuring her, as I'd try to reassure Carol, I said, "There's nothing we can do. His body is at the funeral home. We might as well stay at our own homes for New Year's."

An hour later, Mike, my youngest brother, called, crying. He said the same thing Julie used to say to me every week. "When ya comin' down, Cath?"

Am I needed? I want to be needed. Being needed gives me purpose. His tears went straight to my heart.

"I'll be there in three hours."

Don was unloading the dishwasher and had heard me. We didn't speak. I snuggled my face into his chest, while his muscular arms held me tighter than he'd ever held me before.

Without showering and dressed in jeans that were now two sizes too big, I packed some clothes and my cats and left my husband to celebrate New Year's without his wife. I don't know how he felt about my leaving, but I had no choice. I had tried to convince myself there was nothing I could do. And there *wasn't*, really, but there was no way I could be away from my brothers and sisters either.

I ARRIVED IN KINGSTON mid-afternoon and drove straight to Mom and Dad's to set up Callie and Freddy with litter, food and water.

The phone rang, and Barb said she'd be there in a few minutes to pick me up to take me to Nancy's, where our family was writing Dad's obituary.

Surrounded by her aunts, our niece Leslie sat at the kitchen table typing whatever they were throwing out to her. They struggled to find the right words for announcing Dad's sudden death. Sitting on the sofa in the living room beside Mike, I waited for a pause in their conversations, then said, "I started to write something this morning."

I had been inspired by something my cousin Margie had said to me seven weeks earlier. "I think your mom just couldn't go without Julie, Cath. I think she probably wrapped her arms around her and said, 'I'm taking you with me.'" I'd borrowed Margie's comforting vision and elaborated on it: *Mom wrapped her arms around Dad, Julie took him by the hand and together they took him to be with them in heaven.*

They loved it.

We had twenty minutes to make the deadline to get the obituary in the next day's newspaper. We double-checked what we'd written. Did we list all the children's and grandchildren's names? His siblings? The wake and the funeral times? Charitable donations?

I hadn't read many obituaries or paid attention to their content until after my parents passed, so I didn't realize we should have written about my father's life and character.

We hadn't mentioned that Dad was a competitive curler and had recently been honoured at the Kingston Curling Club with a lifetime membership. That he'd coached kids' baseball and played golf. That he'd been an usher at the church for forty-eight years. We hadn't written about his work or hobbies. But we *had* mentioned his legacy. All of us.

Once we finished, Barb and Mike drove me the few blocks home. The sun had set, and the house was pitch-black. Not even a light on outside. I kissed Mike on the cheek, thanked Barb and got out of the car. I walked up the cracked concrete walkway and entered the lonely house. No Mom to greet me. No background sound of televisions. Even my cats were nowhere to be seen.

I flicked on the hall light and climbed the carpeted stairway to Dad's bedroom. My parents' art deco master suite was the only furniture I ever remember seeing in their bedroom. I sat on the forest green plaid comforter that covered his bed. I looked around the room. Over the headboard hung an eleven-by-fourteen-inch framed photo of his six-foot-three father in full 1930s curling attire. He died at age thirty-six, due to complications from appendicitis surgeries, when my father was only six years old. His obituary read, "Earl Gourdier was a young man of the most likeable disposition, always cheerful." We could've written the same words about Dad.

There were plastic sculpted faces of Jesus and Mary in brown diamond-shaped frames on the wall over his night table, and, on Mom's side, a collage of photos of Mom and Dad with their friends. His sliding closet door was open, suits and shirts crammed into the small space. On his dresser were coins in an antique glass dish and a Black Velvet whisky container he used as a piggy bank. I picked it up. It must have had five pounds of coins in it.

Exhausted, I lay down on the bed, rested back on the pillows and closed my eyes. I knew Dad had wanted to join Mom and Julie, but I wasn't ready to say goodbye to him. I thought of the times I'd sat on the edge of his bed, kissed him good-night and listened to him say, "I can't live without her, Cath." I knew he felt the same about the Julie but couldn't bring himself to say her name out loud.

The sound of a car door slamming startled me. I sat up and peered out the window. Cars were pulling into the church parking lot. I looked at my watch: 5:10. *Of course.* Mom and Dad would have been attending the 5:15 mass. I needed to go. I didn't care that I didn't have any makeup on and was wearing baggy jeans. I didn't want to be late.

I went to the front hall closet, where Mom, Dad and Julie's coats still hung. We didn't want Dad to look at an empty closet, so we hadn't cleared out their coats. I grabbed my long, dark green coat, plopped a wool hat on my head and stepped out into the cold darkness.

Then it hit me.

I have to cross the road.

I could see the yellow glow of light from inside the church. God was right over there, but I was afraid to cross alone. He hadn't helped Mom and Julie get to the other side. And I'd have to walk across the pavement where Julie had lain. I couldn't do it.

I went to Randy's house next door, knocked and nervously waited. I hoped I wasn't interrupting him and his wife. He opened the door.

"Hi, Randy, I'm sorry for bothering you, but I want to go to church and . . . um, would you mind escorting me across the street?"

"Of course not," he said. He grabbed a parka off a hook on the wall and slipped it on over his jeans and T-shirt. I put my left arm through his, my right hand too, grasping his arm.

As we walked, he said, "Every day when I look out the window, I'm reminded of that night, your mom squeezing my hand, her eyes rolling back. I have nightmares about it."

I didn't know how to respond, so I squeezed his arm to acknowledge what he'd shared with me.

When we got to the church steps, his eyes welled up. I embraced him. With my head on his shoulder, he said, "I'm gonna miss your dad."

Once inside, I saw that "their" pew near the back was empty. How conveniently odd, considering the church was quite full. I sat in Dad's usual seat by the aisle. I remained composed during the mass until Father Brennan said, "And we'd especially like to pray for Bill Gourdier."

Some people turned around and looked at me. His obituary hadn't appeared in the paper yet, so I hadn't expected to hear Dad's name aloud, confirming his death. I searched my pockets for a tissue. Tears spilled over my cheeks and down my throat.

After mass, a few people offered their condolences, lightly touching my shoulder. *Sorry for your loss, Sorry about your father.* I thanked them and stepped out through the centre doors. Standing on the church steps, I stared across the road at our split-level grey brick house, unable to move.

A man approached. "Hi, Catherine, I'm your Aunt Lola's nephew, Frank Halligan. Would you like me to walk you back?"

My father must have whispered in his ear.

"Yes, please."

I put my arm through his. Mindful of the cars exiting the parking lot, Frank walked me right to the front door of our house.

Barb, Nance and Mike were inside waiting for me. They'd called the house repeatedly, and when I hadn't answered the phone, they'd grown worried and came to check on me. But when they saw the full parking lot at church, their worry subsided. Their concern made me feel loved. I needed their love. Barb invited me to her house—the same house we'd decorated as a horror house for Julie's party. The same house where we'd had our last Christmas dinner with Dad. I didn't want to be alone. I needed to be with family.

I was disappointed to find that Dave wasn't home. He wasn't with us earlier when we were writing Dad's obituary, so I'd really wanted to see him and feel the protective embrace of his bear hug. But I certainly understood his need to drown his sorrow with his buddies, all of whom knew my father. I don't even know what my other siblings did that night.

With the aid of alcohol I managed to have a good time playing Wii games with Barb and Leslie. We laughed a lot—mostly at me trying to play Dance Dance Revolution, an interactive game where the player has to step on arrowed buttons in time with a chosen song. I was terrible at it. We didn't celebrate the New Year with party favours or champagne, or yell "Happy New Year!" at midnight. In fact, Leslie drove me back to our house on Days Road before the official start of 2010. Usually Deb and I would call each other at midnight, and sometimes I'd call one or two of my other siblings too. And I'd always talk to Mom. But not that New Year's.

Callie and Freddy greeted me. After cuddling them, I went to Dad's room, opened a dresser drawer and found his well-worn blue and white Amherstview Golf Club sweatshirt. The first time I golfed with my dad was on a sunny day in June 1989. On the first tee, in full view of the golfers sitting outside having a beer, I hit the ball 180 yards right down the middle of the fairway. My father beamed to the guys behind us. "Did you see that?" The rest of my game was not as good.

I slipped his sweatshirt over my head and was heading downstairs when the phone rang. It was Dave. We both bawled and said *I love you.* After I hung up, I took my wine into the darkened living room and sat in the loveseat facing the front window. I looked through the window at the streetlights. The lights that hadn't been bright enough to save my mom and sister. In fact, there was a rumour that one light was out the night they were hit, but it was fixed before anyone could make a case out of it. Freddy hopped up on my lap. Thinking about my father's last day, I stroked his fluffy fur and cried until my wine-glass was empty.

Ron had picked up Dad about twenty minutes after I blubbered "I love you" on the phone. They went for their usual Wednesday beer, served by Chuck, who'd been their bartender there for thirty-five years. Dad and Ron had known each other since they were seven years old. They attended the same Catholic schools, played hockey and curled together, and engaged in endless nights of euchre at their kitchen tables with their wives. That last day, Ron had dropped his best friend off at home at 1:15 p.m. Around two o'clock, Dad called my Uncle Don to wish him a happy new year, even though it was only December 30. Uncle Don would later recall being surprised, because Dad had never called him before. Mom always called. And it was not New Year's Day yet. Sometime between two and four, Dad suffered heart failure and passed away in Mom's chair. Nancy, who found him, said he looked like he was napping, sitting up, his chin resting on his chest.

As much as Dad had kept telling me he wished to be alone, that was the first time we'd left him for more than an hour, other than at night, to sleep. But I knew he needed privacy to grieve. I imagine that his heart was so broken as he sat there in his empty, silent home that he spoke to Mom: *Neet, I love our kids, but I can't live without you. Please ask God to take me too.*

Dad had spent the last weeks of his life in agony. He managed to crack the odd joke, but only Mom could heal his heartache. Most thought Dad's death was unexpected. I did not. Dad died of a broken heart. And now he was where he wanted to be. It had been so hard to see Dad in pain that I thanked God for taking him.

I only wish I'd saved his voice-mail message:

Cath, call your dad. Cath, call your dad.

Chapter 8

Once again, my siblings and I gathered in the living room of my parents' home to discuss a funeral. I offered to give the eulogy.

Carol said firmly, "There's no way you'll be able to do it. Karen should do it."

Karen used to live on the corner, right beside us. She was five years older than me and was our former babysitter. When she got married, she moved to the south end of Days Road, about a mile away. She remained close to us, frequently sitting with Mom, Dad and Julie at mass.

A month after Mom's and Julie's funeral, I asked Karen about the night of the accident. I learned her grandson had been with her. In a soothing voice, Karen told me what she remembered.

"We all left together as usual, chatting in the parking lot about the party. I left them to put Austin in his car seat. Your dad was holding

Julie's hand, getting ready to cross the road. That was the last I saw before I heard the whack. I ran to see what happened. People were already there, so I rushed home to send Paul to be with your dad until you all got there. It's still so hard to comprehend."

I thought about Carol's advice to have Karen deliver the eulogy. "Okay, I'll call her right now and ask."

Karen's response was what I expected. "There's no way I'd be able to, but I'll do a reading if you like."

I wasn't sure why Carol didn't want me to speak about our father. It's common for adult children to deliver the eulogy for their parents. Sometimes more than one child speaks. No one else had expressed interest. I didn't know if I could, but as the eldest, I thought it was my responsibility.

Father Brennan was adamant that the eulogy couldn't be longer than three minutes. I finished writing it two days before the funeral. I practised reading it aloud, over and over. I figured if I got used to speaking the words, I wouldn't cry at the service.

At the dinner break for Dad's visitation, the night before the funeral, I had my laptop open on a table to show my family what I'd written. Some asked me to add this, or add that. "Why can't you put that story in?" It wasn't that I didn't want to, but it was already longer than three minutes. I had tried to include each of them or their children, but it was impossible to incorporate stories of twenty-three of us in that time. I hadn't even used a story about me and my dad. And as I would learn later, the eulogy should have included more about the life he lived.

My cousin Margie called that night to offer condolences. I told her I was afraid I'd break down while reading the eulogy. She said, "Get Don to stand up there with you. If you can't get through it, he can finish. But knowing he's there will probably give you the strength to get through."

For Dad's service the next morning, I wore a grey pencil skirt with matching jacket, a Gift of Life pin prominent on the peaked lapel. When I stepped up to the podium, Don followed and stood behind me. My family sat in the front row. I couldn't look at them without breaking down, so before I began to speak, I moved my gaze to our friends on my left.

"Since our father died of a broken heart, it's really hard to talk about him without talking about Mom. Fifty-six years ago, Bill Gourdier asked Wanita Tuepah to dance. He kept asking all night, so no one else could. Dad proposed three times before she said yes, because she kept insisting she was "too old for him." She was three years older. "We're glad he persisted."

I told the story about them dancing at the Oarsman the week before the accident.

"When I asked Dad about that night, he said, 'You should've seen the twinkle in her eye when I asked her to dance. And she wasn't half bad either!' He told Mom that was the most fun he'd had in a long time.

"Dad and Uncle Randy owned the retail store Gourdier Furs. When we were children, sometimes we'd go to work with Dad on Saturdays. We'd play on the 1940s typewriter and ride up and down the rickety elevator. He'd say, 'Make sure you don't take it too high, it'll come off the track.' We always took it too high, and he'd have to fix it. But he never got upset about it.

"Our father was an honest and moral man, always concerned for others before himself. He had an incredibly witty sense of humour. Just try to remember a conversation with our dad that didn't involve a joke. One time when Nancy was out of town for a couple days, he put a sign on the door: "NANCY, WE MOVED. Love, DAD.""

"Dad was a goalie when goalies didn't wear masks. That's how he lost his front teeth. Jake, his grandson, said to me yesterday, 'Papa played hockey with Don Cherry, isn't that cool?'

"He enjoyed teaching Leslie about curling as they watched the Canadian Curling Round Robin.

"When Teresa, Deb, Carol and I made our long drives back to our homes, he'd call: 'Just wanted to make sure you got home okay, better let you go.'

Dad was a sensitive soul. Sitting behind him at Dave's wedding, I tapped his shoulder to talk to him. He wouldn't turn around because he was crying.

"When Mike asked Dad to be his best man, Dad said, 'You're supposed to ask your best friend.' Mike said, 'I just did.'

"People often look in awe at our family. If we have turned out to be fun, caring and loving people, it's because of Mom and Dad and Julie that we are. Mom and Julie are comforting Dad in a way we could not possibly do, no matter how much we tried. So, dance together then, wherever you may be."

Tears blurred my vision as I readied myself for the closing lines.

"How lucky are you, his friends and relatives, to have known him. How blessed and proud are we to have Bill Gourdier as our father and papa."

When I sat down beside Carol, she placed her hand on my leg. "Good job, Cath."

She had no idea how much I needed to hear that, especially from her. I reached into Mom's black patent purse, pulled out Dad's white cotton hanky and dabbed my eyes.

It was brutally cold at St. Mary's Cemetery on Tuesday, January 5. My sisters wore their knee-length wolf fur coats. Dad had allowed us to buy our coats with a monthly payment plan over several years. I'd bought mine when I was twenty-three, but it had been stolen from Dad's store when it was robbed in the early '90s.

On one of our alone days at the house, referring to Mom's full-length silver mink, Dad had said, "You should have her coat, Cath." I do have it, but I can't remember if I wore it the day of the funeral.

My siblings stood around the open grave, crying and shivering. Their spouses and children huddled close, as Father Brennan recited his final blessing for Dad. Don's children didn't attend, making the absence of my sweet Julie even more profound for me. I didn't have a child to comfort nor a child's hand in mine. With my arm linked through Don's, I stared at the shallow mounds of dirt where Mom's and Julie's bodies lay, dead flowers, brown and brittle, scattered over the frozen mud.

At the graveside, we stood in a receiving line formation. Father Brennan offered us his condolences and blessings. I watched as he shook one sibling's hand and then the next. Realizing what was about to happen, I began to feel woozy. Things seemed to be moving in slow motion. I watched Father Brennan grasp Carol's hand. I was next, at the end of the line. I was now the eldest living member of our immediate family. Father looked into my eyes and handed me Dad's wooden cross. Clutching it tightly, I gritted my teeth and pushed my tongue against my front teeth to stop my jaw from quivering.

Slowly we dispersed back to the limos, the snow crunching beneath our feet.

Before getting in the car, I turned back to look at the graves. I could not contain my anguish. I cried out, "Julie!" My knees buckled. Don grabbed me before I hit the ground.

I don't remember what we did after Dad's burial. There must have been another reception at the church and another gathering at the house. I don't remember a thing. A new level of shock had hit. Hard.

But at least Mom, Dad and Julie were together again.

DON HAD TO RETURN to Toronto the next day, to get back to work. Once again, alone in our family home, I sat at the foot of Dad's bed. His closet door was open, and I noticed a clear plastic bag on his shoe rack. There was something rolled up inside. It seemed odd. I opened the bag and pulled out two sweaters. A red one and a navy one. They had been sliced up the middle.

The sweaters Dad was wearing when he died.

I sat on the floor, holding them tightly to my chest.

Since the accident, Dad had lost weight and got the chills frequently. To keep warm, he wore two long-sleeved sweaters, one on top of the other. Apparently the paramedics had left them on the living room floor. Barb had hidden them in the closet. She couldn't dispose of them. That was not a decision she could make.

After I held them in my arms and had a good cry, I took the tattered sweaters and placed them in my suitcase. I couldn't dispose of them either.

Dad, Julie and Mom at the Loyal Oarsman on New Year's Eve.
PHOTO COURTESY OF THE AUTHOR'S FAMILY

Chapter 9

When Barb, my co-executor of Dad's will, and I went to the law office two weeks after Dad died, the first thing the lawyer advised us to do was change the locks on the house.

"I can't do that," I said. "Dave sits at their kitchen table almost every day to do his paperwork. Nancy and Mike drop in all the time. They'd hate me. I can't do it."

He'd heard horror stories from other "close-knit" families in which siblings had gone into the house and taken items without consulting the others. Leaning forward, elbows on the conference table, he reiterated, "You should change the locks."

Confident my siblings would never do such a thing, I refused. And since January was not a good time to put the house on the market, I went back to Toronto.

TO AID IN MY GRIEVING PROCESS, my friend Lina recommended a Reiki clairvoyant named Bonita. Lina had lost her mother tragically, so she knew how grief can overwhelm one's mind and body. Bonita worked occasionally with the Toronto police on missing children cases and had a good reputation. Still, because of an inner skepticism, I made sure to give her only my first name in case she Googled me.

On a crisp, cold day in February, I arrived at Bonita's high-rise apartment at the end of the hall on the tenth floor. An effervescent woman of sixty-ish with long blond hair opened the door.

"Hi, Catherine, come in, dear, come in."

The apartment was cozy but crammed with too much furniture. A single treatment bed was set up in the middle of the living room. She lit a candle on the coffee table and placed several rock crystals on the sofa beside the bed. Then she closed the drapes to block the bright sun. I asked for permission to record the session. When she stepped out of the room to get me a glass of water, I opened my purse and took out the plasticized memory cards of Mom, Dad and Julie. Their smiling faces reassured me that what I was about to do was fine with them.

Bonita called out from the kitchen, "Go ahead and lie down, dear, make yourself comfortable."

I welcomed the warmth of the soft flannel sheets. My eyes were closed, but when Bonita entered, I could hear her as she stood over me taking deep breaths, in and out, in and out. She spoke quickly but clearly.

"I need to read your auras first, the colours surrounding you. You have a lot of blues—periwinkle blue, baby blue, sky blue—and tangerine." She placed her hands lightly on my head. Though she was barely touching me, it felt surprisingly calming. "Blue indicates your heart. Blue is the colour of love. You're coming from your heart. There's a little bit of green—that means you're still healing. Red is what you need to catapult you ahead, to move on. It involves the throat chakra. Talking. You need to talk."

Her hands hovered close over my body. "There's a young woman right behind you. She appears to be in her late teens or early twenties, but I have a feeling she's much older than that." My heart raced. Julie looked half her age. "Your grandmother is here. Your mom's mother and another woman sidled right up beside her. Your grandmother says you have to keep on writing and singing. You haven't been doing that. You love to do it, so you must. And walk, walk, walk. You used to walk with your music. Keep doing that."

Bonita didn't even know my last name. She wasn't aware of my love of music, singing, writing or power walking, but apparently my grandmother was. "Your grandmother is saying something about raspberry jam cookies?" Impressive! Grandma made "jam jam" cookies with raspberry jam and molasses. They were rolled flat and round, with a hole in the middle exposing the seeded red jam.

"Do you have any questions, dear?"

"Could you ask my dad for the nickname he called me?"

"I can put it out there and see."

"Can you go back to the girl you saw?"

She closed her eyes and laid her hands on my belly. "She's still here. She seems to have a bit of a speech problem. Some trouble speaking?"

A tear rolled out of the corner of my eye. Julie could carry on a conversation, but sometimes her speech was difficult to understand. There was no way Bonita could know this unless Julie was talking to her. This freaked me out, in a good way.

"She's trying to say something. She loves you, she needs you, yes, she needs you and needs your love."

Tears slid down my temples and onto the pillow.

Toward the end of the session, Bonita said, "Your Aunt Joan has some health issues."

I hadn't even told her I had an aunt, let alone one named Joan. And AJ definitely had health issues.

I'm Catholic. I believe in heaven. I did not believe in psychics. Until I met Bonita.

A WEEK LATER I was in Los Angeles staying at a boutique hotel in West Hollywood. It was the same hotel my mother and I had stayed at ten months earlier. Don and I have a home in Hidden Hills, on the western border of the San Fernando Valley, but we had rented it out to a rock star. Though I missed our serene neighbourhood, I relished things about the bachelor-apartment-sized hotel suite. Ordering room service and eating dinner on the king-sized bed while watching movies on the big-screen television was a relaxing escape from grief. Since most of my Toronto connections would be getting ready for bed by dinner Pacific Time, there were no distracting phone calls.

Not so in the mornings, however. On February 12, the ring of my cellphone woke me up at six, the caller unaware that I was three time zones away.

It was a producer from Global News in Toronto. She explained that they were doing a two-minute news piece on Valentine's Day about people dying of a broken heart. They'd found out about Dad by googling "Dying of a broken heart." The *Whig-Standard* article about his death came up on the first page: "Local Businessman Dies of a Broken Heart." Global had initially called Aunt Joan, but she'd told them, "You should be talking to my brother Bill's eldest, Catherine," and gave them my phone number.

The article would be a beautiful tribute to my parents' love.

I agreed to the interview but said it would have to be done in Los Angeles. The producer asked if I could send some photos of my parents. I had a few in my computer, so sent them along. A few hours later she called to say she was having a hard time finding a camera operator to meet me in West Hollywood.

"Do you have any other siblings in Ontario?"

"Yes, I have six."

"Really? Wow. Because of the time constraints and logistics, could you see if one of them would do the interview?"

I sent out an email to my siblings explaining what was going on. I got two responses. One from Teresa: "We should just decline the interview." Carol said, "I agree with Teresa." Why didn't they want to do it? The story was a Valentine's Day piece about the power of love. Our parents' love.

I emailed the producer. "Sorry, my sisters don't want to do the interview, but thank you for your interest in our parents."

I thought the interview had gone away, and I no longer had to be concerned how my siblings would react to me doing it.

At seven the next morning, my phone rang again. It was the producer. "We have a camera crew coming to your hotel at eleven thirty this morning."

Uh-oh.

"How many others are you interviewing?" If they had other stories to present, I'd say my sisters didn't want me to do mine.

"Just you," she said.

The piece was airing the next day, and it was crucial for their piece to show photos of an actual person who died of a broken heart. I couldn't leave them hanging. Aunt Joan thought I should do it. I wanted to do it too. I called her, crying.

"Carol and Treas don't want me to do it, but I am. Aunt Joan, I'm scared they're going to hate me."

In her comforting voice, she said, "Cath, it's a beautiful testament to your parents' love—that's why I gave them your number. If they don't want to see it, they don't have to watch it. I think it's beautiful, honey, I do."

I knew Mom would want me to do it too (as long as they showed good pictures of her).

I touched up my makeup while the two-person camera team rearranged the hotel room furniture. The camera operator asked me to find family photos on my laptop so he could film me as I scrolled through them. As the videographer clipped the microphone to my top, he slipped in his condolences. When the reporter, Beatrice Politi, called, we put the phone on speaker for the interview.

Beatrice asked me to explain briefly what had happened. My energy level was low, making it easier to keep a calm demeanour.

"I know Dad died of a broken heart because when I tucked him into bed, he'd say, 'I love you, all of you, but I just can't live without her.'"

The overwhelming emotional response to the loss of a long-time spouse can increase the release of certain hormones, such as adrenalin or epinephrine, which cause symptoms resembling a heart attack. Technically it's called stressed-induced cardiomyopathy, or takotsubo cardiomyopathy, named so by Dr. Hikaru Sato. In 1990, he wrote an article describing an unusual set of sudden, life-threatening symptoms that he and his colleagues were seeing in their patients—chest pain, shortness of breath, an elevated electrocardiogram and elevated cardiac enzyme levels—symptoms similar to those of a heart attack. More tests revealed that their patients' arteries were clear. The researchers theorized that the left ventricle of the heart, which is responsible for pumping, was weakened and mimicking the symptoms of a heart attack. Doctors now accept that dying of a broken heart is not folklore. It is a condition recognized by modern medicine.

To my knowledge, my father did not suffer from any heart ailments, yet he lived only six weeks after burying the love of his life and his youngest child.

While the videographer packed up his things, I wrote an email to Aunt Joan. "Hi AJ, the interview will be on Global's six o'clock news tomorrow. I hope my family will agree that the piece is a way of worshipping our parents' love for each other."

After the segment aired, a few friends and relatives emailed me notes saying they thought the piece was a lovely tribute. I guess it was too disturbing and too soon for my brothers and sisters to see photos of our parents on the news, because I didn't hear a word from any of them.

BY THE TIME I returned to Toronto a week later, I realized I needed professional help from someone who understood grief. I missed my calls to Mom so much. I couldn't talk to my sisters, because they were apparently displeased that I had gone ahead with the Global interview. I assumed my brothers were like my dad and most men—not into talking about their feelings. I had six siblings, yet I felt alone in my grief.

I Googled "Toronto psychologists." After checking the profiles of several therapists, I found Dr. Geri Notham. Being Catholic, I liked that she was a Christian counsellor who specialized in bereavement. We set a time to meet for the next day.

I arrived early at Dr. Notham's house, a mere eight-minute drive from mine. She lived in a two-storey red-brick house with a front porch, not a downtown high-rise. I liked that too. I'd been instructed to enter by the side door. A sign said, "Please enter—wait downstairs."

As I opened the door, a woman around my age with long brown hair poked her head out from the upstairs doorway. "Have a seat. I need a few minutes."

Five minutes later, she came downstairs and led me into a cozy basement room lined with bookshelves, a couple of chairs, a sofa and a desk. I sat on the sofa, and she sat beside me in a wing-back chair. A floral tissue box sat within easy reach on the antique coffee table.

I spilled my story. I told her about the clairvoyant I'd seen and how the messages conveyed convinced me that my parents and Julie were still "alive" in the afterlife.

"I absolutely believe in the afterlife," she said.

A professional, intelligent person believed me!

Then I told her what had happened, or rather what hadn't happened, when my family gathered at our Days Road house a week earlier for a meeting about when to put the house on the market. I'd told them that a few days earlier, I was so distraught, I fell to my knees in my bedroom and cried while shouting "I just want to know that you are together, wherever you are! Please, send me a sign so I know." I told them that a few seconds later, the lights dimmed and then brightened a few times in a row. I was nowhere near the light switch. I said, "It was Mom and Dad telling us they are together!" At least that is what I wanted to believe. How else could that be explained?

I had been sitting in the corner chair; they were on the sofas. Nervous and breathing heavily, I gazed at each of them in turn. Not one of them said a word. Did they think I was crazy? I'd opened myself up with this very personal experience, and no one said a word. Not even *That's hogwash,* or *That's nice, Cath.* Their lack of response made me feel like an alien, instead of their big sister who was only trying to help them feel better about our loss.

I told Dr. Notham my concern about my family's special bond breaking apart. I'd heard that could happen. My siblings were not keeping in touch with me. Neither were Don's children. I was incredibly lonely.

"Your brothers and sisters are too caught up in their own grief to think about you. They'll come around," she assured me.

I reached into my purse and pulled out Julie's photo album. "This was in Julie's birthday gift bag."

She perused the delightful pictures of our summer holiday together.

After ninety minutes of listening to me unload, she said, "I can't believe you got through this session without crying. You're so strong."

I was growing tired of people saying that to me. In reality, I felt so shattered that sometimes I didn't even have the energy to cry.

As she handed me the receipt for my payment, tears rolled down her face. "Catherine, yours is the saddest story I've ever heard, and I've been doing this for many years."

I stepped closer and hugged her. There I was, ending my first-ever grief counselling session by comforting my therapist. In a strange way, it was funny, but I didn't laugh.

A FEW DAYS LATER, I returned to Kingston. I felt less stressed at my parents' house. I liked being able to drive to the grocery store, the drugstore and the bank and be back home in half an hour. In Toronto, the thought of doing errands made me cringe: the traffic congestion, lane closures, dodging bikes, trying to find a parking spot, and then paying to park was exhausting.

At my parents' house in Kingston, I'd be only four blocks from Nancy, six minutes drive to Aunt Joan's and twelve minutes away from my brothers. That knowledge offered the solace I craved. I wanted to live at 491 Days Road, to read and write in Mom's chair, drink martinis with Aunt Joan, watch Sammy and Haley play basketball, meet Dave for lunch and drive my young nieces, Cedar and Marley, to school, the same school I had once attended.

My husband sensed my longing and was afraid I'd leave him to renew my life in Kingston. I didn't have the space in my heart to miss Don. I was too absorbed with the aftermath of my losses. All I wanted was to spend time with my immediate family and Aunt Joan. But as much as I wanted to move back to my hometown, I knew our work was in Toronto. And before I could return to the big city, my siblings and I had to sell our childhood home.

Chapter 10

In 1959, Dad bought Lot 713 on Days Road. He was twenty-five years old. The exorbitant sum of 27,000 dollars included the land and the yet-to-be-built three-bedroom, split-level house. With three children and one on the way, it was time to say goodbye to the two-bedroom low-rise apartment building on Park Street in downtown Kingston where my family had been living.

When we made the move in the spring of 1960, I was three years old, Carol was two, David was a toddler, and Mom was seven months pregnant with Deb. Our Lady of Lourdes Church wouldn't be built until a decade later. There was nothing across the street from our new home except a large, old, limestone house, fenced-in fields, and in the distance, what everyone wants in plain sight: a prison. Collins Bay Institution was two and a half kilometres away, but we could see it from our front porch. It looked like the Sleeping Beauty castle at

Disneyland, only with red turrets instead of blue. I have childhood memories of seeing inmates dressed in grey jumpsuits working in the prison fields.

Knowing spring is the best time to put a house on the market, my siblings and I gathered on a weekend in March 2010 to do the deed of sorting, distributing or tossing fifty years of accumulation.

A friend of my brother's, Gord Johnson, is in the waste disposal business. He dropped off a huge Dumpster in the driveway and included hauling it away as a gift to our family. People don't know what to do or say when their friends are grieving, so they give you things. A beautiful scarf right off their neck, porcelain angels, wine, books, homemade soup. Or a disposal bin.

We made a rule to help with the sorting: if it was something one of us had bought for them, we had the option of keeping it. I had bought Mom a black purse for her seventy-ninth birthday. It was the purse she'd taken on her travels with me. She'd owned it for eleven months. Now it was mine. I unzipped it and, in the inside pocket, found a folded piece of paper.

After our return from California, I'd seen an article in *More*, a magazine for women, titled, "Take Mom to the Big Apple." I'd ripped it out and sent it inside her Mother's Day card, scribbling, *Our next trip maybe??? Cath xox.* I was overcome with emotion. Mom had kept that magazine page in her purse since May. It turned out our next trip *was* to the Big Apple, for the *Amelia* premiere.

I dug deeper and found a piece of paper with a note in Mom's handwriting. *Pick up the cake. Pizzas × 10 – 7:30 p.m.* The back of my neck tingled. *Julie's birthday cake and the pizzas none of us ate.* I left both pieces of paper in the pocket, and there they'll stay until I, the paper or the purse crumble and die.

Under the master bed we found large manila envelopes with each of our names written in black marker. Mine included assorted cards: Mother's Day, birthday, "just because I love you" cards, postcards I'd sent from Italy, France, England, from all over the world. I found a stack of letters I'd written to Mom when I moved to Toronto to take an esthetics and marketing course at Seneca College. There were Sears and Kmart catalogue pages of me modelling pyjamas, shorts and tops. And my Grade One report card from 1963. I have a "Mom" box at my home. The sentiments in her cards and letters to me are also too precious to discard.

Off the veneer wood-panelled basement was a room we called the crawl space. The furnace room, really. The ceiling was so low you had to crouch to move around in there. I'd hit my forehead on the metal heating vent many times. When I was a kid, it was a good place to play hide-and-seek as long as you weren't afraid of running into spiders or getting cobwebs stuck on your face and clothes. The artificial Christmas tree, decorations and wrapping paper lived eleven months of the year in there. Wooden trunks that looked like treasure chests were stuffed with old clothes and shoes. Cardboard boxes and storage bins were filled with seasonal clothes. The closets in the house were small, so every year Mom would put away the fall/winter clothes and bring out the spring/summer wardrobes. The thought of her packing and unpacking seasonal clothes for ten of us was staggering. I found a yellow Rubbermaid bin with a piece of paper taped to it that said "Bill's Winter Clothes." I dragged it out into the family room. Inside it were sweaters, gloves and scarves. I found the sweater Dad had worn to my fiftieth birthday party, blue with black stripes. No one seemed that interested in Dad's clothes, so I decided to keep it. In fact, I emptied the bin, put his sweater back in it and kept the bin too.

Hanging from an aluminum rolling clothing rack in the laundry room were long fancy dresses Mom and Julie had worn to weddings, old coats, and assorted outfits from the '70s and '80s.

We found bills, bank books and original mortgage papers for the house. I turned up their first wills from 1965, when Dad was thirty-two. This part was amusing: "For the children I now have and those that may be born after the date of this will . . ." There were already six of us, but for a Roman Catholic dad, it was a good idea to include that clause.

Our house had one small bathroom. I have a photo of five of us, boys and girls, having a bath together. When Nancy, the seventh, was born, Dad built a powder room downstairs, so at least we had another toilet. At the same time, he added a bedroom upstairs that was large enough for three twin beds and three dressers, for Carol, Debbie and me. The old laundry room was converted into a small bedroom with bunk beds for my brothers, and the laundry room was moved under the new bedroom. In the end, our home had five bedrooms. After all of us, except Julie, moved out, Mom stored her clothes in three bedrooms as well as the closet in the laundry room and the crawl space. (Dear Don, I come by my pack-rat habits honestly.)

Beginning in my old bedroom, my sisters and I sorted through Mom's clothing together. There were two outfits that three of us wanted. Both were ensembles Mom had worn the last time we travelled together. She'd worn her silver and black sparkly outfit to the *Amelia* premiere in New York and had travelled in her comfortable denim-look navy jacket with the sparkly burgundy floral design and coordinating navy pants.

We decided to draw for the outfits: whoever picked out the paper that said *It's yours* got it. I was the third to draw for the silver sparkly outfit, which at the outset was the one I thought I needed to have. My heart pounded when I picked the *It's yours* paper, and I started crying. "I'd rather have the pant suit," I blubbered. "That was what Mom was wearing . . . the last time I saw her."

I'd been acting so jovial that my breakdown caught my sisters totally off guard. Me too. Teresa eased my pain by handing me Mom's travel outfit. I'd flown to Los Angeles and New York with Mom sitting beside me in that suit, sipping champagne. She'd worn it on our walk in Central Park with Uncle Mike, where I'd taken several photos of them that last day.

On a shelf on the wall in Mom's room was a fifteen-inch-tall statue of the Virgin Mary, her arms open and welcoming. Mary watched over us as we pulled out the drawers of Mom's jewellery case, and boxes from her closet, then spread everything on her bed. I watched the sad faces of my sisters as they carefully picked up earrings and necklaces, gazed at them and put them back, each perhaps searching for that piece that held a special memory.

We packed brown stoneware dishes, assorted coffee mugs and glassware, Mom's paperbacks, Dad's golf clubs and Julie's VHS horror movies and country music CDs. Unique items we kept were the antique glass dish used for cranberry sauce at Christmas, 50s-era juice glasses with oranges on them, the glass swan that held the SOS pad by the kitchen sink, and adorable vintage red, white and green felt Christmas shelf elves.

Late afternoon, while wrapping Grandma's china with newspaper in the dining room, I overheard my brothers-in-law talking in the kitchen. They'd found *something* while cleaning out my brothers' bedroom. "Looks like Cork forgot a bag of pot!" They chuckled, thinking they'd exposed a secret. It was good to hear the laughter, but the joke was on them: the tiny Ziploc baggie held my recent purchase of catnip! I stored it downstairs because the cats' food dishes were outside the laundry room.

When I went downstairs, I noticed that Dad's La-Z-Boy was gone. Carol was sitting on the sofa sorting through a box from the crawlspace.

"Where's Dad's chair?"

"We threw it out," she said.

What? I'd bought him that chair.

"It was filthy," she added.

It probably *was* filthy, but it was supposed to be my decision whether to keep it or toss it. I would be living alone there, and I wanted to sit in Dad's filthy chair and watch TV until our house was sold.

I went outside to attempt to fetch the chair out of the bin in the driveway. I hadn't been outside all day and was shocked to find the

Dumpster overflowing. Broken toys, rusty tools, soiled door mats, rickety furniture, et cetera. But not even a hint of the recliner. Buried somewhere in that bin, Dad's chair would have to rest in peace.

I'D BEEN KEEPING the kitty litter box in the hallway downstairs, outside the small bedroom where my brothers used to sleep. Once the house was put on the market, I had to find a less conspicuous place for it. The closet in the laundry room would be more discreet. While cleaning it out, I noticed a green garbage bag tucked in a dark corner. With all of us decluttering all weekend, how had we missed it?

I untied the knot. I saw a big ball of white lace and slowly pulled it out. Mom's wedding dress! The bag could easily have been tossed as garbage. I unravelled the slightly yellowed, strapless gown. Quivering with excitement, I held it up to my body. I had to try it on. I stripped down to my panties and stepped into it. It fit perfectly. I ran my hands over the crumpled lace and wire corset.

It was wrinkled and faded, and the zipper was busted, but it was my mother's 1955 wedding dress, and I had it. I didn't want to tell my sisters. I was afraid we'd have to draw for it, and I'd lose. *What if someone finds me in it?* The front door was always unlocked; anyone could pop in. I took off the dress, put it back in the bag and threw my clothes on. Then I ran outside and tucked the bag in the bed of my truck. No one would find it there.

I'd tell my sisters I'd found it after it was safely in my Toronto home. I'd have it cleaned and repaired, and would hang it in our guestroom closet beside Julie's bridesmaid dress from our wedding. I know I should've told my sisters I found it, but I really wanted it. They'd made lists of "things" they'd wanted. I hadn't made a list at all. Mom's wedding dress wasn't on anyone's list. We could take turns "owning it" would be my response if they were upset with me.

Back downstairs I collected the bags of clothing to be dropped off at local charities. Julie's clothes were in a clear bag. There was her fleece bathrobe, the turquoise one with navy stars on it. I couldn't give her robe away. I pulled it out. As I did, I saw the black-and-white polka dot blouse she'd worn the year before at Dad's seventy-fifth birthday party. I had a picture of her in that blouse sitting on Don's lap. I snatched that too. Holding her clothes against my chest, I slumped, cross-legged, on the concrete floor. I laid her bathrobe across my lap, as if her child-sized body were in it, cradling the collar end in the crook of my elbow. I rocked back and forth, holding her robe against my body, my face nuzzled into the soft fleece. Then I bawled my eyes out.

Chapter 11

At my parents' home, there used to be three televisions on at once: Dad watching *Matlock* or sports downstairs, *Dallas* or *Three's Company* reruns on in Julie's room, and Mom watching a drama series or a TV movie in the master bedroom. After they were gone, I walked past these empty rooms several times a day. The kitchen table, where each day Mom sat down to do the crossword puzzle in the newspaper, seemed lonely too. "Crosswords are supposed to be good for your brain," she would say. Now, our home was eerily silent.

My days of being in my family home were numbered. I knew everything had to be cleared out of the house, but some items were difficult for me to discard. In the bathroom cabinet was an Oil of Olay pump cleanser. It was almost empty, but I didn't want to throw even it away. It was Mom's. I ended up taking it to Woodhaven, our lakehouse, and putting it in my toiletries box on the bathroom counter beside the sink. Even when I eventually pumped out the last drop, I could not throw it away. I liked to look at it.

While I was living at my parents' house, one of my siblings suggested I cut off the landline. But some of our relatives, my parents' friends and my friends in Kingston were still calling that number. Another sibling suggested cancelling the cable television, even though I was staying there alone and had taken the lead in getting the house ready to put on the market. TV shows not only kept me company in the desolate house, they also distracted my afflicted mind. Carol told me I should get my cats out of the house so it wouldn't smell "like cat." But I'd had cats for twelve years, and my homes never smelled. My cats were my "kids." I had lived alone for twenty years before I got married. None of my siblings had *ever* lived alone, so I guess they weren't aware of how lonely it would be without the sound of the phone ringing, an evening escape into a fictional TV show or the comforting companionship of cats.

Did they not realize I had pushed my mourning aside to do executor duties? It was unsettling to open mail addressed to my deceased parents. To respond to the representatives who asked, "Is there anything we can do to keep you from cancelling your credit card, ma'am?" *Unfortunately not. It's my mom's and she died.* That did not roll off my tongue easily.

I didn't live alone long. The house sold in April, three weeks after we put it on the market. Our father would've been very proud, because it sold for the price we'd hoped.

ON ONE OF MY LAST NIGHTS THERE, I'd been invited to join Nance and Pete at their friend's house. We sat in the backyard, on the grass around a bonfire, bundled in sweaters and scarves, drinking. Around ten or eleven, I bid them good-night. That cool spring night, I said I was fine walking the kilometre or so home on my own, but Pete insisted on escorting me. Even though we were both pretty hammered already, when we got to my parents' place, he opened the fridge and grabbed a beer. All the glassware had been packed and was gone. I poured what was left of a bottle of Pinot Grigio into an old coffee mug. The table and chairs were also gone, so we sat on the floor, Pete's back against the fridge, mine against the cupboard door to the Campbell's soup cans that were no longer there.

Between swigs of beer, he told me that he and Nancy had been at the accident scene. That Nancy had seen Mom's and Julie's bodies on the road. That Dad had paced between them. That Dad had said, "Julie was ripped from my hand." For six months, Nancy had kept that inside. Or kept it from me, at least. I wondered if Julie had been conscious. Did Nancy witness Mom getting CPR? Did she see the driver? I wanted to find out, but I could not send Nancy back in time to relive those horrific moments. I couldn't do that. Not until more time passed. But if she needed me to listen, I would be there for her.

That night, I dreamed about Mom. She was standing in the kitchen wearing her turquoise and pink floral lounging gown and extending her arms out to hug me. I could see and hear her so clearly. *I'm still here, honey*, she said.

THE NEXT MORNING, I took down the plaque that said "Bless This House." Using a black Sharpie, I wrote the new owners a note on the back:

Our house was always filled with Love and Laughter. Enjoy making your own special memories in our Family Home of 50 years. The 'Bill' Gourdiers 1960–2010.

Then I hung it back up over the stove.

I went to Costco and had a photo of the ten of us enlarged to an eight-by-ten. It was taken at a family Christmas party in 1990. We're sitting on a sectional sofa in front of a panelled wall in Dave's basement. We had two taken—one of the ten of us smiling, and one of us doing our silly "family photo face"—sticking out our tongues and framing our goofy faces by pointing one index finger at our head and the other at the tip of our chin. Dad took out his front teeth dentures, which made him look even more foolish. I wrote all our names on the back of the smiley one, put it in a Ziploc baggie and tossed it into the attic over the stairs. I couldn't say goodbye to our house without leaving "all of us" in it.

We could never really "leave" our home at 491 Days Road. Our hearts would live there forever.

ON MOTHER'S DAY, my first without my mother, I wanted to be alone with my memories of her. I was so downhearted that I didn't want the company of anyone else, including my husband.

Years ago, I had been invited to a Mothers and Daughters party. I called the hostess and said, "Thank you for including me, but I don't have a daughter." She said, "But you are a daughter, and you have a mother. Please come." And I did. But after the accident, I knew Mother's Day would never feel the same for me again. My sisters would be spoiled by their children. Breakfasts in bed, homemade cards, gifts and cuddles. I couldn't even call my mom anymore.

WHEN I CAME BACK to Toronto a few days before Mother's Day, Don greeted me with the warmest hug he'd ever given to me. "I don't want to lose you, I love you," he said. His manner, which was often abrupt, was now tender. He was more empathetic with his words. He realized it was going to take time for me to heal, and he wanted to be there once I had. I wanted to be with him too.

But not on this Mother's Day.

Don respected my decision and went up to the lake.

It seemed to me an appropriate activity to read everything in the "Catherine" envelope Mom had saved for me. Wearing polka-dot pyjama bottoms and a pink T-shirt, I sat cross-legged on the sofa in the living room and started the process. Mom had saved three of my Mother's Day cards. I placed them on the sofa sideboard cabinet beside the eleven-by-fourteen photo of her and Dad.

I thought of the last time I'd seen my mother, two weeks before she died. It was the day we'd flown back to Toronto from New York after the *Amelia* premiere. She had three hours before her train to

Kingston was to depart, so we went to visit the *Resident Evil: Afterlife* set. The crew were lighting for the next shot when we got there. Don was sitting in a director's chair watching playback on a twenty-six-inch monitor. Mom asked why the video was blurry. He explained that the film was being shot in 3D. "You have to wear 3D glasses to see a clear picture." He handed her a pair of large, black-framed glasses. Rafy, the stills photographer, took a photo of her wearing them, capturing the childlike smile on her face.

The costume designer mentioned there were some jeans and tops I might want to try on (another perk of being the producer's wife), so we headed for the wardrobe department. While checking out the clothes, the gregarious Kim Coates, best known for his roles on *Sons of Anarchy* and *Goon*, showed up for a fitting. Recognizing me, he yelled, "Catherine!" Of course, Mom wanted a picture with the six-foot-tall actor with the gorgeous pale blue eyes. Kim wrapped his arm around my giddy mother. This would be the last photo I took of her.

I asked if she'd like to take something to eat on the train. Emily, Don's assistant, got her a tuna sandwich from the catering truck. Mom held Emily's hand in hers and thanked her.

Wheeling her carry-on bag, I accompanied Mom into the busy massive Union Station. I found her a seat in the departure area, then told her I had to leave, because Aleck, our driver from the production office, was waiting in a no-parking zone. The train was due to board in only ten minutes, but I felt bad leaving before her departure.

Mom said, "Don't be silly. Go on. I'm fine." She thanked me again for "everything."

I hugged her, kissed her cheek, then walked away thinking, *She's so easy to please and always so grateful.* When I was almost out of her sight, just like in the movies, I stopped and looked back. My last glimpse of Mom was her wearing her navy flowered sequined jacket, contentedly reading a Tess Gerritsen mystery paperback, a cellophane-wrapped tuna sandwich resting on her lap.

Now I looked at her cheery smile in the photo. I told her I missed her. That I wished I'd had my own child. How perhaps if I had, I wouldn't feel so lonely. That I regretted not telling Aleck to keep driving around the block, so I could've enjoyed her company for those last ten minutes before she had to board.

Chapter 12

A couple of weeks after the "Dying of a Broken Heart" segment aired on Global News, I received a call from the network's show *16×9: The Bigger Picture*. The program delves into current controversial topics. They were producing a piece called "Too Old for the Road," focusing on recent fatal pedestrian car accidents and collisions involving elderly seniors. Since my family's tragedy involved an elderly driver, they wanted to interview me.

The producer said, "You could get the word out to other families, help prevent future deaths and heartaches." I had to do it.

I told the producer that my brother-in-law, David, enraged about our loss, had come up with the idea of starting an initiative called J.U.L.I.E., an acronym for "Just Undergo Live In the car Exams." They wanted him to participate in the show as well. The consulting producer and host of the show, Mary Garofalo, asked to meet me before the taping, so I invited her to my home in Toronto.

Mary is a voluptuous, smart, ballsy and compassionate woman. I liked her immediately. As I recapped our tragic story and showed her photos of my loved ones, tears sprang to her eyes. She asked if I had any videos of them. "Video footage will better show the audience your family members' personalities."

After Mary left, I searched the bottom drawer of the wall unit in my TV room and found videos of my wedding in 1999 and Dad's sixtieth birthday in 1993.

I set myself up in my bedroom to watch them. Placing a glass of wine and a tissue box within reach on my nightstand, I inserted the VHS wedding video into the Sony player on the dresser and leaned back onto propped-up pillows to begin my mission of finding good clips for the television show. I fast-forwarded until I found Julie, one of my bridesmaids, in a sage green gown, her long brown hair swept into an elegant updo. She grinned as she walked ahead of Dad and me down the aisle of the intimate Newman Centre chapel. Mom was radiant in a long burgundy skirt and matching jacket trimmed with pin-dot sparkles. Hearing their voices, their laughter, I was grateful Mary had reminded me about my precious films.

Methodically I time-coded the footage that I would give permission to air. For example, Dad acting silly holding the bridesmaids' bouquets up to his face—one hour, eight-minute mark. I chose a few short clips, enough to show the essence of their personalities.

As the shooting day approached, I became more and more nervous, but I also knew the information needed to get out there. Our family's catastrophe was proof.

David didn't have time to come to Toronto, so we scheduled the shoot at his home in Burlington. During my drive there, I was so overwrought, I felt sick. Just over six months had passed since the accident. I was apprehensive of my family's reaction to a show featuring our tragedy on national television but assured myself that our parents would be proud.

I'd spent hours on the internet researching seniors' driving accidents and found countless stories of preventable tragedies. Surprising news to me was that those over eighty are allowed to drive without having their ability and vision tested while actually *driving* a car. I know some people in their eighties who are perfectly capable drivers, but I've seen many who should not be behind the wheel. I've watched the elderly painstakingly get out of their cars, pull a walker from the back seat and hobble, hunched over, into the post office or grocery store. Their inability to react quickly is a frightening reality.

In Ontario, Canada, you can get your driver's licence at seventeen years old and never have to get in the car to take another test for the rest of your life, even if you're still driving in your nineties. Since I began writing this book in 2010, thankfully the testing has become more thorough; however, a test that involves getting into a car and driving is still not mandatory.

The 2020 Ontario guidelines state that once you turn eighty, in order to renew your licence you must take a driver's test every two years. You have to take a vision test, undergo a driver record review, attend a forty-five-minute group education session about new traffic laws, complete two in-class screening exercises, learn how aging affects driving and get tips specifically for elderly drivers. If you do well in the "class," you don't have to get in the car and drive at all.

An actress and singer friend of mine, Meg, shared her licence renewal experience with me. Meg is not your average eighty-year-old. She lives independently in her own apartment, swims regularly at the Y, walks daily around her neighbourhood, does the occasional acting job and has rebooted her singing career. She told me that one of the men fell asleep during the group test, and the instructor still passed him. He did not have to get in a car and drive. The ministry also reviews your driving record, but that wouldn't tell you if that man also falls asleep at a red light.

Eye disorders such as cataracts, glaucoma and macular degeneration can lead to reduced vision and are prevalent in adults over sixty years of age. Dusk and night driving are particularly unsafe for seniors. Sunset was at 5:06 p.m. the night of the accident. My mother and sister were struck at about 6:10 p.m. The driver had left home while the sun was setting, and at the time of the accident was driving in the dark.

With the ongoing rise in dementia and Alzheimer's cases, perhaps cognitive ability tests should begin at seventy-five years old, for the safety of the driver as well as potential victims.

BY THE TIME I got to my sister's house, my throat had tightened up and my voice was hoarse. Hoping to ease it, I sipped on some warm water while David and I waited for Mary.

The camera operator arrived first, camera bag over his shoulder and lights in hand. He chose their family room for the shoot, because the big picture window let in lots of natural light. After setting up his camera and lights, he clipped a microphone to the front of my avocado green blouse.

When Mary got there and saw how nervous I was, she hugged me. "You're going to be great."

After a minute or so of pleasantries to test the sound levels on our microphones, we began. David, who was wearing a business suit, often spoke at investment seminars and is the lead singer in a band, so he seemed comfortable being interviewed. Even though I'm not usually shy, I was nervous about this interview.

Mary asked if I believed the driver's age played a factor in the accident.

"Yes, I believe that a forty-year-old driver with better vision and reflexes would've seen my family and hit the brakes."

I tried to get the message across how unfathomable it was that the elderly woman did not see *three* people walking across the road. A driver has mere seconds to react when they suddenly see something in their path. 1. *See it.* 2. *Gasp.* 3. *Hit the brake.* The elderly driver did not see, gasp, or hit the brake. Apparently she hadn't seen a thing.

"My family were jaywalking as they had for forty years, but my point is, they were not seen *at all*."

Mary surprised me by asking what I'd said to Julie. That had not been on the list of questions we'd discussed.

Thinking back to seeing Julie lying comatose, I began to weep. "I told her I loved her."

A FEW DAYS LATER, I met Mary at a Timothy's coffee shop to retrieve my videos and CD of photos.

"Catherine," she said, "I got to know your family so well watching that video footage. My production team all said, 'She's great,' but I said, 'Yes, she was, but I wish I had met the other Catherine. The one in the videos. She was so happy and so funny.'"

I wondered, too, how long it would take until I was that person again.

Even though I wasn't there when it happened, I kept dreaming about the accident. I saw their scared faces in the headlights, Julie ripped from my father's hand. Dad watching Mom roll down the road. I saw Julie on the pavement, whimpering.

David's heart was in the right place, too, but nothing ever came of his idea for the J.U.L.I.E. initiative. So they would not have died in vain and to help me cope with my loss, I would continue my efforts to change the driving requirements for the elderly to avoid preventable deaths.

COINCIDENTALLY, while back in Kingston a week later, I sat beside a guy at the Loyal Oarsman pub who knew the driver's children. He told me they'd been asking her to give up her car keys for months. Apparently she'd said she intended to quit driving on her eighty-fifth birthday. Seven weeks too late for Mom and Julie. But even though she knew she shouldn't be behind the wheel of a car, I knew she did *not* get in the car that day with the intention of killing two people. It was an accident.

I went shopping for an appropriate card to give to the woman that killed my mother and sister. I wanted to help ease *her* pain. And mine. I found one with a bright yellow sun. It read: *Hoping brighter and sunnier days come to cheer you.* On the inside, I wrote:

> *We know it was an accident. A tragic accident. Although our healing process is a difficult one, we are trying to focus on our loving memories . . .*

The other purpose of the card was to let her know about the upcoming *16×9* show on seniors' driving. Mary had asked me several times for the identity of the driver, but I'd refused to release her name. I knew she was suffering too. Everyone in my hometown community knew about the accident. I wanted the woman to know I'd been interviewed about it. I wanted her to have time to tell her family and prepare herself before it aired.

I'd received her name from the police, and the man at the pub had told me her street's name, so all I had to do was check the phone book for the house number. Yellow envelope on the passenger seat, I headed to her house, two and a half kilometres from ours.

Driving slowly along her street in my "inconspicuous" bright orange truck, I saw it, a burgundy brick bungalow with white trim. The curtains in the front window were wide open. I parked across the street where I hoped she couldn't see me.

I held my breath for a few seconds as I looked at the compact, four-door car parked in the driveway. The nose faced the garage, so I couldn't see the damage, if there was any. Was that even the car she drove that night? Should I even be giving her a card telling her we forgave her? Dad had said she should be sending *us* an apology card. I worried that he wouldn't want me to be doing this. But part of *my* healing process was to forgive her.

I scooted up her driveway and slipped the envelope into the wooden mailbox mounted on the brick wall at her side door. Then I hurried back to my truck. I didn't look back, in case she'd seen me. In case she'd opened the door. I buckled my seat belt and drove away as quickly as possible. But I couldn't stop thinking of the poor old woman.

If she had come outside while I was placing the card in the mailbox, I wouldn't have known what to say. If I'd told her who I was, both of us would probably have cried. If she cried, I probably would have hugged the woman who killed my mom and sister.

Chapter 13

Seven months after the accident, I was standing at the stove stirring risotto. A song came on the radio with the lyrics *"maybe the next time . . . save your sister,"* and I thought of Julie lying on the pavement. I started crying.

Don, heading to the fridge to get ice for his Scotch, asked me what was wrong.

How could he not know what was wrong?

My husband had no idea how I felt. He couldn't see my imagined visions of "that night" and the "what if" thoughts that streamed in my head all day. He couldn't feel how much I hurt. He only knew that I was sad all the time. The woman he married—*poof!* Gone. I wished I could transport him into my head, so he'd understand how grief had overwhelmed my mind and sucked the life out of my body.

Sobbing, I said, "The song says, '*save your sister.*' I couldn't save her."

"Oh gawd," he said.

How could he say that? Why didn't he hug me? I wanted him to feel, just for one minute, what I felt. He didn't say anything more. He just sat on the sofa drinking his Scotch and reading the newspaper. Later I found out that the lyrics were actually "*save your scissors.*"

Sometimes I forgot they were all dead. I got back to living my life. At the Whistler Film Festival, Don and I had the pleasure of dining with one of my longtime actor crushes, Bruce Greenwood. I was so excited, I wanted to tell Mom. At a Jay's game where they slammed the Yankees, I wanted to call Dad and boast about it. I wanted to phone Julie and tell her that her "brudder-in-law" was making another scary movie.

"I picked up the phone to call Mom this morning . . . I forgot." I had called her every weekend for over thirty years.

Don said, "How could you forget?"

"Your kids don't live with us, so if one of your kids died, you'd probably forget sometimes."

He stood up and yelled, "I would not! How could I forget something like that?"

"I just did."

As much as he loved me, he had no idea how I felt, or how he might feel, because it didn't happen to his family. It happened to mine.

AFTER I HAD HEARD Bonita's messages from the other side, I left the meeting feeling lighter, less depressed, so I saw her again in June, four months after our first session.

This time instead of my lying on a bed, we sat in deep cushy chairs. Candles and rock crystals in assorted colours adorned the walnut coffee table in front of us.

Right off the bat she said, "Your sister is behind you right now. She likes it when you wear her clothes." I was six and a half inches taller than Julie, so her pants and sleeves were short on me, but I'd wear them sometimes. "She misses your singing too." Happy goose-bumps crept up my spine.

"I see red this time," she said. "It represents the anger that'll help you get out."

I assumed she must mean my anger about the laws that allowed elderly seniors to drive without proper testing of their competence. And a township that had yet to install a crosswalk on a dangerously busy street.

She closed her eyes. "There's writing here for you. You haven't finished? Write. I'm getting: *Finish it off.*" I had *not* told her I was writing this book.

"You're in this warrior state now, all about taking back your power, and the power for your family. Justice. There's so much going on. You're thinking, is what I'm doing a good thing? Absolutely. Your mom says you need help. You have no support."

The insecure warrior took a sip of water.

"This needs to go into levels of government. There's a story to be written. You're dealing with too much. It rips your heart apart every time you talk about it, but you do it. Do you know a Leslie?"

I smiled. "Yes, my niece."

"She might help you. Your mom keeps talking about a silver coat?"

"The mink my dad bought her."

"Your husband's feeling very sad. There's a change around him. I see him leaving your home but coming in another door. A change in behaviour is what I'm sensing." It had to be difficult for him to live with Mrs. Grief.

"He's worried about something and doesn't want to bring it to you. He's transitioning. You already have. You know who you are. He doesn't know where he should be. You have the whole load on your shoulders with all that's happening with the outcome of your loss. Your mom says you try to do too much on your own. You're alone too much."

Got that right.

"You have beautiful energy. Keep going over the hurdles. There's something very special in your kitchen, where the sun shines through."

A silly wooden plaque had hung at our family home for over forty years: *No matter where I serve my guests, they seem to like my kitchen best.* It's in my kitchen at the lake now.

"I see you helping children and women. Writing will be a big part of your future. You're so connected to the other side and to angels. The angels will feed you information; you just need to write it all down. Your mom says, no matter what anyone says, be who you are. Don't change for anyone."

Thanks, Mom. I needed to hear that.

"Helping change laws, going through the process, will help you and help others. I see you helping people, Catherine."

IN THE LATE 1960S, there were only a few stores at the strip mall. Three blocks away from us there was no housing at all, only fields and a quarry. Our Lady of Lourdes Church was still being built. I'd easily stroll across the two-lane road to the Dairy Queen to purchase my ten-cent soft ice cream cone with the curl on top. Dad smoked when he drank, and sometimes he would use his charm to get me to go across the street to buy his Player's smokes.

"Cathy, I bet you can't get to the store and back in less than ten minutes."

Even at nine years old, I loved a challenge. Proudly, in front of his beer-guzzling buddies, I'd say, "Oh, yes I can!" I'd easily run across the road and be back in eight minutes.

In the 1980s, Mom had been struck by a car when she crossed Days Road to go to the bank on the corner. A few years later, a neighbour, who lived on Abdo Road, the street behind us, was hit and killed while crossing there.

By 2009 the strip mall had grown to more than thirty retail outlets, and the sprawling fields a few blocks west of our home were bustling with new housing developments. Days Road had become a high-traffic zone, yet a quarter of a century later, there was still no crosswalk or streetlights. Not even "Caution" or "Slow down" signs.

Dr. Knight's dental office has been at the corner of Days and Castell Roads since the early 1970s. He was my dentist when I was a teenager. I called him to speak about the dangers of that stretch of road. He informed me pedestrian crossing had gotten so bad that he had his receptionist escort the elderly seniors across the street to return to their cars in the church parking lot or their apartment behind it.

The night of the accident, Father Brennan had told the local newspaper reporter, "Cars travel quite quickly along there. It's a bad road for people to get across."

The church was less than a one-minute walk from our house. It was so close we'd leave just a few minutes before the service began. With Julie between them, Mom and Dad would hold her hands crossing the street. When I was home, I'd walk in the middle and hold Mom's and Julie's hands. Dad, with his long stride, would walk ahead of us to open the church's big oak door. In the last few years, as his Parkinson's slowly advanced, his gait had become more of a shuffle. I never let on that I noticed. He was a proud man, not happy to have developed the debilitating disease so soon after his retirement.

Dad told me the stream of traffic had increased so much, it could take him three or four minutes to back the car out of the driveway. His friend Ron stopped entering the driveway to pick him up for their weekly beers for that reason. He'd pull up to the end of the driveway and honk his horn instead. The traffic issue bothered me, but I never spoke to my parents about my concern for them walking across the road.

What could I have said? Tell Dad to drive to church? Tell Mom to hike to the corner streetlight and back, more than half a kilometre, to cross the street safely? Would they have listened? I didn't know what to say, so I'd said nothing. After all, they'd crossed safely for over forty years.

The summer after the accident, I attempted to document how bad it was for pedestrians crossing that stretch of road. I parked my truck near the corner of Castell and Days Roads. Dr. Knight's dental office was to my left. In front of me was the entrance to the strip mall and the church, our family home was to my right, the second house from the corner. From my vantage point, I could look into our back-yard. The trees, which had been only saplings in 1960, now towered over my old playground. It was a foreign feeling, being so close yet not being able to go inside our home.

Feeling like a spy, I took out my iPhone and put it in camera mode. I looked up just as a young man pushing a baby carriage ran across. *Snap.* A group of young teens skittered in front of three oncoming lanes of traffic. *Snap.* Two women in their sixties stopped, looked both ways. *Snap.* They waited, started to go, saw another car, stepped back, waited, then finally crossed, walking as fast as they could. The scary thought of someone falling while dashing across in front of oncoming cars crossed my mind.

Four lanes in a sixty-kilometre-an-hour traffic zone (most drivers drive faster than the speed limit), and yet there was no crosswalk or traffic light. Why hadn't the community asked for a crosswalk years ago? What I witnessed took place in approximately fifteen minutes on a sunny day in June 2010. I wonder how many more wary pedestrians I would've seen if I'd sat there for a couple of hours.

To attempt to get approval for a crosswalk, I sent my report to Dorothy Hector, the local councillor for my parents' neighbourhood at that time. She said that not enough people walked across Days Road to justify the cost. I'm sure many people didn't walk across the four lanes of traffic because they were afraid of being hit. But I bet a lot more parents and their kids would walk to the store to pick up bread and milk if there was a streetlight to stop the traffic. And what about safety for the ones who did venture across without a crosswalk or lights?

MY FRIEND ALICIA, a production designer I'd met when we worked together on the horror film *Wrong Turn*, became worried about my well-being. By the end of June, I still couldn't work, and my usually bubbly personality had not resurfaced, so she introduced me to a NeuroModulation Technique (NMT) therapist, Deborah Frenette. I had never heard of such a treatment, but Deborah had healed Alicia of a debilitating allergy, so I wanted to see if she could make me feel better too.

Since I was at the lake, we arranged a phone session. I set myself up in my cottage chair. I had a pen, paper, glass of water, mini-cassette recorder and phone on the cherry-wood end table beside me. I looked around the great room. The floor-to-ceiling windows and hexagonal structure allowed a full view of the spruce, cedar and maple trees, the blue jays visiting the bird feeder, my cats sunbathing on the deck and the glistening lake below.

As I gazed at the photos of Mom, Dad and Julie on the sideboard, the phone rang, startling me so much I jumped in my chair.

Deborah spoke quickly in a cheery voice. "Hello, Catherine! Are you ready for this?" I was so ready. "I call it 'weird science.' It could be therapeutic for you to keep a journal of our sessions."

After our family house sold, I'd started to write about my grief journey for therapeutic purposes. With her permission, I recorded our session, so I could refer to it later.

"I'm going to be talking to your brain, or as I like to call it, your Natural Control System. Nothing, not physiotherapy or surgery or psychotherapy, can heal you if your brain is not accepting the message. I'll be asking you to 'tap and breathe.' When I do, I want you to tap the base of your thumb with your fingers and take a deep breath."

She was muttering so quickly I couldn't decipher most of what she was saying, but I was open to any alternative method that could heal my shattered heart. "Am I supposed to understand what you're saying, or are you just doing your thing?"

She laughed. "I'm doing 'my thing,' but I don't want you to hang up and say, 'Oh, she was talking gobbledygook.' If I'm going too fast, let me know." Slower now, she continued her introduction to neuro-modular therapy: "I'm coaching your system to work with me. I'm removing any blocks that are stopping your system from working with anyone—not just me, anyone."

Interesting.

"Let's tap and breathe—reinforce the system so it's ready to do the job. Repeat after me: 'I believe I am able, one hundred percent able, ready and willing to be healed.'" With my left wrist resting on the arm of the chair, I tapped and repeated her words. "We're going to do some wrist balancing now," she said, "to bring all the energy back into your body. You know how some people say they're scattered?"

"Yeah. I've been like that a lot lately."

"That's because your energy is physically scattered. We're energetic beings. The energy can get scattered, especially when there's a lot of trauma. By pressing your wrists together, you complete an energy circuit in the body. We bring all the energy back into your body. Put your wrists together at the pulse points, your right hand over your left hand; say your full name, and today's date."

"Catherine Helen Gourdier, June 21, 2010."

"Say, 'I'm in my conscious, rational decision-making mind now, and I fully occupy my body.'"

I said it.

"It really does help people to be calmer. Repeat it several times and mean it. Visualize all your good energy coming back to you. Remember to breathe."

Come on back, energy!

"Here's some homework. Write this down."

I grabbed a pen and paper.

"'I am able, willing and worthy of one hundred percent healing now.' Repeat this several times during the day, have fun saying it, but really mean it. Convince your mind you can do this. We're reinforcing that you're going to be healing with your mind. Turn the mind's attention to healing and away from trauma and stress."

She began her rapid talking again, as though speaking to someone else. It was bizarre. She asked if my brain was accepting and open. Apparently my mind was 97 percent open to this therapy.

"People think our bodies are healed by cutting them open or taking a drug, but that's not true. Mainstream drugs have a lot of side effects and can cause people a lot of trouble. Let's tap and breathe."

I tapped and took deep belly breaths.

"As often happens with people who have had trauma, there's some fragmentation in your system. A lot of what I do is based on a blend of science and spirituality. I modulate your system so your system can heal you. So that even after you've left me, your system keeps healing you."

Apparently we have neurosystems in the stomach as well as the heart, which function like a brain. Was that why seven months after the accident I still had anxiety in my gut every waking moment?

"Let's tap into the system's ability to heal. Breathe, Catherine."

At the end of the ninety-minute session, I felt depleted, but calm.

It was a hot summer day, so I put on my bathing suit, watered the planter boxes surrounding the deck, lay in the sun for twenty minutes, showered and then masturbated. I hadn't had sex with my husband since the accident, let alone pleasured myself. I hadn't been able to go to that erotic place in my mind. Feeling horny was a sure sign I felt better. Weird science was working!

In our second session, I shared how my husband had no idea how to comfort me. That he'd said some hurtful things.

"He just doesn't know," Deborah replied.

Thankfully Don had been there the weekend of the accident to help us. He collected the bereavement information brochures, got the police constable's contact information, drove us where we needed to go. But I don't remember him holding me. I don't remember Don in the room with Mom's body at all. When I walked out of Mom's bay and found Julie, I was alone. Was he behind me? Was I in too much shock to notice? Or maybe he looked at my lost, sad eyes and was afraid to approach me, because there was nothing he could do to make me feel better.

"He's probably never experienced anything even close to what you're feeling," Deborah said.

"Hopefully he never will," I replied.

Don had not experienced the sudden death of a loved one. His parents and his first wife were ill for weeks or months before passing. At least he had had a chance to say goodbye.

"It was a real shock to him as well. He's never seen you like this, things just 'came out' of him. He doesn't have a clue what's going on inside you."

She was right. I listened as she continued to defend my husband.

"It's difficult for most men to cope with emotions on any day, but when something like this happens, it's very difficult. Can you forgive him for not understanding what you're going through?"

"I want to. I bought the book *Don't Sweat the Small Stuff in Love*."

"I wouldn't call this small stuff, Catherine."

A devilish laugh escaped my lips. "I know. I put it on his night table." I didn't ask Don to read it, but he did.

"I'm not going to minimize the fact your husband wasn't as supportive as he could have been, but we're trying to understand why. Focus on letting go of the resentment and replace it with loving forgiveness. Tap and breathe. Imagine you're breathing in love and breathing out resentment."

I breathed in as she continued talking to my brain. "Depression is robbing you of vitality. Depression is often described as anger turned inward—have you heard that?"

"Nope."

"Keep that in mind. You did your best under the circumstances. Remember that."

I tapped, and listened.

"We're powerful spiritual beings. If we have positive beliefs, it will be a lot easier to cope with life in general, especially traumas."

I leaned back and put my feet up on the ottoman. In a quiet voice, she fed me more information about her healing process.

"We're working with the cells and DNA to release the genes that are inappropriately activated by stress. We're talking about spiritual powers of manifestation. About you as a spiritual being. Okay, let's tap and breathe."

The tap-and-breathe exercise continued to have a pleasant calming effect.

"Let's imagine you're bringing your system to a place where it can accept the beliefs. Visualize getting on a boat and being transported somewhere where you realize you're a spiritual being; you can manifest leaving the conditions that cause the depression and the fear behind on the shore. You're heading out to sea, to a place of letting go."

I had my own vision: "I'm on a horse, on the beach."

Excited I was so into the therapy, Deborah said, "Get on that horse and ride to freedom!"

I closed my eyes and pictured myself riding bareback on a palomino, his white mane and my blond hair blowing in the wind as we cantered across a sandy oceanside beach.

Deborah snapped me out of my daydream. "It's important that you're releasing, not running away."

Interesting observation. I'd felt like running away from my life a few times.

"We're going to do some work on your neurological system now. The internal reality is what's real within us, our connection with the source or God. The external reality is something that's more unreal— the world that we see with our eyes is less real than our connection with God. That's sort of how we think of it in this type of work."

I was taken aback when she mentioned God in the same breath as her work. I was still struggling to understand why God had allowed my sister and mother to be taken so horrifically.

"It could very well be that your cranial rhythm has been upset by this trauma. Ha! I'm getting a 'yes' on that!"

Hogwash! How could my "system" answer her? She sounded a bit zany. Yet her method seemed to be helping me.

The next day I didn't get out of bed until I'd repeated my "homework" lines three times:

"I'm in my conscious, rational, decision-making mind, and I fully occupy my body. I am able, willing and worthy of one hundred percent healing now."

Missing my mother later on that day, I felt my anxiety creeping back. To curb it I began to sing my mantra like a rap song while I vacuumed the mats in the hall. I hadn't felt like doing housework in months, and there I was singing as I swept the kitchen floor. Making up a melody, I sang, *"I'm able and willing and in full control of my body, yes I am, so I'll be happy today, oh yeah!"*

One bereavement counsellor had said that talking about the accident was part of my healing process. "You should aspire to get to a place where you can talk about it and not get upset." I kept stepping into the pain. I had to do things to help me heal. Like trying the zany but effective NMT therapy.

The next day there was more trauma ahead.

FIVE DAYS BEFORE THE ACCIDENT, I'd adopted the cutest longhaired, grey-and-white kitten. He had a quirky personality and behaved more like a puppy than a cat, following me around the house and coming when he was called.

Julie didn't get to meet him, but since she was supposed to help me name him, I'd sat in her room to get inspiration. Sitting on a shelf on the white wall unit in her bedroom was a Freddy Krueger mug. He's the killer from *A Nightmare on Elm Street* who uses a gloved arm with long razors for fingers to kill his victims. That series of horror films was a favourite of Julie's, so I named the kitten Freddy.

Freddy would poke his head through the banister rails at the top of the stairs or climb into Christmas gift boxes while I wrapped them. Once I found him napping in one of Don's shoes. He made me laugh every day during the saddest time of my life. Fearing something might happen to them, some cat owners never let their pets outside. I do, because they like to sunbathe, chase chipmunks and catch mice.

That day I'd let Freddy out, then gone into town to get groceries. When I returned an hour later, he was nowhere in sight. At five, it started to pour rain, and there was still no sign of him. I wanted a drink, but instead I repeated my NMT mantra over and over. When the sun set at 7:30, I became more anxious. I put on rubber boots and a hooded slicker and walked around the outside of the house calling "Freddy!"

Nothing. Scared, I prayed to God. I hailed Mary. *Please tell Freddy to come home.* At eight, I went outside in the pouring rain again. I looked under the deck, crying while calling his name. He'd never been out for more than an hour. I was afraid of finding him dead.

I phoned my friend Barbara, the one from whom I'd adopted him. We had met on the set of *Once a Thief* in 1997, soon after we'd each made a career change into the film business. We both had cats and no kids, and quickly became friends.

Sobbing I said, "Freddy's been gone four hours, now the fishers are out, and they've probably killed him." The carnivorous fisher is the second-largest member of the weasel family.

Barbara said calmly, "He's probably hiding from the rain. Call for him again, okay? Take out a bag of treats and shake it."

I grabbed the bag of treats and approached the door to go outside. Suddenly, there he was! Walking down the hall toward me. Either a miracle had happened, or Freddy had been sleeping soundly somewhere in the house the whole time. I didn't care which it was. I was just happy he was alive.

I picked him up and held him like a baby in the crook of my arm, close to my heart.

Chapter 14

In July, several days before the *16×9* show aired, the reporter, Mary, called me. I hadn't told her the name of the driver, so she did some old-fashioned investigating. She asked around the neighbourhood until someone gave her the name and address of the woman. Mary now had what she needed for a more powerful story: an interview with the driver.

She asked if I wanted to hear everything she'd found out.

I told her I did.

This is what I remember her telling me about what allegedly happened:

The elderly woman and her husband were driving back from the drugstore. When they passed by our house, they heard a thump. A few days earlier, teen boys had tried to steal her purse while she was shopping. She thought the thump was boys throwing a pumpkin at her car. She stopped the car, but she didn't have a clue what had happened until she stepped out and saw Julie's body.

She cried out, "I've hit a young girl!" She asked the "girl" what her name was. Julie's speech was garbled, so she didn't understand her. Then she saw another body.

My mother lay about three metres away, in a fetal position, facing down the road.

THE DAY THE SHOW AIRED, I encased myself in Mom, Dad and Julie's clothing. I wore Mom's yellow bowling T-shirt with *Neta* surrounded by black bowling pins printed on the left front chest and the name of her sponsor, *W. F. Gourdier Furs*, on the back. I put on Julie's grey jersey pants that she'd worn during her holiday with me. They were capri length on me but otherwise fit. The striped blue sweater Dad had worn to my fiftieth birthday party was wrapped around my shoulders.

Don didn't know what to do or say as I prepared to watch the show, other than, "Can I get you another drink?" At least I'd had his support in agreeing to do the TV show. Mom would've supported me too. If I hadn't believed that, I wouldn't have done it. I turned the volume up.

Mary introduced the show. "Too Old for the Road. When *are* we too old for the road?" Don handed me a glass of liquid courage, then sat on the sectional sofa a few feet away from me.

The program included a reenactment of a case in which an eighty-two-year-old woman ran a red light in Brampton, Ontario. A young mother named Mrs. Mendoza had been pushing a baby carriage, crossing on a green light, when she suddenly realized the driver of a car that was approaching wasn't going to stop. Frantically she pushed the carriage out of the way. Her baby was thrown, but survived. Mrs. Mendoza died, leaving her husband and two young children behind. That elderly driver was caught on film, driving, the very next day. When approached by a reporter, she yelled, "Get that camera out of my face!"

Our segment opened with photographs and video clips of Mom, Dad and Julie. Seeing my family looking so alive on the screen was surreal. Next they featured a close-up of the elderly driver who had struck my family. There she was. A frail, sad, obviously remorseful old lady. I shifted myself closer to Don so our shoulders touched.

The woman showed Mary the card I'd dropped off in her mailbox. "I thought they must hate me. I couldn't believe it when I got this card."

We know it was an accident. A tragic accident.

"If I didn't have my husband to care for, I thought I might kill myself," the driver said.

I felt sorry for her. This old woman would never intentionally harm anyone. She was suffering too. This message needs to get to the adult children of elderly seniors, I thought, so they can help their parents with the tough decision of putting away the car keys. Drivers involved in car accidents that cause fatalities grieve too.

At the end of the segment, Mary asked the driver if she had anything she'd like to say to the viewers. Using a tissue, the elderly woman wiped tears from her eyes as she pleaded, "If you feel uncomfortable at all, stop driving. Just stop driving."

Whether I was in agreement or not about Mary interviewing the driver, the old woman's raw presence had made for a more gripping story and sent a clear message to her peers and their children.

Relieved the show was over, I curled my legs up onto the sofa and sobbed. Don wrapped his arms around me.

"You did a good job," he said.

Over the next couple of days, three friends called to say that after watching the show, their mother or father had put away their car keys. Other friends told me they were in the process of convincing their parents to stop driving. Aunt Joan, Uncle Mike, cousins and friends sent me emails saying they were impressed by my courage to tell our story on national television in order to help make the streets a little safer.

I'd hoped my siblings would be proud of me too. But I guess it was just too hard for them to watch, because to my dismay, once again, I don't recall hearing a word from any of them.

Chapter 15

Early in 2009, Nancy suggested the fabulous idea of hosting the next Sisters Weekend at my lakehouse. We would have more time to visit, and Julie could join us.

Usually the sisters got together in Toronto, where, over the years, Julie had been included in only one of these weekends. The tradition had originated as a day of shopping, lunch at a pub, then back to my house for dinner, drinks and games. After the first couple of gatherings, Teresa mentioned she'd prefer to go downtown bar-hopping and dancing instead. She had moved to a small town and had young children, and didn't get out much, so I understood her desire to get a little wild in the streets. Besides, we all love to dance. But Julie didn't like loud, thumping music, so for the next few years we had to have Sisters Weekend without her.

We had a blast at the clubs, but those evenings involved less visiting with each other and more dancing and flirting with men we didn't know. One time we got hit on by an entire British soccer team, all in their twenties, which was flattering to us, as we were all over forty.

It was sunny and dry on that June 12 and 13 Sisters Weekend just five months before the accident. Not tropical hot, but at 21 degrees Celsius, warm enough to sit on the dock. Saturday afternoon we lounged on dock chairs in our colourful bikinis sipping Bud Lights and margaritas, eating tortilla and potato chips. We laughed and chattered over one another. When the sun disappeared behind the clouds, we got chilly and moved to the hot tub up on the deck.

As we relaxed in the warm water, pop music blaring, drinks in hand, Julie giggled, "Cath and I go naked in the hot tub!" True. We sang Katy Perry's song about kissing girls and liking it at the top of our lungs. Julie began to snicker as her bathing-suit bottom floated to the top of the water. Guffawing at how brazen she was, I took my suit off and flopped it over the side of the tub. Then all of my sisters joined in the frivolity.

As we drank more, our voices became higher pitched and louder. Julie said, "We should jump in the lake!"

Teresa said, "Why not? We won't do it when we're sixty."

I was pretty sure I would skinny-dip in my sixties. I was only eight years away from that milestone compared to her sixteen.

With our naked bodies wrapped in beach towels, the six of us walked down the winding wooded path to the water. Without a moment's thought as to whether anyone across the lake would see us, we stood holding hands along the edge of the dock. Squeezing each other's hands, we screamed, "One, two, three, tequila!" and plunged into the chilly water.

Our youngest sister had given us our most memorable escapade together.

That evening, I gave each of my sisters a white tank top with *CANADIAN GIRLS DRINKING TEAM* printed across the chest. They put them on immediately. We had a delicious dinner, and then spent the night in the games room singing upbeat karaoke songs. After playing pool for a while, Julie left her tipsy sisters to watch a horror movie in the house. The rest of us danced, sang and drank until well after midnight.

After Julie died, Treas asked to have Julie's "drinking" top. I have an adorable photo of Julie wearing that top, her left hand on her hip, mustard smeared on her top, a bit on her cheek, her right hand elegantly holding up a flute of bubbly as she beamed at me behind the camera. It had been my gift to Julie, and I desperately wanted to keep it. I didn't want to wash out that mustard stain. Ever. But my eldest sibling syndrome kicked in, and I let Treas have it.

Though I'd mentioned a few times that I missed them and that I wished we would all get together again, my sisters perhaps weren't ready to come back to the place where we had so much fun with Julie. I don't know. All I know is that nine years later, we still hadn't had another Sisters Weekend.

I LIVED ALONE at the lake all week, until Friday at around five, when Don would arrive for the weekend. I have friends in the city, but because they were working, they were unable to make the two-hour-plus drive to visit me. I wished I could work, but my brain wasn't ready yet. No one visited. My siblings Dave, Deb, Mike and Nance worked full time, and Treas and Carol had young children at home.

In late June I called Treas to ask when my goddaughter could come for her annual vacation.

She said, "We have a pretty booked summer. We're only doing things as a family this year."

Ever since Abbey was three years old, she had come for yearly sleepover visits with me in Toronto. After we bought the lakehouse, she'd visit for a few days during the summer holidays too. I felt really hurt by Treas's response. I hadn't really thought about it before, but I guess once a woman has kids, her siblings aren't her "immediate" family anymore.

Since they knew I was alone during the week, I thought my siblings would check in on me. But except for the occasional call from Nance, they didn't. One had said, "You don't have to talk about Mom, Dad and Julie all the time." Why not? I missed them, so I wanted to talk about them. But maybe that was why they didn't want to talk to me or see me. Or maybe we hadn't spoken to each other as much as I thought before the tragedy, but I hadn't noticed because I talked to Mom and Julie once or twice a week. And then there was the fact I used to work fifteen hours a day.

I did call my siblings, but invariably it was never a convenient time. They were driving their kids to soccer practice or grocery shopping or were on the way to the bank or with their friends. I never seemed to catch them when they were available to talk.

I suppose I felt more isolated because I didn't have children like they all did. And Don's adult children seldomly reached out to me.

I grew more lonely and depressed.

I'd never had suicidal tendencies before, but the more lonesome I became, the more I thought about dying. I'd be driving along the country highway and think, *What if I just drove full speed into the rock wall on the side of road?* Once, on Highway 28, a car was driving straight for me but veered off and crashed into the ditch. That scared the crap out of me. I pulled over and called 911. The driver survived. She'd fallen asleep; she hadn't been trying to kill herself.

For a less messy death, I thought about taking thirty lorazepam with two martinis. I'd fall asleep and never wake up. I could be with my parents and Julie. And I wouldn't be lonely or in pain anymore.

Our lakehouse doesn't have air conditioning. It's nestled among trees, so it's usually cool enough for most of the summer. But summer of 2010 was a different story. It was a sweltering, 30-plus-degrees Celsius for a few weeks in a row. The afternoon sun, shining through the windows of the house, had brought the indoor temperature to 31 degrees.

But the lake was a perfect 25 degrees.

One day I stripped off my shorts and top and slipped into Julie's bathing suit. To hide the scar on her belly, Mom always bought Julie one-piece bathing suits. A couple of summers earlier, I'd taken Julie shopping for a two-piece tankini suit. That style would cover her scar and be easier to take off than a wet, clinging, one-piece bathing suit. Julie followed me around the store as I held up one suit after another, finally finding a size small. The bottoms looked like denim short shorts, the top had turquoise, pink and navy flowers on a white background.

I walked down the winding path among the trees to the dock. I looked to the spot where, ten months earlier, Julie had sat on a bright orange beach towel, sunbathing, smiling at me, sipping lemonade from a flowered plastic cup. I sat on the edge and dangled my feet in the temperate water. The sun gave the lake a magical effect. I could see Julie swimming the dog paddle, kicking and splashing, holding her head above the water. Bonita, the clairvoyant, had said, "Your sister says she needs you." Why tell me she needs me, when I'm on this side and she's on the other? I'd have to die to be with her. Step by step, I descended the ladder into the lake.

At the last Sisters Weekend, Julie had climbed up that ladder, and reacted to the cold water by saying *fuck* for, I think, the first time. The night before, we'd watched the romantic comedy *Forgetting Sarah Marshall*, in which the *f*-word is uttered often. Carol was not amused by Julie's "new" swear word, but I thought it was hysterical when Julie said *fuck*. She obviously knew when to use that kind of profanity. She was thirty-nine years old, after all.

As the refreshing water cooled my body, I thought, *I could join my sweetie pie Julie.* I'd heard that drowning was one of the quickest ways to die. The first couple of breaths would be hard, but if I could hold myself under, breathe water into my lungs, I'd pass out and drown. Then I'd be with Julie and my parents.

I submerged my head and looped my arms and legs through the ladder to keep me below the surface. That worked, but I couldn't bring myself to breathe in the water. Drowning is easier to plan than execute. I squeezed my eyes shut, continued to hold my breath and thought of Aunt Joan. She'd had heart surgery two days after Dad's funeral. She loved me. If I died, she could have a fatal heart attack from the shock of it. Don loved me too. I untangled my limbs and popped out of the water, sputtering and crying. Grabbing a towel, I ran back to the house.

I took a bottle of wine out of the fridge and filled Julie's Tim Hortons wineglass up to the rim. I walked over to the sideboard to look at the photo of her sitting on the towel on the dock. She was smiling at the photographer. Me.

As lonely as I was and as much as I missed Julie, I knew I didn't want to die.

DEBORAH FRENETTE'S NMT healing therapy always improved my mood. Three days after my failed attempt to drown, we had another phone session.

"Your system is showing sadness regarding 'fertility,'" she said.

I was surprised she mentioned this. At fifty-three, it was too late for me to get pregnant, so I'd been thinking about adopting, but I hadn't shared that with anyone.

Don's twin girls were eight and his son was ten years old when I met them, and I was happy to welcome them into my life. Though

I'd consistently tried my best, my relationship with them had not worked out the way I'd dreamed it would, for a lot of reasons, some beyond my control. Being a stepmother can be a complicated and challenging role to play.

Though Julie was my sister, and an adult, loving her was the closest experience I'd had to what it might feel like to have a child of my own. She had fulfilled some of my maternal needs. With her in my life, I experienced what it could be like to have someone to look after. Someone who looked up to me and who loved me unconditionally, as I loved her.

But since Don was almost sixty and I was still grieving, eventually I decided to focus on charity work instead of adopting a child.

BECAUSE I WAS STILL so sad and skinny, my friends were concerned for my health. One suggested an alternative healer, Dr. Everett, who practised out of his home near our lake. He had doctorates in osteopathy, Chinese medicine, acupuncture and natural medicines. I agreed to check him out. I believed that if I went headlong into all types of therapy, eventually my pain and anxiety would go away.

Arriving at his house, I entered the small screened-in porch and knocked on the door. A silver-haired man invited me to take a seat in the treatment room. There was a massage table in the centre of the room, a desk on the right side. I sat down on a black vinyl and chrome chair in the corner.

As I did with everyone, I showed him the memory cards of Mom, Dad and Julie. I needed him to see whom I'd lost. He said, "Sorry for your loss," then asked me to lie down. I flopped onto the table and thought of Jesus on the cross: "Into your hands I commend my spirit." *Please, God, take me or help me heal.*

While pushing and prodding to realign my body, he suggested a test that would target specific areas. It could "help the healing move along more quickly."

It was called an electro interstitial scan, or EIS. An EIS is a computerized method that applies detailed algorithms and proprietary formulations to generate 3D representations of the body's organs onto a computer screen.

Since my insides were an anxious mess, doused in too much alcohol and not enough food, I agreed to the test. The scan was a simple process. I sat on a wooden chair in front of a fifteen-inch computer screen, my bare feet on glass mirror plates underneath the desk, my hands on two smaller plates on the desk, and two monitor patches, like those used for cardiograms, stuck to my forehead. Piece by piece, the screen displayed a woman's body—my body, which quickly turned a gorgeous shade of royal blue. I soon found out that blue was not a good sign. Blue meant my internal organs were inflamed and severely acidic. Sorrow can cause physical changes in your body, it seems.

He printed out a bar graph displaying the results. The graph showed that my sodium was low, potassium was high, insulin was abnormally low, and there was an imbalance in my thyroid. My cortisol level, or, as he called it, my "coping mechanism," was in the basement, practically not functioning at all.

Grief was sucking the life out of me.

He was concerned that my serotonin level was so low, in the negatives. Low serotonin levels promote feelings of sadness. Serotonin, a neurotransmitter, apparently plays a key role in regulating our feelings of happiness or depression, anxiety and overall mood. It also affects our sleep patterns and plays an important role in wound healing.

I was wounded, and my wounds could not heal.

Every organ in my body was low on oxygen. My blood didn't have sufficient levels of oxygen to carry to my organs, resulting in fatigue and shortness of breath. To kick-start my serotonin, I'd forced myself to work out daily, even if it was just twenty minutes on a StairMaster. Twenty minutes hadn't kicked it hard enough.

"I'm shocked you can even find the strength to go out in the world to do anything at all. You must be really strong when you're well," Dr. Everett said.

Yet another person amazed at my strength to get out of bed. If they could experience one day in my heart and head, perhaps they wouldn't think I was so damned strong.

It was suggested by this healer and Deborah that I cut out alcohol, sugar, gluten and dairy. No more daily piece of chocolate, no more bowls of ice cream on hot summer nights, no wine with cheese and crackers. Four "comfort foods" banned. Because I didn't want to take anti-depressant drugs, abstaining from booze was never going to happen. I switched to vodka. Less sugar than wine.

I tried to cut back on drinking by making tea and coffee dates with friends instead of indulging in cocktail hour. I was a grief-aholic, not an alcoholic. I didn't have a bottle of vodka in my bed-side table. I had foot cream, several books including a bible, laven-der spray, K-Y lubricant and a vibrator. When alone, I managed to get my drinking down to one or two drinks per night, but when friends arrived, my willpower galloped away on that palomino. Drinking is social. Drinking is fun. It helped me put my tragic loss aside and laugh.

The health practitioner said a skinny body with lots of sugar in it could be a breeding ground for cancer. I was 104 pounds, eating ice cream and chocolate, drinking wine. Telling me I could be giving myself cancer was just fabulous news. Of course, I wanted my physi-cal body to get better, but mostly I needed my mind and heart to be at peace. To be able to sleep without pills and booze and not wake up every day with anxiety rippling through my core.

When I spoke about the accident, my voice would go hoarse. I asked why.

Dr. Earl said, "If you remember back to your initial reaction to hearing about the accident and the deaths, you were probably speechless." I was. "Have you heard of chakras?" I had. "Well, the grief chakra is located here"—he placed his finger on the base of my throat—"and here"—he touched the back of my neck. "That chakra closes right up. So, you see, it makes sense when you know this, that you lose your voice when you bring back the pain of that night."

It made a lot of sense.

I MISSED MY REMAINING FAMILY so much, but they had all returned to their busy lives. Maybe I was being overly sensitive because I was alone so much. But unlike the two years before, when four of my siblings and their children had come to the lake throughout the summer, that year by mid-August, no one had come to visit. And no one had invited me to their cottage either. Was I being selfish, wanting them to think of me? To come visit me?

I didn't know what to do about my feelings, so I hoped another phone session with Deborah Frenette, the NMT therapist, would once again make me feel better.

"Maybe they don't want to be around you because you talk about it. And you're trying to do things to heal yourself that they can't, because they aren't there yet," she said.

She told me not to take it personally. But I didn't know how to *not* take it personally.

At the end of our session that day, Deborah spoke compassionately. "Remember, Catherine, you are a leader in your family, and they need you."

Then, I did what all leaders do. I hung up the phone and cried.

Chapter 16

Julie had a TBI, traumatic brain injury. TBIs are one of the top five causes of death in North America. A person can be conscious initially, but fade quickly into a coma.

Most victims don't die right away. They can survive for days or several weeks.

In the hospital, I had looked at Julie's chest rising and falling, and said, "She's alive, she's breathing."

The nurse replied, "The machine is helping her breathe, dear. She can't breathe on her own."

I had read an upsetting article that said some patients come out of comas, which made me temporarily second guess everything we did for Julie. The article said the brain, over time, somehow regenerates and can in some cases heal itself. It can take years, and the victim usually ends up partially mentally or physically challenged, but in rare cases, they do wake up.

Something else concerned me. When did the doctors realize Julie had Down syndrome? Her most distinguishing feature, her eyes, were closed. I wondered if her doctors had ever read the brain waves of someone with Down syndrome. Wouldn't their brain waves differ from a normal brain? I was worried that maybe the doctor had made a mistake. What if she wasn't brain dead? What if she was just unconscious?

I Googled and found an article that said scientists and doctors had done very little research on brain imaging and people with Down syndrome. There had been one study, and it described how the brain scans of people with Down syndrome were different from those without. Another study found that "slow wave" brain activity is a major characteristic of Down syndrome brains. Slow wave brain activity means higher activity of the brain in low frequencies and lower activity in high frequencies.

Now I was *more* worried. What if the doctors had read "slow waves" as a sign that Julie was brain dead? Since some TBI victims do recover, I had this grand delusion that Julie's brain would have regrown its cells if we'd given her more time. I didn't know the difference between being brain dead and being in a coma. I needed to understand that difference in order to accept why we'd agreed to let her go twenty hours after the accident.

Evidently "not being able to breathe on your own" is the deciding factor. Yet I couldn't help thinking about the "what ifs."

I remembered turning away from the nurse and holding Julie's hand, and saying, "You're still alive, aren't you, sweetie pie?"

Six months after the accident, I was home alone, watching an episode of *Grey's Anatomy* about a man whose partner was on life support. All medical shows have advisers in the writing room and on the set to make sure medical equipment is set up properly and displaying the correct readings and that official medical terms are used. In fact, *Grey's Anatomy* has inspired many students to train for a medical career.

In this episode, the character Dr. Yang told the man he had to "let go" of his partner, who was "clinically brain dead." Exactly as I'd done, the man asked, "Why is he on life support if he's dead? How can he be breathing?" Dr. Yang showed him brain scans of someone in a coma but not brain dead, so he could see the difference. The man argued that people wake up all the time.

Then I heard what I'd been needing to hear:

"But those people were not declared brain dead. His EEG brain scan shows his brain activity as flat, whereas the person in the coma shows lines going up and down."

Julie had indeed been brain dead. Her organs were in perfect condition, but her brain could no longer send messages to her lungs to breathe, to her heart to beat or to her eyes to open. I had tried Googling *brain dead* and *coma* but didn't understand the difference until I saw this show. And I am not embarrassed to admit I have learned a lot from television.

Finally, I accepted it had been the right decision to let Julie go.

DEBBIE WAS THE FIRST of us to have a milestone birthday party after the tragedy, her fiftieth. She's the middle child, fourth of eight.

For Debbie's fortieth, I'd planned a surprise trip. I had asked her to pack an overnight bag, and on a warm July morning, I picked her up at her home. We drove to Stratford, Ontario, to see the musical *My Fair Lady*. We enjoyed our getaway together so much that I wanted to do it again for her fiftieth. This time I let her choose the show. She chose *Evita*.

I booked a charming room atop a restaurant, with two queen-sized beds covered in cabbage-rose bedspreads, a fireplace, kitchenette, sofa and a bathroom large enough for us to apply our makeup side by side in front of the mirror. After we changed into floral dresses, we sat on the sofa and snacked on cheese and crackers. Chilled champagne bubbles danced in our glasses as we yakked about girly stuff. Between our sips and giggles, my thoughts shifted.

"I'm writing about *it*," I said.

She stood up abruptly and snapped at me. "You're just writing for yourself, right? You're not going to do anything with it, are you?"

It had never occurred to me that writing about my grief journey was wrong. But then, Deb doesn't like to share her personal issues. Because I need reinforcement, I do.

When we'd all gathered to begin the purging process at our parents' house, I'd gently made suggestions to my siblings to help them heal. I placed some grief books on the coffee table in the living room: *Chicken Soup for the Grieving Soul*, *Hello from Heaven*, Alison Dubois's book *We Are Their Heaven*. I explained that these books, bereavement counselling and psychic mediums were helping me with my grief.

One of my sisters responded, "Everyone's grieving process is different."

Another said, "I'm not going to talk about this to a stranger," as if the whole world of psychotherapy and grief counselling didn't exist.

I told them I'd read that after four to six months, the shock phase of grieving starts to wear off.

Nancy said firmly, "There are no rules. There are no schedules."

She was absolutely right. *There are no rules.* So why did my doing what worked for me garner such a negative reaction?

It devastated me to see my family in so much pain. I just wanted to help.

Grieving alone was agonizing, so I had turned to writing for consolation. My intention had not been to rile Deb, but to gain her support in my chosen path to healing. I had expected her to say, *Good for you, Cath, I hope it's helping*, as my friends, Aunt Joan and therapists had said. Before I had a chance to respond, she sat back down.

"Well, as long as you don't make it into a movie." (Aunt Joan had suggested just that. "I think a film would be a wonderful tribute, honey.") To hide my disappointment, I changed the subject.

After a delicious pasta dinner, we walked a few blocks in the warm evening air to the theatre, the mention of *it* forgotten. Our seats were third row centre, close enough to see even subtle expressions on the actors' faces. As the black drapes slowly parted, the haunting score began.

When I realized what was coming, I almost gasped, worried about Deb. I turned to see her completely still, staring straight ahead.

Sitting centre stage was a casket covered in flowers.

My plan in coming to Stratford had been to push aside our grief, but I'd forgotten the opening scene was Evita's funeral.

After the show was over, we walked down the street to a bar called Down the Street. While sipping our wine, we discussed how much we admired the voice of the handsome actor playing Che. Despite the unwelcome surprise of the casket scene, the show had been a welcome distraction from our grief.

Chapter 17

Over several months, I'd left messages at the police station asking when I could get my mother's and sister's clothes back. I didn't get a response, so at the end of August I headed to Kingston to speak to someone in person about it.

An hour into the drive, I called Dave and Nancy to see if they were free for lunch. My other brother, Mike, couldn't join us, because he worked shift hours. He was either at the hospital or sleeping. But Teresa happened to be in town. It was a Wednesday, so I picked up Dad's friend Ron too. Ron, always a comedian, still joked with me, but he'd lost the sparkle in his eyes since my father passed away.

Ron and I were the first ones to edge up to the bar at the Portsmouth Tavern (known as the Ports by its regulars), a laid-back bar for beer drinkers and students. Chuck, the bartender, plunked a bottle of Molson Canadian in front of Ron. I ordered a vodka soda with lemon, refreshing for a hot summer day. My sisters arrived moments later. Teresa wore a '50s-style, yellow floral full skirt, her usually straight hair a mane of bouncy curls. Her light blue eyes twinkled when she said hello. (I have green eyes, while the rest of our family have hazel.) Nancy was in a brown T-shirt dress, coordinated with a brown sparkly bracelet and headband. Her dark blond hair cascaded down to her waist. They looked too lovely to lunch in an old pub.

Wearing faded blue jeans and a jersey golf shirt, Dave sauntered in. He shook Ron's hand, then hugged and kissed each of us. We sat at the wraparound corner of the bar, chatting about the weather and other grief-free topics.

Before we had a chance to order, Chuck brought out a huge tray of wings, quesadillas, cheese balls and fried zucchini. Dad had been a favourite customer of his for over thirty years, so the food was his treat. *People don't know what to do, so they give you things.*

An hour passed quickly. Dave had to get back to work. We hugged goodbye, saying "Love you" as we pecked each other's cheeks.

When I dropped Ron off at his house, his wife, Barb, invited me in for a cup of tea. I politely declined, telling them I was heading to the police station.

"What for?" Ron asked.

"To try to get Mom's and Julie's clothes back."

They looked concerned.

"Are you okay going by yourself?" Barb asked.

I answered as steadily as I could. "Yes. I don't know if the police will call when they're finished investigating. I'm afraid they'll call

Nancy. She was there. She saw Mom's and Julie's bodies on the road. I haven't been able to talk to her about it. I'm afraid of upsetting her."

After an uncomfortable pause, Ron asked exactly what my dad would have asked: "Do you know where the new police station is?"

"Yes, thank you." *Across the street from my laid-to-rest family.*

The closer I got to the station, the more anxious I became about my task. Driving by St. Mary's Cemetery, I glanced at the old stone pillars at the entrance, almost directly across from the Kingston police station.

With trepidation, I got out of my truck and went inside. The receptionist at the front desk directed me to the Police Records window.

A woman in her forties sat at a long desk in a glass-enclosed office. It had a small opening so she could hear me. She looked up from her computer.

"Hi. Can you tell me if the police report is finished on my family's accident? It's been almost nine months."

"Do you want it for insurance?" the clerk asked.

"No."

"For the lawyers?"

"No." *Why is it any of her business?*

She kept on. "Who's asking for it, then?"

"I am. I want their clothes back."

Once I started talking, I couldn't stop. "My mother and sister were killed November 7, and we still don't have their clothes back. I'm afraid you'll call my sister, Nancy, who saw their bodies on the road. That could upset her more. I can't stomach the thought of their clothes being burned or thrown into a trash bin. I'm sorry, but I just want them."

She just stared at me.

"Is Constable Mahoney in? He's the investigating officer, I think."

She tried his line. "I got his voice mail."

I could tell by the change in her tone that what I'd said had affected her.

"I can also try the Properties Department."

She got voice mail again. She wrote something on a small piece of paper and slid it through the opening. "Here are the extension numbers if you'd like to leave a message yourself. You can call from over there." She pointed to a phone mounted on the wall across from the reception area.

I tried the numbers, but no one answered, so I left voice-mail messages for them.

I went back to the Records window. "Who is Constable Mahoney's boss? Could I have that number too, please?"

Keen to help now, she said, "Sure. It's Sergeant Benson." She wrote down his number and handed the paper to me.

I returned to the phone and called again. This time the sergeant answered. I explained the situation, then implored, "Sergeant, I need their clothes back. It's been almost nine months. Please, sir."

The sergeant said that Constable Mahoney was on holiday but he assured me he'd give our case priority upon his return. That sounded promising.

Afterwards, I went to the gravesite. Since there was no headstone yet and the mounds of dirt had levelled off, the burial plots were harder to find. I glanced around for them, then I blurted, "Oh, I'm right on top of you. Hello! I'm trying to get everyone to agree on what to put on your headstone, so it can be here for the one-year anniversary. It's going to be beautiful." I said a prayer, blew a kiss and got back in my truck.

After an enjoyable dinner of reminiscing with my high school friend Laurie at a gourmet pizza restaurant downtown, I headed back to Dave's house in Amherstview, a twenty-five-minute drive west of downtown Kingston. But because it was dark by then, instead of going straight to Dave's, I headed for the accident site, to test out how far ahead I could see with my headlights at that crucial spot in the road. I stopped at the red light at the intersection of Days and Bath Roads, one long block from our family home. I lowered the left-turn indicator and anxiously listened to it *click, click* while waiting for the green left-turn arrow.

As I drove toward our house, I stared into the path of oncoming headlights. In my estimation, I could see about five car-lengths ahead—surely enough time to brake. Dogs run out onto roads. Cats. Deer. Garbage pails are blown by the wind. Most aren't struck, because the driver sees them and hits the brakes or swerves.

The driver who hit Mom and Julie didn't see them, brake or swerve.

AUNT JOAN NEVER HAD CHILDREN. That was just one of the reasons we had a special bond. Unlike her, I eventually married, of course, but at the "spinster" age of forty-two. We'd shared our broken engagements and heartbreak stories. She opened up to me about everything: her old beaus, her regrets, her fascination with true murder crimes, mischievous escapades, even her sex life. The only thing she wouldn't talk about was the lives of inmates at the Prison for Women, where she worked for twenty-five years, initially as a guard. Eventually she was promoted to a management position, but being a people person, she preferred working on the floor with the inmates. I'd beg her to tell me inside stories, but she'd always say, "I'm not allowed to, Cath."

At five foot nine, with a sturdy build and a loud, direct manner of speaking, she could be intimidating. She'd share her opinion whether you wanted to hear it or not. But she had a big heart and a generous soul. Even though she didn't have money to throw around, Aunt Joan would tip the Chinese food delivery guy ten bucks and her hairdresser twenty, because "they don't get paid much, sweetie, they really don't."

After the tragedy, we grew even closer. On one of our martini evenings at her one-bedroom apartment, she'd fanned her arm around the living room and said, "Look! I have so many photos, they're cluttering my apartment." Framed photos were crammed together on her dining table, hutch, china cabinet and bookcase, and there were a dozen more on side tables in her bedroom. With grandnieces and grandnephews getting married and having babies, there was no end in sight to photos from our huge family. She was running out of space. So when I saw collage frames that said FAMILY on sale at my local photo shop, I bought a few for her.

The next time we spoke, she invited me to sleep over. I had never stayed overnight before, because my parents' house was close to her apartment. She loved my idea of taking the photos out of their frames and hanging collages on her wall. It was an easy solution to free up some space.

Aunt Joan had the TV on sixteen hours a day. News, soaps, crime shows. That night we had two hours before our favourite drama, *The Good Wife*, started.

Like me, AJ was a vodka drinker. I'd bring a bottle of premium vodka whenever I came to visit. "You spoil me!" she'd say. I poured several ounces into a cocktail shaker, added ice and, using a tiny atomizer, a breath's spray of vermouth. I shook hard for fifteen seconds, then poured the liquor into martini glasses. The floating shards of ice glistened in the ice-cold vodka. I added picks with three colossal olives to each glass. I prepared a tray of cheddar cheese and crackers too.

We clinked our glasses carefully, so we wouldn't spill any of the precious spirit.

"To family," I said.

AJ took a sip. "Damn, that's good."

I sat on the living room floor to remove photos from the frames, Aunt Joan chattering while I worked. Her black and white cat, Holly, would occasionally pay a visit, stepping across the splayed photos.

"Bill used to visit me every week while Neta went shopping at the 'Cat' Centre." That's what we called the Cataraqui Shopping Centre. I wasn't aware Dad had visited Aunt Joan that often. "We'd watch the Blue Jays games together, over the phone. He'd call me right after a good play or a stupid play by 'my Jays.' Julie and I talked on the phone every Tuesday and Friday. She told me about the *Y & R* and about the crush she had on her dentist, Dr. Chan."

Later she said, "I used to drive Neta to the States to go shopping. One time we stopped for a drink on the way back and were quite late. Your dad was furious." She laughed heartily. "We just lost track of time, but, oh, Bill was not very happy with me leaving him so long with all you kids!"

I was sipping my drink when she said this and almost spit vodka on the photos. Her stories warmed my heart. It made me realize how close she was to all three of them. Mom, Dad and Julie had played a significant role her life.

Long after *The Good Wife* ended, I was still creating collages, photos spread all around me, sorted into piles for the families of each of her siblings—Sylvia, Randy and my dad, Bill. It was one in the morning by the time I finally finished. AJ, a nighthawk, was still wide awake. She didn't have a guest room or even a full-sized sofa, so I took cushions from the loveseats and placed them on the floor.

Aunt Joan emerged from her bedroom in blue floral pyjamas. She handed me sheets and a pillow.

"Do you need any Tylenol or anything to help you sleep, sweetie?"

"No, thank you, AJ," I said, while putting together a makeshift bed on the floor.

"I think of Bill, Neta and Julie all the time, Cath, and I can't get to sleep. You're so lucky you don't have to take anything before you go to bed."

I didn't tell her I'd already taken my homeopathic grief anxiety meds, as well as a lorazepam. On top of a couple of martinis.

"Ya know, I felt Bill sitting at the foot of my bed one time, Cath. I really did, honey."

Smiling, I said, "I've felt them too." I really had.

Dad, Aunt Joan and Julie at 491 Day's Road, 1980s. Photo courtesy of the author's family

Chapter 18

My parents had bought burial plots for themselves and Julie, but not a headstone. Getting all seven of us to agree on the design aspects of the monument—shape, colour and dedication—turned out to be my most challenging role as co-executor, physically and emotionally.

I had put the process in motion in March, when we cleared out the house. Again, we all gathered in the living room at my parents' house. First we discussed the colour of the granite. Rose was mentioned, so was silver; Carol wanted black, so the script would be easier to read; some couldn't even think about it. My two cents: black was morose and silver too bland. I suggested charcoal grey. They accepted that. Agreeing on the stone would be the easy part.

Next we had to decide on the style. I'd seen a headstone with three hearts intertwined and loved the idea of their names in each of the hearts. Mike liked it too. The others didn't. We settled on an extra-wide, traditional rectangle headstone. After that, we had to decide on the everlasting dedication. We quickly agreed to etch an inscription along the base of the stone: *Loving parents of Catherine, Carol, David, Debbie, Mike, Teresa, Nancy and Julie*. But getting everyone to concur on the wording and other adornments was not so easy. Weeks turned into months of back-and-forth emails. Some wanted flowers in the corners, others crucifixes or bibles.

At the end of July, I practically begged them to make a decision so the headstone could be installed by November 7, 2010, the one-year anniversary of the fatal accident. One suggested *forever in our thoughts*; another, *forever in our hearts*. I offered *loving you always*; Teresa suggested *remember you always*.

I felt like a salesperson trying to close a deal. To help, I sketched a drawing of the granite slab, with a ribbon adorned with flowers flowing through a heart and the words *Love you forever, remember you always* across the top with crosses in the bottom corners. Centred on the base were the words *Families are Forever*, with all our names listed. Then I emailed it to them.

Six months after our discussions began, they finally approved.

My sisters and Mike accompanied me into the sales office of Kingston Monuments. Putting my fifteen years of sales experience to use, I treated the whole process as a business transaction. My family sat or stood in a semicircle around the reception desk. They listened as I took the lead once more.

I suggested adding the Gift of Life logo above Julie's name to further honour her and promote organ donations. I said to the sales-person, Isabel, "If the ribbon is two inches, that's an okay size, right? And we could put the trillium on it too." The Gift of Life logo is a trillium with a green ribbon.

Resignedly, she said, "I'm sorry. It'll be too small. We'll only be able to do the ribbon."

Of course sandblasting tiny flower petals on granite would be a disaster.

"How big can it be?" Fighting to keep a calm demeanour, I said, "I want it to look nice . . . for her."

She pointed at the diagram on the desk. "I measured from Julie's name to the bottom of your family name—GOURDIER—and there are four inches."

I said, "Okay, the logo should be two inches high, centred above her name, with an inch above and an inch below."

I turned toward my family, hoping they agreed. I don't recall whether any of them gave an opinion. They looked so sad. This task was tough for us to comprehend.

I signed the purchase order and gave a deposit. Then I took a deep breath and exhaled as the sales representative in me melted away. I surprised Isabel by suddenly hugging her. Her hands rested lightly on my back. I held her a beat longer than a casual hug and felt my eyes well up.

I gave a quick kiss goodbye to my sisters and Mike, all of them tearful too, and we went our separate ways to privately absorb what we'd just done. Sobbing, I hurried to my truck.

I cried because the ultimate confirmation of their death, the order to sandblast our beloveds' names in granite, was finished. I cried because my executor duties were almost over. I cried because that was the last decision my whole family had to make together. I cried because I was afraid their regular correspondence with me would stop.

AFTER MONTHS OF PUTTERING, on the one-year mark since I'd last seen her alive, August 31, 2009, I finished Julie's Woodhaven Holiday Collage.

We have two oblong dining tables at the lake, so I had made one my desk for the summer. A poster-sized picture frame and dozens of photos of Julie were scattered all over it: Julie swimming, singing, walking a dog, sunbathing, floating in a raft, playing pool. I cut out words written on cardboard that came with the frame and made my own phrases—*My Angel, I love you so much, I miss you, Sis.*

I cranked up the CD player and belted out "Proud Mary" while arranging the captions around the photos.

I was so happily engrossed in my Julie memories that I managed to make it to six before even thinking of having a drink.

THE BOX CONTAINING Mom's and Julie's clothes arrived at my home in Toronto the first week of September 2010. I had known that at some point in my life I'd see my mom in a coffin, but I had never expected to see her clothes in a box with a sticker reading, "Police Seal. Do not break without authorization."

I was anxious about opening it alone, but I couldn't open it in front of my husband. I didn't want to burden him with the awkward task of comforting me if I crumbled.

I knew that Mom had worn her black leather jacket that evening, the one we'd shopped for together, because I hadn't seen it in her closet. I wanted that jacket. I wanted to see what my sister had worn for her fortieth birthday party. I had to satisfy my longing to hug their clothes, then place them with the sweaters Dad had been wearing when he joined them on the other side.

But I wasn't quite ready to open the box.

LATER THAT MONTH, I found a large manila envelope sticking out of my mailbox. It contained the hospital records of my parents and Julie. It must have weighed a couple of pounds.

I'd been in such a daze on that tragic weekend that I hadn't asked the doctors any questions. Then I read Joan Didion's *The Year of Magical Thinking* and found out she had requested her husband's hospital records. Knowing she had done so, I didn't feel odd doing the same. Retrieving the information surrounding their deaths made me feel like I was doing something for them. I would finally have all the facts.

But I couldn't bring myself to open the envelope either.

I would read details of their deaths and open the box later. When I felt stronger.

Maybe in a year.

Or two.

Surely I'd feel better by then.

IN LATE SEPTEMBER, Barb suggested it was time to close the estate account and distribute the inheritance to my siblings. I thought I should let them know their cheques would be arriving in their mailbox soon, so they could prepare themselves for yet another hard reminder that our parents were gone.

I called each of them.

Number one said, "Thanks for letting me know, Cath." Number two talked about how she still couldn't absorb information too well, and that she'd driven straight through a stop sign. Number three related the story of a man who had asked her how she felt about getting her upcoming inheritance. She said it made her feel sick. The man replied, "Yes, that's the feeling I had. Sick." Numbers four and five just said, "Thanks, Cath." Number six was Dave, Barb's husband.

A week passed, but I still hadn't issued the cheques. I'd sit down every day, look at the bank statement and think, *Okay, I should send the cheques today.* And then couldn't. I'd study the balance, enter the total in my calculator, divide by seven. Every time I did it, I'd stop to think, *How many of us are there again?*

Closing the estate account meant that my official duties as co-executor were finished. I didn't want to let go. Taking care of family business gave me a purpose. I glanced over at a framed photo of my parents. They seemed to be smiling at me, not at the church's portrait photographer. A floral fragrance lingered in the air. Mom wore White Shoulders and Liz Taylor's White Diamonds. The colour white in a spiritual sense represents goodness, purity, sincerity, faith . . . my mother. Mom was with me. I picked up the pen.

Tears wet my face as I wrote the cheques: *Pay to the order of: Carol . . . David . . . Debbie . . . Mike . . . Teresa . . . Nancy.* And me. Seven.

Number eight was in heaven.

LINA, THE WOMAN who'd recommended the clairvoyant, Bonita, revealed that the group sessions at Bereaved Families of Ontario had helped her too. Still forlorn eleven months later, I decided to give it a try.

I arrived early at the Victorian house, smiling as I passed people I assumed to be fellow mourners smoking on the front porch. The counsellors, a middle-aged man and woman, told me to write my name on a stick-on badge and to feel free to take a seat or get a coffee. The furniture looked like garage sale goods, faded and worn. Three mismatched sofas formed a horseshoe around the square coffee table. A floral tissue box and a glass donation jar sat in the centre of it. Chairs for the counsellors were at the head.

The springs had lost their support, so I sank deep into the old couch by the door. From there I observed the disparate crew of bereaved individuals entering the room. A girl in her twenties; a sophisticated-looking silver-haired woman; two middle-aged women, one in a business suit, the other in jeans; and a skinny man who sat to my left.

I felt confident, ready to get the show on the road, like I was attending a fundraising committee meeting, not a bereavement session. The counsellors passed a pamphlet around and asked each of us to read one of the guidelines aloud.

The rules stipulated that we were not allowed to touch, hug or even pat each other on the shoulder, or do anything without first asking permission. The pamphlet pointed out that while one person may be trying to offer some comfort, the other might not want it or be ready for it.

We were also instructed not to tell people what to do just because it was something that had worked for us. For example, we weren't allowed to say, "You have to read this book." Instead we had to say, "I read this book and it helped me."

We were then asked to tell the group about our loss in a few sentences.

One of the front porch smokers, a thin, middle-aged man, spoke first. He cried as he told his story. Not only had his sister not let him know their mother was dying, so he could have a chance to say goodbye, but she'd also refused to give him any of his inheritance. Not even one token object to keep as a memento. A woman in her fifties fought back tears as she told the incredibly sad story of her twenty-one-year-old daughter who had suffered a severe case of postpartum depression and killed herself, leaving the woman with a three-month-old grandson to raise. I shouldn't say it was good to know there were others who felt as sad as I did, but in a way, it was. They understood.

After forty-five minutes, we took a break from the stories. I went to the coffee room for a cookie and herbal tea. The skinny man entered.

I said, "May I hug you?"

He nodded, and I gave him a hug, holding him close for a few beats even though he smelled like an ashtray.

When I broke away, he said, "Thank you. That felt really good."

It had felt good to me too.

When we returned to the room, people recounted more tragic stories. A twenty-year-old girl lost her sister to cancer, another lady's sister had a botched operation and died, leaving two children orphaned. The woman beside me lost her ninety-two-year-old mother eight months earlier, yet still wasn't able to go back to work. I couldn't help thinking, *You're so lucky—you had your mom twelve years longer than me.*

When my turn came, I began with a smile on my face. "It was the night of my sister's surprise party . . ." That's all I got out before I started crying. I could *not stop* crying. My sudden loss of composure seemed to shock everyone, including me. I'd felt so positive when I arrived that evening. I'd put ten bucks in the donation jar. I'd hugged that man!

The woman beside me handed me a tissue, and I sobbed through the whole recounting of the accident and my father's death.

At the conclusion of the meeting, one of the bereavement counsellors asked if we had anything we'd like to add. I did.

"I had many days where I'd do nothing but look at photo albums, photos on my computer, go online and find the newspaper articles on the accident and my dad's death, reading them again and again, even rereading the sympathy cards. I moped. After a couple of months, I assigned myself at least one thing to do each day, even if it was to go to the store to get milk. Even when I don't feel like it, I walk every day for at least half an hour. I've read several grief memoirs and books on the afterlife too. I've started to write my own book. These things have helped me cope, and maybe they could help some of you."

The counsellors told us that session was one of the most touching they'd ever experienced.

AROUND THAT TIME, the police report was finally finished. I don't know why an investigation into an accident in which two people were killed by an elderly driver, and no charges had been laid, had taken so long. I wondered if things would have moved faster in a case where charges were being laid, for example if the driver had been a texting nineteen-year-old.

To move forward in my healing process, I was determined to have a discussion with the officer overseeing our case.

Constable Drew Mahoney was a specialty officer, a collision recon-structionist. His job was to find out how a collision occurred. What had happened in the few milliseconds leading up to the accident? What happened after? He gets a call only if the victim has been killed or is suffering life-threatening injuries.

When I drove once again by the stone gates of St. Mary's Ceme-tery, I said, "I have to do this, Mom."

I pulled into the parking lot and backed the truck into the parking space, so it faced the police headquarters. I stared at the intimidating glass and stone building for a moment. Then I took a deep breath and stepped out of my truck. I walked slowly to the entrance and pushed open the heavy glass door.

After checking in with reception, I paced the lobby, awaiting the constable's arrival. When I heard footsteps approaching, I looked up to find a tall, dark-haired man in his late thirties heading my way. He shook my hand.

"You and your family are pretty popular. Everyone seems to know you. People are always asking me how the investigation is going."

"Oh?" It was nice to know so many people cared about my family, but we also have cousins who are Kingston police officers.

He escorted me into a bleak, windowless interrogation room and motioned me to sit at the table. It felt dreamlike, as if I were in a cop show.

"The day it happened my whole family was in town for my sister's surprise party," I said.

The look in his eyes confirmed that he already knew.

In a deep, comforting voice, he explained his scientifically deduced conclusions. The main reason for the accident was something called *contrast sensitivity*. Meaning the colour of Mom's and Julie's clothes was so similar to the dark sky that the driver couldn't differentiate between them.

Arguing politely, I said, "But what about her headlights? That's what headlights are for, to see what's in front of you. There are streetlights too. How could she not see three people walking?"

He explained again that it was because of contrast sensitivity. But I had a hard time accepting it.

I told him I had coincidentally met the driver's neighbour at the Oarsman. He'd said the elderly woman knew she shouldn't be driving. She'd promised her children she'd quit on her eighty-fifth birthday, seven weeks after the accident. Constable Mahoney dismissed the woman's age, no matter how many times I raised the issue.

He went on to explain more about the accident. "The driver did not hit the brakes. Even though it was a 60-kilometre zone, we could only prove she was driving between 37 and 43 kilometres an hour." Slow enough to brake, if she'd seen them. "That doesn't mean she wasn't driving faster; it just means that's a speed range I can prove according to the evidence."

"What do you mean by 'evidence'?" I asked.

He paused. Our eyes met. "Julie's shoes."

A sick feeling washed over me. I'd taken Julie shoe shopping once. She giggled as the salesman slipped the shoes onto her tiny feet. Only four foot eleven, she wore a size three shoe.

I didn't say a word, but Constable Mahoney must have noticed the change in my demeanour. He could tell I didn't quite understand.

He added, "Where her shoes were found, compared to how far their bodies were thrown."

Thrown. That word again. The thought of their bodies being thrown into the air and smacking down on the pavement made me nauseous.

"They were found six feet apart, both in the fetal position facing down the road, both of their heads in the same position."

Mere steps from the end of our driveway.

He laid out his diagram of the accident scene on the table. Marked on it were numbers 1 to 5.

"What are the numbers for?" I asked.

My heartbeat accelerated as he spoke gently while moving his tanned index finger slowly from one number to the next.

"Number 1 is Julie's shoes . . . Number 2 is her feet . . . Number 3 is her head."

My jaws clenched tighter with each reveal. My left elbow on the table, I tapped my lips with the knuckle of my index finger. He looked deep into my eyes to make sure I was okay. I wasn't, but I gave him a slight nod anyway.

"Number 4 is your mom's feet, and Number 5 is your mom's head."

The details were hard to hear, and I'm sure I was given more information that I couldn't retain after picturing their bodies on the road, Dad walking aimlessly between them, not knowing whether to comfort his wife or his daughter. But the meeting gave me closure.

Once we were finished, Constable Mahoney walked me back to the lobby. I did something I'd seen my mother do several times. I held his right hand with both of mine and uttered a sincere thank you.

I DROVE FROM THERE directly to the cemetery. Over the summer, the dirt mounds had been levelled and grass had sprouted. I placed a Porter Airlines water bottle filled with bright pink roses on their graves. I'd kept that bottle for ten months. It was from the flight Mom, Uncle Mike and I had taken back from New York a couple of weeks before her death. I hadn't been able to throw it away, because it was another memento from the last day I'd seen her alive.

Our wedding anniversaries were one week away, so I'd written on the bottle *Happy Anniversary, miss you, love you, Cath xox.* My parents were married on October 15, 1955. When I was a teenager, I thought it would be a special tribute to get married on the same date. In October 1999, I did just that.

I asked Mom, Dad and Julie to send me a sign they were there. "I won't be frightened if I see you," I said aloud.

I didn't see them, but I knew they were with me, because the anxiety of the police interview floated away and was replaced by the warmth of their love.

IN OCTOBER 2010, almost a year after the accident, I was in Los Angeles, the week of the wedding anniversaries, dealing with issues at our rental property. It was the first anniversary I couldn't call my parents and say, "Happy anniversary" to them, and the first time in eleven years I wasn't with my husband. Don was producing the hockey comedy *Goon*, in Manitoba. I had been alone more since we married than when I was single. Even when Don was with me, he spoke more to his damn BlackBerry than to me. The tragedy had taken a toll not only on my heart but also on our marriage.

The rock star was still renting our home in the valley, so I'd booked a room at Le Montrose Suite Hotel, the same place Mom and I had stayed six months before she was killed. The hotel staff knew me, which was somewhat comforting, but I still wasn't feeling myself.

The morning after I arrived, wearing sneakers, a casual cotton dress and a fedora-style hat, I made the thirty-five-minute jaunt to a jewellery store to get my rings cleaned. It was the same store where Don had purchased my wedding ring.

Sima, a saleswoman in her sixties who wore her jet-black hair swept up in an elegant bun, greeted me. I knew she "knew" about the deaths in my family when she hugged me, something she wouldn't ordinarily do. She had met Mom when we dropped in to repair a necklace. They'd hit it off immediately.

"My dear, dear Catherine. I'm so sorry. Don said for you to pick anything, honey, anything."

I had no idea he'd called her. Perhaps my dear husband was trying to alleviate his guilt at not being with me on our anniversary. But I was moved by his chivalrous gesture. If only I were the kind of woman who wanted to spend thousands of dollars on jewellery. I wasn't in the mood to shop until Sima piqued my interest.

"Honey, do you like crosses?"

The first time Mom and I flew to Los Angeles, she wore a sparkly cross around her neck. She looked at me and said, "Oh! You fly wearing a cross too." I was wearing a black cross with green stones that I'd picked up in Mexico. I always wear a cross when I fly.

Sima led me to a display case filled with sterling silver, bejewelled and heavy metal crosses. Then I saw *the* one. A stunning filigreed bronze cross with white and champagne diamonds. The piece would honour my parents. It was the perfect gift for this particular anniversary.

I also knew Mom would have kicked me if I didn't buy anything. *Are you kidding? Choose something!* she would have said.

That night I went on my own to a restaurant Mom and I had been to, BLT Steak, on the Sunset Strip, a luxurious and spacious place with white tablecloths, a mix of booths and tables and a long bar with an earthtone granite countertop. We'd gone there the second night of our holiday.

At one point that night, upon my return from the restroom, I'd found a thirty-five-year-old hunk sitting beside Mom.

"I leave you for two minutes and look at you," I said.

Mom laughed.

"She was alone, so I thought I'd join her for a minute," the man replied. "I'm Paul. If you need anything, let me know. Have a good evening, ladies." He stood up and left. It turned out he was an executive from the BLT head office.

Mom leaned toward me and whispered, "I told him we were celebrating my eightieth birthday."

I smiled.

Tittering, she added, "Well, we are, even though it's not today. That's what this trip is for, right?"

Indeed, it was. She loved the restaurant so much, she insisted we return a week later, on our last night in Los Angeles.

Now, walking into BLT on my own, I knew it would be the perfect place to celebrate both our wedding anniversaries. I glanced over at the bar and headed for the corner seats where Mom and I had sat for our before-dinner bubbly. Mom and I loved our champagne. I perused the cocktail menu. They didn't offer champagne by the glass, so I ordered a bottle of the Laurent-Perrier 1999. I was never that extravagant, but 1999 was the year I got married, *and* it was my anniversary. I texted Don and told him.

He texted back: *That was a very good year! Enjoy. Dx.*

I wished he were with me.

I was wearing an olive-green V-necked top, black pencil skirt and black pumps. I crossed my legs, my high-heeled foot moving in sync with the pop music playing over the sound system as I sipped my bubbly and observed the crowd in the dining room.

Maarten, a theatrical lighting designer I'd worked with when I was co-producing our friend Dina's one-woman show in Toronto, dropped in to offer his condolences. "I'm so sorry. I just don't know what to say."

"That's the right thing to say," I said, and hugged him.

I didn't really want to go there, but I couldn't help myself. "Did Dina tell you that we were waiting at my brother's house in zombie costumes?"

"Yes. Maybe it was good that it happened then? Somebody up there made the decision for it to happen while you were all there."

Good? No! Somebody "up there" had made a bad decision. Maarten meant well, but that idea of us "all together" did not give me any comfort.

Twenty minutes later, he had to leave to attend a play, but it had been kind of him to stop in and offer his condolences.

I was left alone listening to David Clayton Thomas of Blood, Sweat & Tears singing about how he wanted to *die naturally.* Julie and Mom didn't "go naturally." That was what made accepting their deaths so hard. Next up was Dido's song, "Thank You," about someone giving her the best days of her life. Her melancholy lyrics crushed me.

I gestured to the bartender to come over so I could pay the tab. I had to leave before I embarrassed myself by crying in a restaurant full of people enjoying themselves. But as he approached from the far end of the counter, I felt Mom send me a message: *Don't cry, honey. Have some champagne for me!*

Instead of asking for the bill, I ordered the tuna tartare appetizer.

I sat up as straight as a ballerina while the bartender poured more champagne into my flute.

I couldn't leave half a bottle of champagne. My mother would kill me if I did that.

FRIENDS CONTINUED to invite me for tea, to dinner, a walk, cocktails. But I didn't always call back. I couldn't. I should have. I needed them to know it wasn't them—it was me.

I'd talk for ten minutes, then think, *That's all I can manage.* It would be the same conversation every time. How're you feeling? You doing okay? I'd say I was fine when I wasn't. Some days I didn't want to pretend I was okay.

I got calls for work too, but I couldn't take the jobs. I wished I could. It would get my brain focusing on film production responsibilities instead of missing my dead family and my living family. A job would give me a reason to put on street clothes instead of wearing yoga pants all day.

But I wasn't ready to coordinate a cast and crew of two hundred. I couldn't accept the responsibility of giving the cast their call times. What if I forgot to call someone? It had happened to me once. I had twenty-two dancers to call for rehearsals for *Chicago*. I'd put the list in front of me each night and tick off their names as I punched in their numbers. A crew member must have called me over the walkie-talkie, distracting me after I'd checked off the dancer's name and started dialling her number. Afterwards, I forgot to call her back. The next day, Catherine Zeta-Jones's dancing partner didn't show up. Not a good experience for me. I didn't want to screw up ever again.

People didn't understand that I needed more time to get my brain to function properly. They *couldn't* know, because they weren't members of the debilitating sudden-death grief club.

Chapter 19

It was November 2, 2010. A year had passed since I'd called Julie on her fortieth birthday and heard her sweet voice say, *I'm drinking champagne, Cath*. I missed her so much that I put on her sweatpants and matching pink and grey jacket. I grabbed Dad's blue striped sweater, a floral top of Mom's and Julie's Tim Hortons wineglass, and I walked over to Tequilaville.

Attached to our games room at the lake is a library with pine bookshelves that go almost to the ceiling. That's where I kept Julie's VHS horror movie collection. It included the complete series of *A Nightmare on Elm Street*, *Hallowe'en*, and *I Know What You Did Last Summer*, 1 and 2. Also three seasons of *Melrose Place*, a series she'd started watching the year she passed. Season 3 was in cellophane, unopened. It had been in my fortieth birthday gift bag to her, along with a bottle of bubbly, the photo album of her summer vacation, a green top and night cream.

Since her skin had become drier in her thirties, I'd been buying her face cream for several years Mom said she would never remember to put it on. The nights I was with her, she'd try rather sloppily to apply it, then I'd take over. She would smile adoringly at me as I smoothed the cream on her cheeks and forehead. Skin dryness and irritations are common in those with Down syndrome. She had atopic dermatitis, or atopic eczema, on her elbows and backs of her arms. Rough, red, dry skin easily treated with a steroid cream. I would massage lotion into her hands and feet too.

At four thirty, I turned on the *Young and the Restless*, her favourite soap opera, but kept the volume on mute. Julie adored country artist Randy Travis, so while I placed her VHS tapes, her wineglass and my parents' clothes on the bar, I sang a verse of his song "I'm Gonna Love You Forever." Searching through the stacks of karaoke DVDs, I found the '60s pop music we liked to sing. I made Sunburn Margaritas, the same drinks Julie and I drank the summer before. Tequila, cranberry juice and lime blended with crushed ice. I poured the mixture into the blue and red margarita glass for Julie and the lime green one for me. I put her drink on the bar beside the birthday shrine and took a selfie.

Julie and I had spent a lot of time in our games room, playing Wii bowling, pool and shuffleboard, and singing karaoke. Gazing at her collage board photos, I sang some of our favourite '60s tunes. Whenever I sang "My Guy," Julie would be my backup singer and would repeat "*my guy.*" She liked classic musicals and once asked to sing "Oklahoma." I have a photo of her, head thrown back, singing her heart out. It perfectly captures her heartwarming personality. When we sang "Leader of the Pack," I'd sing the lead, and Julie would shout out the "*down, down*" and "*town, town*" parts. We'd sung that song a dozen times, but I'd forgotten that it ends with the boy from the wrong side of town crashing his motorcycle, dying. Now I couldn't sing the rest.

I sat on a bar stool, looking at Julie's birthday shrine. I guzzled my drink, then picked up her margarita too.

In my early thirties, I'd been shattered by the surprising end of a relationship. Seeing how sad I was, my BFF Kirsty said, "You like to sing. You should do something with that." I ended up producing several charity cabaret shows as fundraisers for the Ontario Rett Syndrome Association (ORSA).

Rett syndrome is a rare genetic neurological and developmental disorder that affects the brain. It afflicts girls almost exclusively. They are born seemingly healthy but eventually lose the ability to speak, walk and eat. Breathing may also become difficult.

I'd initially become involved with ORSA through a fundraiser at my fitness club. I was moved after meeting a couple of the girls with Rett syndrome and their parents. My "production team" was just me, with a cassette tape of prerecorded music, a microphone and several glamorous costumes. My repertoire included Broadway hits, songs by Marilyn Monroe and Patsy Cline, and for fun, Madonna's "Like a Virgin."

On opening night, the classy dining room of the Yorkville restaurant the Bottom Line was packed with friends and family. I was quite nervous throughout my performance, but the support I felt in the room helped to calm me. Near the conclusion, I began singing "Over the Rainbow." Looking out into the audience, I got distracted by someone walking across the room and forgot the lyrics. Not wanting anyone to know, I looked at Julie in the front row and said, "Hi, Jule." Then, in my short, tight, red-sequined dress and high-heeled black patent pumps, I carefully sat on the edge of the stage, my gaze down as I desperately listened to find my place in the music.

When I started singing again and raised my eyes, I realized that Julie, of her own accord, had come up to the stage. She sat beside me, her right hand clenched in a fist using it as a microphone, pretending to sing along with me. When the audience applauded, she put her arm around me, lightly patted my shoulder and kissed my cheek. Fortunately I have this tender moment recorded on a VHS tape.

Several months after the accident, I found out that a pregnant woman, Shannon Murphy, had sung "Over the Rainbow" to Julie as she lay on the pavement. Shannon told me "Julie was whimpering," so she lay down beside her, held her hand and sang to her. I was thankful Julie had Shannon with her, but I wished it had been me comforting her. Now when I hear that beautiful song, I think of sweet Julie lying on the road.

Was I acting normal for someone who was grieving? Making shrines, pouring drinks for someone who wasn't physically present, talking to dead people, singing with my deceased sister? I certainly was living up to my sisters' proclamation that *Everyone's grieving process is different.* And *There are no rules.*

Sometime that night at Tequilaville, while singing another of our

'60s songs, "It's My Party," I lost it. My wail travelled through the screen door and into the woods, where no one but the wildlife could hear me. I had to cry now, because I'd be seeing my family in a few days at the one-year anniversary. I always felt I had to stay composed in front of them.

MY FAMILY GATHERED at Our Lady of Lourdes Church on Saturday, November 6, 2010, for the 5:15 mass, the same mass as the night of the accident. It felt unsettling to pull into the church parking lot rather than the driveway of our home across the street.

Don and I sat in the same pew that my family had sat in for over forty years. The second-last row, on the right side. I fondled the Gift of Life pin on the lapel of my coat as I scanned the room, smiling at the large turnout of my extended family from my father's and mother's sides. My cousin Diane McCormick told me she'd always come over "to give Uncle Bill a kiss on the forehead." Our friend Karen, who had sat with Mom, Dad and Julie that fateful night, joined us. I had started to refer to her as my *big sis*. Sometimes I needed a big sis, instead of always being one.

Father Brennan announced, "This mass is in memory of and for the repose of the souls of Bill, Neta and Julie Gourdier."

Even though I had known it was coming, a year later this reality was still hard to comprehend.

After the service, several parishioners asked how I was doing. Putting on a happy face I said, "I'm good, thank you, I'm fine."

Outside on the steps, I looked across the street and saw lights on in "our" house. New drapes. An unfamiliar car in the driveway. A shadow passing by the front window. A new family lived there. I hoped they were as happy as we had once been.

Friends and family joined us at the Oarsman. We packed the cozy pub. There were a few tears, but mostly we drank beer and wine and laughed a lot.

Near the end of the evening, a high school friend said, "So, now you've got all the 'firsts' out of the way."

He had no idea. I wanted to say, *You're so wrong. Tomorrow is the 7th, the actual date of the accident. The next day, November 8, is the day we had to say goodbye to Julie. The day we had to make the decision to take her off life support and donate her organs. There is my first Christmas without any parents, then December 30, the one-year anniversary of Dad's death, and January 5, the one-year anniversary of his funeral.*

Instead, forcing a smile, I gave him a hug and said, "Thank you so much for coming." Then I gripped the stem of my wineglass and went to the back of the room to join the rest of my boisterous family, who were also pretending to be okay.

THE NEXT MORNING, on the one-year anniversary, I drove to the accident site. Holding a pot of pink flowers, I stepped out of my truck and placed the flowers by the post near where my mother's body had lain. I stood at the curb and looked down at the manhole cover.

Mom had been thrown to that spot. Julie's body, only two metres away, had been closer to our driveway. Though sickened with the vision of them lying there, I kept staring at the pavement. I believed in stepping into the pain to come out the other side, but there was a point when it was too much for me.

I got back in my truck, thinking about how horrific it must've been for my father to witness their deaths. How terrifying for him to be so helpless. As I reached for the tissue box in the back seat, I was startled by a sharp rap. It was an elderly woman. I lowered the window.

In a matter-of-fact tone, pointing at the flowers, she said, "Are you with this?"

"Yes," I said.

I expected her to say, *Sorry for your loss.*

She yelled, "You did that TV show! You said all seniors are stupid! I didn't like the slant of that show at all, calling all seniors stupid! Do you know how busy this road is? That poor woman, you blamed her, it wasn't her fault!"

I tried to interject, but she yelled over me. She would not listen, just as she had not listened to the message of the *16×9* show. No one had said elderly seniors were stupid.

Finally I said, "I sent the driver a card saying we knew it was an accident. Do you recall seeing that in the show?"

The woman continued ranting. "I had guests here a while ago who wanted to walk to church. I wouldn't let them. That road is too dangerous to walk across. I drove them." I couldn't believe what this callous woman said next, to a grieving daughter. "You should have driven your parents. You never should have let them walk across that road."

She might as well have stabbed my heart with a butcher knife. I started to quiver.

"It was a surprise party—"

"I know it was! But you should've driven them."

"Lady, I'm grieving here. Please stop yelling at me."

"My parents are dead too, you know!" She looked to be in her eighties. Of course her parents were dead.

She returned to the TV show. "How dare you say seniors are stupid!"

"I did not say that. No one said that. The driver didn't see my family at all. That's my issue." I struggled to appear calm despite my tears. "There was another story on the show, about an eighty-two-year-old woman who ran through a red light and killed a mother pushing a baby carriage. Did you see that?"

She stopped yelling. "No."

I now questioned whether she had seen the show at all.

"I'm trying to do something to make this road safer to cross. You'll see. I hope."

She finally huffed away, revealing a small dog tugging at his leash to get her moving.

How cruel of her to speak to me that way. She didn't even know me.

I blew my runny nose and sat for another moment, glancing at the church, our home, the road. I took one last look at the flowers on the roadside, took a deep yoga breath, turned the key in the ignition and then did a U-turn over the section of the road where their bodies had lain.

THE THOUGHT OF MY SISTER'S eighty-seven-pound body lying on an operating table while surgeons cut out her heart, liver, lungs, kidneys and eyes made me feel sick, but still, I wanted to meet the people whose lives she'd saved.

Was the heart recipient still alive? Who was breathing with Julie's smoke-free lungs? Who got Julie's eyes? It's not as portrayed in the movies. I couldn't look into the recipient's eyes and see Julie's hazel eyes looking into mine. Only the corneas are donated. Since she was small, I wondered if she'd saved any children's lives.

A couple of weeks later, before I had a chance to enquire about writing to them, we received a letter from Trillium Gift of Life. The cover letter said, "Enclosed is a letter from the recipient of Julie's lungs." The recipient's letter was on white paper in Bradley hand font in Tiffany blue ink.

Dear Donor Family,

The question of how to begin this letter and how exactly I am going to achieve thanking you have been on my mind since the moment I woke up from surgery. It's true when they say there is no way you can thank someone for saving your life. No words can amount to the gratitude you feel toward a perfect stranger, a stranger who saved your life without even knowing it. Your loved one has saved me.

I know how you can thank me, I thought. *I want to meet you, hold you. Look into your eyes.*

I was born with cystic fibrosis. I am now in my early twenties, recently being able to celebrate another birthday. When I was sixteen, my health began to slowly deplete until a year ago, when I was put on the waiting list for my first double lung transplant. I was on oxygen twenty-four hours a day and couldn't do much at all. I waited five months for the call and received it while trying to fight off a lung disease. Doctors thought I only had a couple of months left, I was so fragile and weak, they were amazed I was here at all.

I received my double lung transplant on November 9, 2009.

November 9. The day after we'd said goodbye to Julie.

Julie's memorial card had read, *November 2, 1969, to November 8, 2009.* But that was not true. Julie was kept on life support until the next day. I'd missed all those hours I could have been holding her warm hand. Had I known they weren't going to perform the surgery until the next day, I would have lain with her that night, especially since I'd spent most of her last day alive driving to and from Toronto. I'd assumed the surgery was going to take place that evening, so her organs would be in the best possible condition. Was it delayed because they had to target or transport the recipients before organizing the transplant surgeries?

It tormented me even more after I read books on near-death experiences, about how people's spirits supposedly hover above their bodies while they're still alive. How they float in the corner of the room and look down at their loved ones crying. I had dated a guy who was bitten by a shark and left with a huge scar across his back. He told me he'd floated in the corner of the operating room and watched his surgery being done. It ripped me apart knowing Julie had been alone her last night in her body.

The letter went on.

> My family and I consider it the best Christmas gift I could ever receive. It was the first Christmas in years that I was able to fully enjoy without worrying about antibiotics. It was also the first Christmas in years that I was guaranteed to be home (before I alternated between spending Christmas or New Year's in the hospital fighting infection). The next gift your loved one has given me is the chance to *dance* once again.

A common thread between us. Julie's love of dancing, hers and mine.

> About three years ago I had to give up my love and passion. I've missed it so much and think of your family every time I get closer to being able to dance again. I cannot express how sorry I am for your loss. The thought that someone else has been going through pain while I've been given a new lease on

life saddens me. I hope this letter helps—even in the smallest way. My family and I are extremely thankful for the gift of time you have given us all.

We held a fundraiser/celebration and lit a candle in honour of and in memory of your loved one. We will continue to do so every Nov. 9th. Without you, the possibility of a bright and happy future was not available. Thank you for giving my family and I more smiles, memories and time together.

As much as I wanted to meet the recipient, the Gift of Life Association does not allow this. But I was permitted to write back. So I did.

Dear Dancer,

You expressed your love of dancing and how much you're looking forward to dancing again. So, that is what I choose to call you rather than "recipient."

I was thrilled to know that my beloved one's sudden death has given life to a wonderful young person. I think you're a girl?

You expressed that you didn't know how to thank us. You have. Your heartfelt words are warm and comforting.

The rules say we can't meet, but being able to meet you would console me. Thank you for keeping my family in your thoughts and prayers. I will think of you each year on my sister's anniversary, November 8. Cheers to your one-year anniversary with your new lungs!

I'll look forward to, as well as cherish, continued correspondence. So, young person, dance, then, wherever you may be. Dance for my beloved who now dances in the heavens.

Sending love and prayers that you will live a long and happy life.

MY BODY NEEDED A TUNE-UP, so I went to visit my brawny osteopath massage therapist. He even has a brawny name. Vlodek.

While soothing spa music played, I breathed in the scent of the aromatherapy candle and undressed. My feet get cold when I have a massage, so I keep my socks on. I choose unusual ones specifically because Vlodek finds them amusing. He'd been treating me for several years, initially for neck and shoulder pain, but also to keep my body in alignment.

Into Buddhism, yoga and good health in general, Vlodek is a mind and body healer in one package. As he ran his strong hands across my bony back and shoulders, he said, "How do you keep your weight off? You're even smaller now."

He'd forgotten.

"Grief," I said.

"I didn't mean to go there," he said apologetically.

He'd been one of the recipients of my drunken email blast about my dad's sudden death. This was the first time I'd seen him since.

As he massaged and manipulated my body, he said, "Breathe, Catherine, breathe." He explained that in the Western world, we focus on our physical being, our physical life, rather than on what will happen after we die or what happened before we were born. He told me that my physical body's condition was in the top 5 percent for a woman my age and that I should focus on the healthy part of me. Directing my negative thoughts into positive thoughts would help me heal mentally and physically. His studies taught him that we suffer a great deal in our physical life and that our physical life is merely a preparation for the beautiful place we go to after we die.

Lying on my stomach as he massaged my lower back, I felt the tension in my body float away.

"If we could let go of the sadness when someone dies," he said, "and instead focus on where they are now and believe they are truly in a better place, we'd be able to live happier and more fulfilling lives."

I believed him, but their deaths would be so much easier to accept if Mom could say, *Don't cry, honey. It's beautiful here. The shoe stores are awesome, your dad plays golf every day, Julie's got her own karaoke machine, and we met Elvis.*

Before I left, I showed Vlodek the small photo album I carried with me. The one I'd made for Julie, mostly of photos of her vacation with me at the lake. He turned the pages slowly, taking in all twenty pages.

"I can see how much Julie loved her life," he said.

Tucked in the back of the album was one more photo—of me with all of my siblings taken at my father's seventy-fifth birthday party in our local pub.

"Wow. You're lucky to have such a big family."

Yes. I am. Sometimes I miss them so much. I've often wondered how different my life might have been if I hadn't moved to the big city when I was only eighteen, so far away from my happy-go-lucky family.

Chapter 20

I am usually crazy for Christmas. Even when I lived alone, I would buy a six-foot pine Christmas tree and lug it up to my apartment all by myself. I'd hang mini-lights and festive decor everywhere. I'd put out festive hand towels, red candles and mugs with poinsettias painted on them. I threw annual Christmas cocktail parties and always wore red or green. I loved Christmas shopping. And I especially looked forward to coming "home" for the holidays.

I wasn't looking forward to Christmas in December 2010. Where was that damn Grinch when I needed him to stop Christmas from coming?

I fretted, feeling anxiety flow through my entire body at the thought of the approaching holiday season. Except for spending the festive holidays twice in California with Don's parents, I had always celebrated with my parents and family at our house on Days Road. In fact, the first time I spent Christmas in California, the year we got married,

I'd invited Deb, my brother-in-law Dave and their kids to join us. I couldn't imagine celebrating Christmas without any of my family.

Don's parents were deceased, and his children, which he had with his second wife in the late 1980s, always flew to California to be with their mother for the holidays, so this year, for the first time Don and I would be alone to celebrate Christmas.

I knew my siblings were struggling with their own sense of loss while trying to make Christmas as normal as possible for their children. It was completely understandable that they had no room in their anguished minds to realize Don and I had lost our "Christmas home" and family, but that was all my grief-struck mind could think about. Still, I prayed we'd get invited to one of their homes, at least for Christmas dinner.

Without the company of any siblings or my nieces and nephews, it wouldn't feel like Christmas at all. We wouldn't be going across the street to 5:15 mass together. There wouldn't be a fun-filled Christmas Eve party at my parents' home with my family and the friends and neighbours who would drop in for some cheer. I wouldn't be sitting on the floor in my red and green plaid PJs beside our artificial tree with the antique angel on top, handing out gifts one at a time, in our birth order, as I'd done since I was twelve years old. I'd miss the delight on Julie's face when she opened her gifts and her hugs that would follow. My nieces and nephews wouldn't be opening their presents we'd brought from Toronto. Mom wouldn't be sitting in her corner chair, sipping decaf coffee, smiling proudly as we blissfully unwrapped our gifts.

I wished we could go back to when we were kids. That one more time we could all sit together on the floor of our panelled basement wearing matching PJs and watch *The Magical World of Disney*, play Yahtzee or Barrel of Monkeys, or click the Pop-O-Matic dice for a game of Trouble. My prayers didn't work, unfortunately.

Since I couldn't bear the thought of Christmas without my family, I asked Don if his kids could spend Christmas with us. Once they turned eighteen, the arrangement was supposed to be one year with their mother, the next year with us. Now in their early twenties, they had never been with us on Christmas Eve or for Christmas dinner. If I had to start a new Christmas tradition, why not invite them to stay with us at the lakehouse?

While driving north, four days before Christmas, I realized I'd forgotten the box. The one holding Mom, Dad and Julie's clothes. I couldn't leave "them" alone in Toronto. I called Don on hands-free mode.

"Can you please bring the box with you?"

"What box?"

"*The* box."

"What's in it?"

"Um. You know."

It hit him. "Oh. Okay."

I turned up the radio and sang loudly along with Lady Gaga's hit "Bad Romance." Glancing in the rear-view mirror, I could see Freddy and Callie watching me from their crates on the back seat. The look in their eyes told me they thought I was nuts.

AT OUR LAKE COMMUNITY, I was surrounded by people who cared, and a priest who knew me. The Sunday before Christmas, I asked

Father Joachim if he would offer Christmas mass to my parents and Julie. He agreed.

After the accident, some of my siblings seemed to turn away from God. I was disappointed with God too, but I still went to Him for comfort. That first year I went to church almost every week—much more often than my previous dozen times a year. My parents were devout Catholics. My mother even had her own missal with *Neta* embossed on it. Dad went to mass every day during Lent. I realized I felt closer to my departed family at church.

Yet I hadn't spoken to our priest since May, when I'd broken down during mass while conveying what had happened and asked the congregation to pray for strength for my siblings.

"I don't know how you cope. You've been so strong. God comes to us, and we find strength within us when we need it," he said to me at the time.

God certainly had his work cut out for him.

LATE AFTERNOON THE NEXT DAY, as it was getting dark, I turned on the lights that I'd hung on the floor-to-ceiling windows of two walls of the great room. The reflections of the green, blue, red and yellow lights in the other windowed walls created a festive wonderland.

One of my Christmas traditions was to put on a sappy, predictable made-for-TV Christmas movie (I think I've seen every one ever made), mix a rum and eggnog, sit on the carpet and wrap presents. I'd taken Mom's leftover bag of Christmas gift wrap and boxes from the crawl space in their house. In it I found a gift tag written in Mom's elegant old-school penmanship, *To Bill, Love, Neta.* Then came a rush of delight when I saw another tag: *To Mom,* signed in juvenile printing, *Ju L ie.* Julie could not read or write, but she could print her name.

I was trying hard to feel okay without my family. But I wasn't. Laying their Christmas stockings over the back of a chair beside the tree made me feel a bit better.

After I finished decorating the living room, I baked treats Mom used to make for the holidays. Noodle cookies are like mini-chocolate bars. The recipe is so easy, they don't even have to be baked. Melt chocolate chips, stir in some peanuts, add crunchy Chinese noodles, stir the mixture some more, then drop tablespoons of it onto a cookie sheet. Stick it in the fridge to harden. Easy peasy. Except, making them made me miss my mother more, blurring my brain so much that I forgot to pour the melted chocolate chips in the bowl first. I put the peanuts and the noodles in and added the chocolate last. While stirring everything together, the noodles snapped into pieces. I had screwed up the easiest recipe ever! They looked messy, but at least they still tasted good.

I wanted to make Mom's banana bread too. I didn't have a loaf pan, so I poured the batter in a muffin tin instead. A new Christmas tradition. Banana muffins.

The next day, my husband and his twenty-two-year-old twin daughters, Caitlin and Erin, arrived. Though they're identical— petite, blue-eyed and golden blond— their career paths and personalities are completely different. They did share some common interests though: Jane Austen, movies, boys and puppies.

Having finished stringing lights on the eight-foot-tall spruce tree, Don relaxed on the sofa reading a magazine. While Michael Bublé sang Christmas carols in the background, the girls and I had a holly-jolly time trimming the tree with shiny red, blue, silver and gold bulbs. We carefully draped countless strands of silver tinsel on the branches the way my mother had taught me, one strand at a time.

When Don's twenty-five-year-old son, Brendan, arrived at dusk, his behaviour toward me clearly demonstrated that he didn't want to spend time with us. My holly-jolly feeling gradually floated up and out of the chimney.

THAT NIGHT, Christmas Eve, after the kids went downstairs to watch a movie and Don went to bed to read, I stayed in the living room. Earlier, when no one was looking, I hid the "box" under the Christmas tree. Now I knelt down, pushed a few gift-wrapped boxes aside and eased it out. I laid my hands on top of it, closed my eyes and spoke to my parents and Julie: "It doesn't feel like Christmas without you."

Lonesome for my family, I drank far too much wine that evening. The booze made me even more emotional. I ended up crying myself to sleep, floppy Freddy lying on my chest. At three in the morning, I awoke to the fresh scent of the spruce tree. The room had gotten cold. I must've been dreaming of Julie, because I cuddled Freddy and called him "Jule."

I looked over at my parents' and Julie's Christmas stockings lying flat and empty over the chair. At fourteen I had a part-time job at

Londry's Variety store, making a dollar an hour, but by the time I was sixteen, I made a whopping $2.75 an hour. My parents didn't have stockings, so I saved up to buy them red felt ones with *Mom* and *Dad* written in green sparkly script on the white bands, and I would stuff these myself. Among other things, I'd put Alka-Seltzer in Dad's for his morning-after stomach.

This year I had purchased stockings for Don's children too. I printed their names on them with a red Sharpie. Stuffing the girls' stockings with lipstick, nail polish, chocolate, hand cream, socks, panties and a toothbrush cheered me up because it made me think of Mom. She used to put items like these in my stocking and I'd put similar items in hers. I'd given Brendan travel-sized deodorant, after-shave, a toothbrush, a Canadian Tire gift certificate and chocolate. I was doing my best to make this feel like a "normal" family Christmas.

I walked barefoot down the cold stone hallway and climbed into bed. Don was snoring softly. Freddy jumped up beside me, while Callie slept in her corner bed in the window, purring away. I squeezed orange spongey earplugs into my ear canals to try to get a couple more hours of sleep.

At seven, I got up and prepared a tray of muffins, bagels and cream cheese. I covered it with cellophane and put it in the fridge beside the orange juice and Prosecco. I changed into a full-length purple velvet gown and slipped a cross around my neck. At 8:45 a.m., we all went to church.

Our quaint white clapboard Catholic church, St. Mary's of the Purification, seats at most sixty parishioners. It was built for 800 dollars in 1870 and is a short kilometre-and-a-half drive on a gravel road from Woodhaven. The previous Christmas I hadn't been able to sing at all, but this year I sang "O Come, All Ye Faithful" in a full voice and looked down the pew at my husband and his kids. Then Father Joachim announced, "Today's mass is offered for the repose of the souls of Bill, Neta and Julie Gourdier," and my sorrow floated back to the surface.

We were back at the house by ten, and even though it was a bright day, I turned on all the Christmas lights. A sparkly silver reindeer on the sideboard by the tree twinkled in the morning sunlight.

Red candles and poinsettia placemats adorned the coffee table on which I'd placed the tray of muffins and bagels. After pouring mimosas for the girls and myself, our gift exchange began.

Later, bowing out of dessert and before we'd all finished our main course, Brendan left to drive back to Toronto. First thing the next morning, Don drove the girls back to the city too. His children were flying to Los Angeles for the remainder of the holidays. I had hoped they'd stay longer, but I completely understood their desire to go "home" for the holidays. Until that day, I had never been so envious of my siblings, who were fortunate to have their own children.

DON WAS STAYING overnight in Toronto and driving back up in the morning, so I was alone again. While I was sitting in my cottage chair, feet curled up beneath me, gazing at the Christmas tree and feeling sorry for myself, an idea hit me. I would invite all my siblings and their children to the lake. I didn't know how many could make it on such short notice during the busiest time of the year, but as it turned out, Christmas really is for visiting family.

Two days after Christmas, twenty-one of my thirty immediate family members—siblings, nieces and nephews—gathered for a day of hiking on the snowy trails, playing pool, karaoke and darts, and hot-tubbing. As soon as they arrived, I felt better. Everyone was having so much fun. Don was a real trooper helping the children figure out the Wii games and setting up the pool table. For dinner we served a couple of huge bowls of pasta, one with chicken, one with sausage. And of course, wine and beer. A dozen sat at the dining tables, three kids at the kitchen bar counter, the rest on the sofas with their bowls on their laps. We have four bedrooms, a blow-up bed and two pullout sofas, so everyone stayed overnight, with some of the young ones snuggling in sleeping bags on the carpeted floor in the basement.

With all the hustle and bustle, chatter and giggling, it finally felt like the "season to be jolly."

DON BOOKED A LAST-MINUTE vacation for us at a resort in Mexico. Our "family day" had cheered me up for a while, but it hadn't been a relaxing Christmas for either of us.

On the day we left, while sitting in the noisy, crowded departure lounge, I received a text from my friend Alicia: *Thinking of you today.*

Huh? I'd been so busy preparing for my much-needed getaway, I'd forgotten it was December 30. One year since Dad died.

That was Don's reason for planning the holiday. To help me leave my grief behind. He didn't understand that taking me to a five-star beach resort would not stop me from thinking about my deceased family, but tropical surroundings and meeting new people would certainly be a welcome distraction.

On our arrival, a young Mexican man welcomed us with rum punch cocktails in the spacious open-air reception area filled with palm trees and tropical flowers. Via water taxi, we were taken along a foliage-lined canal to our suite. As the boat skimmed the turquoise water, I cuddled closer to Don, my head on his shoulder.

Thank you for scooping me away to this tropical paradise. Alone with you, with this view and the warm sun on my skin, I really do feel better.

For the elaborate poolside New Year's Eve party, I dressed in a cocktail-length green and silver beaded sleeveless dress and strappy silver two-inch heels. Don wore a black silk Tommy Bahama shirt, dress pants and leather sandals. We arrived to find that the pool deck had been transformed with brightly coloured fiesta decorations and lights. An hombre wearing a sequined sombrero handed us a shot of Mexico's signature drink, agave tequila. A woman plunked a wedding veil on my head and asked us, "Would you like to get married?" Laughing, we grabbed the opportunity to exchange our vows again and to get the silly photo op.

Following the four-course Mexican dinner and show with brightly costumed dancers and musicians, Don sat on the deck with an after-dinner Scotch watching his fifty-three-year-old wife burn up the dance floor to Lady Gaga and the Black Eyed Peas. Dancing made me happy. After all the booze and exercise, I had no problem sleeping that night.

I had booked myself a facial for New Year's Day, figuring it would be the perfect way to recover after a night of partying. Wearing a cotton robe and flip-flops, I walked along a tropical-tree-lined stone pathway to my treatment room, a hut by the canal. Serene music played as I lay on my back, a white sheet draped over me, and the esthetician's fingers began lightly massaging my face. Still, I couldn't calm my mind.

Before leaving our room, I'd checked my email, only to learn that my ailing Uncle Don had been moved to palliative care. As the fruit mask tingled my cheeks, I thought of my visit with him at the hospital before Christmas. He had seemed frail, but his infectious laugh was still robust. I kissed his forehead as I bid him goodbye, thinking that would probably be the least time I'd see him.

A few minutes later, the esthetician laid a robe across my body, saying quietly, "Ma'am, take your time getting up. I'll wait outside."

When I got back to the suite, I checked my email. My uncle had died. Perhaps that was the reason I couldn't stop thinking of him. My family would say goodbye to our Uncle Don on the one-year anniversary of my father's funeral.

Though that week in paradise didn't prevent me from thinking of my losses, I'd had a good time and, best of all, I got to "marry" my husband all over again.

Chapter 21

More than a year had passed, but I still wasn't ready for the all-consuming job of filmmaking. I had to find something to keep my mind off missing my family.

On Wikipedia, I read that there are five identities of grievers. S. A. Berger wrote about it, coincidentally, the year my family died. A *memorialist* is committed to keeping the memory of their loved one alive. A *normalizer* focuses on recreating a sense of family. An *activist* takes the focus off their own grief to help others who are also grieving. A *seeker* incorporates religious and spiritual beliefs into their lives. A *nomad* runs from grief instead of resolving it.

A memorialist and activist. That was me. To learn to live with my grief, I wanted to accomplish three things: to keep Julie's memory alive, to get a crosswalk installed on Days Road, and to have the regulations for driving tests for elderly seniors amended.

I arranged to meet with a woman named Stephanie, coordinator of the Kingston chapter of Special Olympics Ontario (known as SOOK), at the Tim Hortons where Julie had worked for seventeen years. When I got there, I sat in the middle of the bustling restaurant sipping Earl Grey tea while I waited.

Stephanie, an effervescent woman with a charming Scottish accent, arrived a few moments later with an iPad in hand. I told her I'd decided to organize a fundraiser in Toronto for her Kingston chapter, in memory of Julie, with the hopes of raising at least 15,000 dollars. In her own words, she was "gobsmacked." Apparently, their in-house fundraisers, mostly bake sales or selling merchandise at tournaments, typically brought in only a few hundred dollars.

I also asked Stephanie about doing something in Julie's memory within SOOK. Concetta, their twenty-something head basketball coordinator, later came up with the idea of an annual award in Julie's name that would be given to a player who exuded Julie's outgoing personality and passion. With that in mind, we called it the Joy of Julie Award, inspired by Barb's description of Julie's singing as "joyful noise."

I ordered five large poster-sized photos of Julie from a print shop in Toronto to display at the tournament. One was a shot of her kissing a gold medal she'd won, another showed her dribbling a basketball in Nancy's driveway. When I was paying for them, I said to the printer guy, "These are for a basketball tournament in memory of my sister." He gave me 40 percent off. A kind gesture from a stranger who'd seen the grief in my eyes.

The tournament took place in January 2011, and that day posters of Julie's smiling face on the walls in the school auditorium made her seem so alive that I thought Mom and Dad might walk in with her any minute. Some of Julie's friends, who were wearing their basketball uniforms, were hanging out in the auditorium waiting for their turn to play. I recognized a few of them: Nathan, Daniel, Coreena, Leonard and Anna. Coreena cried when she saw me. Nathan spoke quickly, animatedly, obviously excited about the big day. I hugged them, then introduced myself to some of the parents.

Julie's team didn't win or place in the tournament, but if you've ever watched a D-Level Special Olympics game, you will know it doesn't matter whether they win or lose; it truly is about how much fun they have playing the game.

When it came time to hand out the Joy of Julie Award, I asked Sammy to do it, because she'd coached Julie's team. The plaque featured the photo of Julie showing off her medal. It was engraved with a touching tribute written by Concetta:

> *This award is presented to a D Level Athlete whose love of basketball is seen on and off the court. Your dedication, enthusiasm and sportsmanship keep the Joy of Julie Gourdier alive, in our hearts and in our spirit. Congratulations to our recipient!*

The boy who won it played for an out-of-town team, and he was so excited that he surprised a blushing Sammy by running up and giving her a big hug.

Initiating an annual award named after Julie helped me accept my loss, and, more important, the Joy of Julie Award brought happiness to "Julie's friends," who were very much alive.

TRILLIUM GIFT OF LIFE had sent me a newsletter in October 2011 about the creation of a quilt honouring organ donors in Ontario. Participants were asked to make a patch that captured the essence of their loved one. I don't know whether any of my siblings also received the notice. None of them lived near me, and remembering how many months it took for us all to agree on the headstone, I didn't ask. We each had our own relationship with Julie, and I knew that for me, making the memorial patch would be another piece in the puzzle of my healing process.

I'd quickly come up with the idea of creating my patch out of the top Julie had been wearing when she died. But it took me four months to find the courage to open the box to retrieve that top.

One winter night in 2012, Don was downstairs watching PBS, while I was upstairs in my TV room. The sealed box sat in the corner. I knelt down, slid it toward me and, using scissors, slit the tape. I had been warned by the police that I might see blood. Quivering, I slowly pulled the flap open.

Mom's black leather jacket was on top. I lifted it out. It had been destroyed. To administer CPR quickly, the paramedics don't take the time to undo buttons. They had sliced the leather alongside the whole row of buttons. It broke my heart to see her beloved jacket like that, but it also brought back a treasured memory.

For Christmas 2008, Dad had wanted to buy Mom a black leather jacket but knew she would want to choose her own. Instead of giving her money, I suggested we buy one, so she'd at least have a gift to open. She could exchange it if she wished. So that's what we did.

On Boxing Day, Mom and I went to the leather store to find a style she preferred. The place was crammed with bargain hunters. Mom tried on one coat after the other, at least ten different styles. Each time she'd look in the full-length mirror: "This one is too long," "This one doesn't cover my boobs," "I don't like the gold buttons." Until finally she found the perfect one. Nehru-collared, supple black leather with etched silver buttons. It fit her perfectly. Mom never did up the buttons of her blazers, but she buttoned up the leather jacket, because it was more flattering that way. "I look pretty sharp in it!" she said. She did.

The soft leather flopped in my hand as I placed the cut-up jacket on the butter yellow carpet.

Next I pulled out a small orange cotton jersey top with ruffles down the front. Julie's. It was cut up, too, but otherwise appeared brand new. Not wanting to ruin the surprise party, my parents and Julie hadn't worn costumes that night.

I wasn't ready to see blood, if there was any. And I wasn't mentally prepared to go through everything in the box, so I placed Mom's jacket back inside. I grabbed the envelope with the hospital records, pressed it down on top of the jacket, then I closed the flaps.

I hung Julie's top in my closet with Mom's suit and Dad's tie. "You can stay there for now," I said as I hugged their clothes. "I miss you so much."

The next morning, I laid the top on the left corner of my desk and took a plastic ruler out of the drawer to measure the quilt square. I'd made the decision to cut the square out of the back panel and leave the ruffles down the front undisturbed.

Even though the paramedics had already slashed the top diagonally across the front, I couldn't bring myself to cut out the square required for the donor quilt. Once I cut it up, it wouldn't be Julie's special top anymore. It would be a demolished piece of orange fabric that was once a cute top worn by my baby sister the night of her surprise fortieth birthday party.

Weeks passed. I just couldn't do it.

AFTER TWO YEARS, I shouldn't have been a rookie at grief anymore.

One night while watching TV, I was in the midst of one of my crazy grief days, wishing we hadn't allowed Julie to go so soon. Why *did* we let her go only twenty hours after the accident? I didn't remember a discussion about taking her off life support. I was absent for six hours the day after, fetching my cats, car and clothes in Toronto. I didn't have any idea what was discussed. Did the doctors ask us to let her go that soon so they could harvest her organs before they were damaged? Had we let her go so she could be with Mom? Or did we concede because our minds were slush, and we would have agreed to anything?

I learned later that family is usually asked if they want to be with their loved ones when they are taken off life support. I don't remember anyone giving us that choice. I absolutely would have stayed with

Julie. Maybe it was because when the organs are being donated, the surgery has to start immediately after the patient dies. Maybe they didn't ask my family because there were so many of us.

If we'd been with Julie, it would've been hard to ask all my sobbing family members to vacate the room so they could rush her body to the operating room to ensure her organs would remain viable.

How did she die? Did they pull the plug and let her fight for air? Since she was brain dead on a respirator, did she even breathe a last breath? Did they disconnect her from the machines, and then her heart stopped beating? Did they inject her with a fluid to put her to sleep the way vets put animals out of their misery? I wondered how long it took before she was completely gone. Did she suffer? Damn it. I didn't know because I was too stunned to ask if I could have stayed with her and held her hand until she took her last breath.

Sometimes I had to say out loud, "They're dead, they're dead, they're dead." Because I still couldn't believe it.

ALCOHOL WAS STILL MY GO-TO FRIEND. My husband, my family and friends—they were busy. Wine, vodka and tequila don't have kids or work fourteen hours a day. They sat on a shelf saying to me, *I'm here for you.* I read a passage in Eckhart Tolle's *A New Earth* that explained why I went to booze to feel better. He basically states that having a drink or two helps your mind relax. You become more carefree and jolly. You might show your cheeriness by dancing or belting out a song. Alcohol can help you let go of the problems in your head, allowing you to feel happy for a few hours. Thus the term *happy hour.*

Being less burdened by my mind was what I needed, so drinking enough to fall below my disturbing thoughts became my goal. I didn't down a twenty-sixer of vodka. I drank until I'd killed enough brain cells that my mind became comfortably numb. It seemed to me that the brilliant Eckhart Tolle was giving me permission to do so.

I didn't drink during the day unless I was on a beach vacation. I'd rise at about seven in the morning and, while working at my desk, drink three cups of green tea with fresh lemon juice squeezed into it. Apparently this mixture helps cleanse the organs of toxins. I would drink at least six glasses of water throughout the day. After cleansing with tea and water, alcohol would be my treat to curb my anxiety.

I made a purposeful attempt to cut back on drinking after my birthday in February 2011. I said proudly to Don, "I only had three ounces of wine today!" *Instead of three glasses.* I was hoping for a pat on the back.

I didn't get one, because to Don, a couple of drinks a day was a non-issue. He didn't realize how hard it was for me to stop at three ounces, with twenty-three more ounces in the bottle.

I was beginning to heal. That was my point.

FOR THE FAMILY DAY long weekend in February 2012, I was home alone. Again. Don was on a location scout in Manitoba.

Family Day seemed an appropriate day to work on the patch for the Gift of Life quilt. Julie's top still lay untouched on the corner of my desk, the plastic ruler across it. I needed accessories for the patch that would express Julie's interests, so I went to a craft store. I walked up and down the aisles that displayed buttons, stencils, art supplies, paint, beads and party decorations. Then I saw the stick-on aisle. Stick-ons would be easy. No sewing involved. There were stick-ons of everything Julie loved: *Happy Halloween*, a basketball, the word *giggles*, a teacup, a margarita glass, a television, a remote control, a CD, a microphone, an ice cream cone, the letter *J*, cowboy boots for her love of country music, and angel wings surrounding the words *Sweet Sister*. I bought far too many to place on a small square of fabric. It would take the whole damn quilt to show the essence of Julie Christine Gourdier.

Back at home, I picked up her top from my desk and caressed the shiny ivory buttons alongside the frill. I moved it to the brighter, spacious kitchen table and plugged in the kettle. Julie and I were the tea drinkers. The rest of my family drank coffee.

I poured the boiled water over the teabag into the floral mug my mother had given me for my forty-fifth birthday. While the tea steeped, I went to the stereo in my adjoining office and put on Julie's favourite music—a *Best of Country Music* CD.

Smoothing the fabric with my fingers, I finally made the cuts. Then I laid the stick-ons out on the polycotton square. I centred the largest piece in the middle, the silver sparkly word *Angel* with wings underneath and a white halo above, then surrounded it with the smaller pieces. The colourful novelty designs made it look cheerful.

Once finished, I checked the instructions one more time: "Whatever you use for your donor patch should be sewn on, as the quilt will travel. You wouldn't want your loved one's patch to lose the items you placed on it."

Sewn on? I'd screwed up! Why hadn't I absorbed that vital information? Because my mind was mush!

Panicked, I called Georgina, my friend the costume designer. She was at my house within thirty minutes and knew exactly what to do. She sewed a fine clear mesh over it. You could still see the stick-ons, but the mesh would keep all the pieces intact.

Julie's patch was now ready to go, but *I* wasn't ready to *let* it go.

In March 2011, I finally took on a non-paying gig producing a short film. Working helped alleviate my depressed mood.

One evening on my way home from the production office I met a singer-composer friend of mine, Shane, at Hemingway's in Yorkville. I arrived first and found a seat in the cozy library area. While waiting for Shane, I looked around the landmark bar I'd been going to for over thirty years, thinking about all the men I'd met here in my twenties and thirties.

Shane whizzed in, greeting me with a bear hug and "How are you?" Unlike others, who use it as an automatic greeting, he really wanted to know.

"Okay," I said.

He flagged down the waitress and ordered us each a glass of shiraz, then said, "But how are you really? Are you seeing someone? I know you're doing all this shit, producing a short film and charity stuff, but have you dealt with it? Aren't you fucking angry about it? Man, how does one wake up in the morning and deal with something like this? How do you do it?"

Wow. He said things that no one else had dared say to me. I took a sip of wine before answering.

"I saw a therapist and a medium. I'm doing a fundraiser in Julie's memory, and I've coordinated with Special Olympics Kingston's basketball division to honour her with an annual award, the Joy of Julie Award."

Shane leaned in, eyes wide. "And?"

I thought he meant what else was I doing, so I said, "I'm trying to get a crosswalk for where they died."

"Great. But, are you okay? *You.* Are you dealing with *your* grief?"

"*This* is how I'm dealing with it."

"Really? And you're okay?" He raised his voice. "How can you lose three loved ones and just say you're 'dealing with it'?"

His probing look frightened me a little. I couldn't respond, because he was right.

I wasn't okay at all. I was the great pretender. I'd been telling myself over and over, *I'm the eldest, I have to be strong. I'll cry later. When I'm finished dealing with it.*

In October 2009, Charlotte, a publicist who worked on some of my husband's movies, had asked if I'd help organize a tribute to be called The DC100 Event, honouring Don for producing one hundred films.

I had agreed to help, but then the accident happened. The tribute was not discussed again until June 2010.

I presented her with my terms: "Don's sixtieth birthday, April 16, falls on a Saturday next year. I'd like it to be a combo, the DC100 & 60 Event. I want to do it as a fundraiser for Special Olympics in Kingston, in memory of my sister. We can also donate a portion to the Canadian Film Centre as a scholarship."

"The press aren't interested in his sixtieth birthday," Charlotte said flatly.

I don't give a shit about the press.

But I needed to keep busy. Eight months of planning began.

Among other things, I wanted a comedian for the emcee. I had met the warm-hearted and hilarious Colin Mochrie once at an awards event. I called his agent and *voilà*.

We sold out three days before event day.

I should have been excited, but all I wanted to do was crawl into a hole where no one could text, email or call me. My phone rang constantly. "Are there any seats left?" "Can I pay online?" I hadn't set up an online process, because I didn't know how. I didn't hire anyone to help—because I wanted every cent possible to go to charity. I'd put myself in the position of being the *only* one to contact to order tickets. What an insane idea! I'd organized fundraisers in the past, but nothing of this scale.

The day of, I was completely overwhelmed. Except for my friend's daughter, Diana, creating the floral centrepieces, and my film industry friends Georgina and Dan Yarhi setting up the thirty-five tables, I pretty much did everything else. I handled sound-checks for the singers, oversaw the dancers' rehearsal, met the videographer, numbered the videos, picked up a DVD from the editor, answered catering questions, decorated the lounge, finished the cue sheet for the emcee. And because I'd added last-minute tables, I hadn't yet finished assigning the seats.

I asked Charlotte, the person whose idea it was in the first place, for help, but she wasn't available. My stepdaughters showed up but only stayed for about an hour. One of my volunteers for the check-in table called to say she couldn't make it.

Three hundred and thirty industry colleagues, actors, friends and family would attend. As much as I wanted the event to be a success, I was so nervous that I couldn't wait for the night to be over.

I squeezed in a quick blow-dry in the hotel salon, faster than styling my hair myself. When I returned to the ballroom, I found Brendan dropping off display cases for his father's awards. Yay, help was here! But he couldn't stay either. I was still arranging awards in the cases when the bartenders and waiters arrived.

At 5:45 p.m., a volunteer let me know guests were arriving. *It isn't six yet!* I was trying to find a place to display a large photo of Julie sitting on Don's lap when the double doors opened. The party had officially started. I had to get changed.

It was an industry event for film, and I felt like I was *in* one. I just couldn't figure out if I was the lead in a comedy or a drama.

Passing the elegantly attired guests, I walked briskly through the lobby in my jeans and T-shirt, trying to be inconspicuous. I wasn't. I heard "Hi, Catherine" coming from all angles. To ease my stress, I joked, "Like my designer gown?" Laughter surrounded me.

While I waited for the elevator, the zombies arrived. Yes. Zombies. Because Don had produced so many horror films, Charlotte believed they'd garner publicity. She wanted zombies, even though I'd told her that my family had dressed as zombies for Julie's party-that-never-was. Glancing at the ghouls, I wondered how my siblings would react. Should I have warned them? But Julie would be the first one in line for a photo with those frightful-looking dudes. Horror movies didn't scare her; they made her laugh. I hoped my siblings would have the same thought process.

The hotel had comped us a lavish one-bedroom suite, I didn't even have time to shower, let alone appreciate the space. Frantically I put on my makeup, slipped on my new sequined turquoise dress and sparkly silver shoes, and headed back down. The elevator doors opened to a reception area packed with television and film colleagues. They were happily mingling, or amusing themselves in the photo booth.

I entered the cocktail lounge, my eyes darting from one side of the room to the other. The first family member I saw was Mike. He usually wore rock band or music-themed T-shirts. Not that night. He was sporting a dark suit and silver tie. Beer in hand, he wove through the glamorous crowd toward me, leaned in and said, "I want to tell you *now* how great this is, what you're doing, before the night gets started. I just wanted to tell you that."

His tender words affected me so much, I felt like crying. The event had barely begun, but I knew I'd remember that as one of the most special moments of the entire evening. I would treasure Mike's words of support forever.

Looking dapper in his black suit, my brother Dave grabbed my hand and pulled me into the photo booth. With his muscular arm holding me close, I felt his love and pride.

I didn't see my sisters. They were with their families somewhere in the crowd.

I wouldn't even get a photo booth shot with my husband. He was too busy being famous.

Dancers started the party boogying to "Knock on Wood." Don and I had both worked on a film about the Studio 54 discotheque, so I'd selected some disco tunes. Elaine Overholt, the vocal coach from *Chicago*, sang "When You're Good to Mama." I'd changed the chorus to *"When you're good to Don . . . Don is good to you!"*

The Special Olympics representatives, Stephanie Beauregard and Glenn MacDonnel, introduced a video tribute to Julie. Stephanie had filmed Julie's athlete friends and coaches saying a few words about her. "She was funny, she was a joy, we miss her, we love her." My family and others in the room sniffled and got teary-eyed.

Colin then introduced me as "the wife of D.C." I'd been too busy to prepare a speech, so I muddled my way through, but at least I was wearing a fabulous dress. I couldn't say Julie's name or speak about the tragedy, because I would have cried, and then my whole family would have cried too. The pain was still so fresh.

Before exiting the stage, I said, "Happy birthday, Don. Roll it, guys!"

I'd wanted to sing live, but knowing I'd be too stressed, I made a music video instead.

Elaine had helped me create my version of "My Husband Makes Movies," putting the song in my key, with my intonations and new Don-related lyrics. I'd gone to her husband Glenn Morley's studio to record it. Standing alone in the glassed-in recording booth, I thought of how much I missed my parents. How much my mother would have loved to attend such a glitzy event honouring her youngest child and son-in-law. My daydream was disrupted by Elaine poking her head in, instructing me to put on the headphones so Glenn could communicate with me.

"Are you ready, Catherine?" he asked.

"Remember to breathe," Elaine said.

I closed my eyes, listened for my cue, and began singing . . .

"*My husband . . . makes movies . . .*"

I tightened my grip on the music stand. I was enormously proud of my husband, but as I sang the line about my husband never coming to bed because he'd rather make movies, I thought of my lonely life.

Now the audience watched me on the big screen. And I watched them. My husband smiled from beginning to end.

When the video finished, I headed back to my seat. As I scooted by my family's table, Deb grabbed my arm. "Good job, Cath." She had no idea how thankful I was to hear that.

Since I was chairing the event and had to keep my wits about me, I only had one glass of wine all night, but after the party ended, we raided the minibar in our suite. Don passed out on the king-sized bed. I slipped on a negligee that would not be seen by the birthday boy. Climbing into bed, I lay on my side facing away from Don and sobbed. I missed my parents and Julie so much. I really needed my Mom to comfort me.

Eight months of organizing had kept my brain focused on my passions: music, singing, writing, dancing, film, Don and Julie. I hadn't had time to feel lonely or sad.

But the next day, the void hit me again. And I hurt like hell.

A FEW WEEKS LATER, Stephanie invited me to attend the annual Kingston Special Olympics banquet to present the cheque for the money we'd raised at the DC100 event. Nancy, Mike, Sharon and four of my nieces joined me.

The banquet took place at the army barracks in a big mess hall. There was a buffet dinner and several rows of long oblong tables for the athletes, their parents or caregivers, and coaches. The organizers played a video collage of the previous year's sporting events in the Kingston area. I kept expecting to see photos of Julie playing basketball. Nancy stood leaning against the wall opposite me, watching the screen. Her tender smile did not mask her sadness. With the knuckle of her index finger, she wiped away a tear sliding down her cheek.

After the video and sports awards presentations, Doug Jeffries, a local sports anchor at CKWS, introduced me. Trembling, I looked out at my family and the athletes. To keep from breaking down, I silently encouraged myself, *Don't cry, smile.*

"I only had the pleasure of seeing Julie play basketball twice," I said, "but I could see how much she loved the game and making new friends. I'm so happy to help you, her friends, with this cheque for 35,000 dollars."

Stephanie rose from her seat in the front row. I handed the cheque to her and sat down. Then Stephanie took the microphone and started to talk about me. *What?* How I was drawn into fundraising because of the sudden loss of one of their adored athletes. She surprised me by calling me back up to receive a plaque for the year's biggest fundraiser. Award in hand, my eyes brimming with tears, I wished my parents had been there, but was extremely grateful Nance and Mike were with me.

Next was the dance. The athletes love music and dancing and apparently the only Special Olympics event throughout the whole year where all the athletes could dance together was at their annual banquet. I winked at my niece Haley, slow dancing with a young male athlete who obviously had a crush on her. I was enjoying myself so much that for a flicker of a moment I thought I saw Julie dancing.

Coreena came over and said, "I wish Julie was here. She loves to dance."

I put my arm around her shoulders. "She certainly does. Let's dance, honey!"

Dance I did, with Julie's friends, to Lady Gaga, Bruno Mars and Michael Jackson. We even did a conga line to the Baha Men's "Who Let the Dogs Out?"

It was an alcohol-free event, and I had a blast.

Chapter 22

After I told Nancy that hearing personal messages from mediums helped me feel more at peace about our losses, and that the messages sometimes made me laugh, she booked a reading with one too. A woman named Veronica Hart in Kingston.

Afterwards, Nance shared her experience with me. She told me one thing after another that rang spookily true, especially when Veronica knew the details about the accident. We laughed till we cried when she told me Veronica "saw" Dad clicking his front dentures up and down in his mouth, then holding them out on his tongue. *Dad did that!* The psychic couldn't have made that up.

Nancy's reading inspired me to book a reading with Veronica too, though my session didn't take place until more than a year later.

It was a crisp, bright day in late spring 2011 when I pulled into the driveway of Veronica's suburban brick bungalow. I was a few minutes early, so I leaned back on the headrest, closed my eyes and talked to my parents. "Mom, Dad, please, talk to her when I get in there. Please. I miss you."

I got out of the car and walked to the door, which was answered by a peppy, middle-aged, woman with long chestnut brown hair. Hearing the lilt of her charming Scottish accent made me smile.

"Hello, Catherine!"

I hadn't given her my surname when I booked the appointment.

She invited me to sit in her kitchen. The sun shone through the window onto the table, casting a beam of light across her shiny silver laptop computer. Because of my sensitive eyes, I sat with my back to the sun. She fetched me a glass of cool water.

Veronica recorded the reading onto a CD through her computer. The following is the remarkable edited-down version of the one-hour-plus session.

"Has yer mum crossed?"

"Yes."

She closed her eyes. "I like yer mum, she comes in very soft, she has a lovely *pear*sonality. She's creepin' up on me, givin' me goosebumps. She gives me a very loving feeling. Was she very close to you?"

"Yes."

"There's a feelin' of tightness. She has an overwhelming energy, yer mom, an awful lot of love that comes out of her. Was she the type of person that her heart was just, *whoosh!*—she would do anything for people?"

Proudly, "Yes."

She pondered. "Yer mum has to be bringing someone else in with her, because if she wasn't sick, there's something letting me know they're happy to be on the other side—this lets me know they weren't doing well before they crossed, okay."

I opened my mouth to speak, but she put her hand up to stop me. Some mediums want to be fed information; Veronica did not.

"Your mom's shouting a name, she's giving me an *M* name—Mary, Margaret, Martha? Who'd have the *M-a-r* name?"

I have cousins named Margaret, Marilyn and Mary, and a niece Marley. But I said, "Mary is my mom's first name, but she didn't use it."

She lit up. "Pearrfect! They don't come to me and say, 'My name is Josephine,' that's not how they do it. They make their messages unique."

That threw me. Why would they want to make their messages unique? Why wouldn't Mom say "Neta" or "Wanita"? Veronica noticed the change in my demeanour.

"It's okay. Loosen up. This is going to be fun. Your mum's got a very strong pearsonality."

I'd never really thought of her that way, but yes, she did.

"Your mum keeps shouting, 'Catherine, Catherine, Catherine,' so that means there should be someone else with the name Catherine in the family. Who else has that name?"

"I don't know."

Veronica persisted. "She keeps saying it, so there's someone else with that name."

Grandma Gourdier was Kathleen, not Catherine.

Veronica raised her voice. "Are you sure? Because she's flashing it. That means there *has* to be someone else with that name."

"I can't think of anyone."

Veronica wanted to move on, but Mom wouldn't let her. "Your mum is a strong woman, she knows what she's telling me, she knows what she's saying, she's still shouting, 'Cath, Cath, Cath!' So, to me there would have to be another—hmm, she's saying 'no' to Catherine."

I smirked because it dawned on me what my mom was trying to tell her.

"Do you go by Cath?"

"Yes!"

We burst out laughing.

"Yer mum was so adamant, flashing her hands, opening and closing, flashing, 'Cath! Cath! Cath!'"

I hadn't been called "Cathy" for over thirty years. When I began my sales career at twenty-one, my sales manager suggested that "Catherine" would be more professional on my business cards. Since then, I have never introduced myself as Cathy. Occasionally my dad or brothers would call me Cathy, but Julie knew I preferred the *y* dropped. I got a kick out of listening to her correct people who called me Cathy. "It's *Cath*," she'd say proudly.

Veronica concentrated for a moment. "Your mum's very good with dates the way she's going to my calendar and flipping the pages." There was a calendar on the wall beside us. "What would you have in the month of December?"

I smiled again. "Mom's birthday."

"Who lives in Barrie that just had a birthday?"

"My Uncle Mike. His birthday was yesterday."

"Your mum's very accurate! She's funny too. It's like she's in charge of me. A very lovely pear-son. I don't know if your mum passed with heart failure or if she's trying to bring someone else in. Who would have had heart failure?"

"My dad."

"Did your dad have heart trouble before he crossed?"

"Not that I know of."

"It should be someone that had heart trouble before they crossed."

"Mom had angina."

"Absolutely, pearr-fect, that's it. Yer mum's sayin' someone is seventy-six. Who's that age?"

"My dad was seventy-six."

"I feel as though your dad's there, but your mum's talking for him." That fit pear-fectly.

"Are there other people you want to come through?"

"Whoever is there."

She took a breath. "Sometimes they'll give me the pain. This feels like 'head.' I don't know if it's an aneurysm or a stroke, but somebody had something with their head. Was it yer mum, or somebody separate?"

"Separate," I said.

"I'm feeling a head injury. This feels different. I know what yer mum feels like and yer dad's heart—this is a totally different feeling. This person with the head injury, um, was it quick?

"Yes."

"I have a different feeling for this person, rushed, as though it was an emergency. I think it's separate from your mum and dad, because it comes in totally different. Does that make sense?"

I didn't answer. "So, it's separate from yer mum and dad?"

I still didn't answer.

She got adamant and snapped, "Is it separate from your mum and dad? Is it?"

It was and it wasn't. She could tell I wasn't sure how to respond.

"Um, yes."

"Mediums get stuff in bits and pieces, like reading a book—you don't know the ending until you get there. This is how your family is coming in. I have to be careful, because if I say 'accident' . . . hmm, okay, now that's what's coming through. Was this an accident?"

"Yes."

She closed her eyes again. "I don't want you to give me information, but would this person know yer mum and dad? Because they're at their side, they're not behind them; this person is right at their side. It's Mum, Dad and this person, all together, they really know each other."

They sure do.

"Was this very quick? They're showing me—" She snapped her fingers. "One, two, three! The way they're showing me, I feel dizzy, it's a feeling like I'm drugged, it's a feeling I get when something happens quick, someone crosses very quickly, and I cross quickly. Do you understand? Did this person cross at the scene?"

"No."

Veronica was surprised.

"Hmm. Really? Because I get, one, two, three. The only other way I get that is that this person is taken to hospital and they're keepin' them alive. Do you understand?"

I sure did. Eyes closed, she put her hand on her neck.

"Ooh, my neck and my head, the energy is really strong. Ooh, they're keeping their hand up, they're being very cagey, so when I'm doin' this, I ask them questions, they're just kinda ignoring me. I don't want to just say something, because I don't want you to think I'm asking you for information, I want them to show me, if they can."

I waited anxiously.

"Was the only person that passed that day that person?"

"No."

Disappointing sigh from Veronica.

I wanted to help. "Can I give you a little information?"

Defensively, "No, I don't want you to tell me who it is, no, no, no."

"I won't tell you who—"

"No, no."

"Can I say one thing?" I didn't wait for her response. "One was one day, and one was the next."

She did not get upset with me for that tidbit.

"Okay. I definitely had the feeling one passed that day. So, this was an accident that happened very quick. Sometimes when it's that quick, they can't show you it because it comes out of the blue. Fast!" She smacked her hands together.

"The energy is overwhelming, someone is sayin' 'Dad.' I'm getting sixteenth, seventeenth, does that mean anything to ya?"

Yes. "The sixteenth is my husband's birthday, the seventeenth is my dad's."

"Is your husband still here?"

"Yes."

Veronica took some deep breaths. "I don't know why that one person is not coming in strong."

Julie might not have been able to convey "messages" to Veronica.

"They're giving me a name now, like a Joanne or a Joe, something like that."

She got the *J*, so I helped her out. "Julie, my baby sister."

Long pause again. She leaned forward, elbows on the table, her eyes closed, fingers at her temples. "I keep getting this feeling of the head. Did someone have a head injury?"

I said, "Yes, but I don't know how much you want me to say."

"I don't want you to give me too much. I don't want to get too graphic either. This feeling can mean a few things, so I have to be careful."

I wanted to hear whatever she was getting. "You can throw anything at me." I took a sip of water, wishing it had a splash of vodka in it.

"It's a feeling like it's from my chest area and up. I feel sedated, I can't speak. I want to speak, but I can't. There's nothing coming."

Julie would get frustrated when she couldn't find the words to convey what she wanted to say, but Veronica could have been referring to when she was unconscious and on life support. Veronica held her head with both hands.

"I feel sedated. My head—I'm so weak. Does that make sense?"

"Yes." Veronica had absolutely convinced me she was communicating with my family. I began to feel woozy too.

She took a deep breath. "I feel as though someone was kept alive by machines. Was there somebody that was 'let go'?"

As a tear trickled from the corner of my left eye, I nodded.

"There's a feeling of 'I'm floating away,' 'I'm tired,' and then I just let go. There's also a feeling of somebody saying, 'Let that person go.' Does that make sense?

I clenched my hands. "Yes."

She took several huffing breaths. "Your family is very different, how they're coming through. I'm hesitant to give information, because I don't want to sound cruel, but it's the way they're showing me it. It's a feeling of internal injuries, of bleeding."

Changing the subject, she gave verification messages. "One of them is singing 'Country Roads.'" Do you live in the country? They're showing me trees and a long driveway."

"Our lakehouse. We have a long driveway lined with trees."

"They're sayin' 'sisters.' You have four or five?"

Smiling, I said, "I sure do."

Veronica paused the recording and asked if another family member had come to see her. When I said yes, she understood why her information was incomplete. Mom had given it to her before.

Animatedly, Veronica said, "It happens all the time! I been thinkin', why aren't they tellin' me? I bet someone else has come to see me, and they've told me it already. Now I know why they were being so cagey!"

She didn't mention anything about Nancy, so I doubt she remembered her.

Veronica got back to business. "They're showing the name Haley?"

"My niece." Validation. Another name too uncommon to just pull out of a hat.

She raised her hands and clenched them together. "We're happy to be together! They're like this, so tight! I feel as though I have just one, even though I know there's two, but the way they're showing me is that they're very close together."

That statement and the "Cath" message were more than I could have hoped to hear. I would have given up vodka and chocolate for a year to hear that. The hour was up, so I thought we were finished, but she kept going.

Hesitantly, "Were they hit? It feels like it's something oncoming, something that's coming to them, a feeling of 'We're getting hit!'"

I could barely speak. "Yes."

"I don't know if they're in a vehicle or out of a vehicle. There's a feeling they don't see this comin', right?"

"Yes," I whispered.

Veronica paused for what felt like five minutes but was probably five seconds. "The person in the vehicle, were they ever charged?"

"No."

I could tell Veronica was trying desperately to get the right information. "So why are they saying charged? It's not that they're saying this person is to blame . . . they're trying to take the responsibility away from themselves. They want you to know it wasn't their fault."

It was an accident.

She let out a deep breath and sat up taller. "It feels like we're going somewhere to have fun, a feeling of 'I'm really happy, la da dee da dee da, we're going to have a good time!'"

The party. We'd all had the fun feeling. Until the fateful call.

Veronica asked me to talk to my father, because he hadn't said a word. I closed my eyes and sent a silent message. *Hey, Dad, show me a sign you're here, okay?*

A moment passed, then, "Were they going somewhere to have a drink? 'Cause your dad has a six-pack of beer!"

I laughed. "Now he's talking!"

"So, the beer makes sense, then?"

"Oh, yeah."

Serious again: "Every time your mum and dad try to come through, I feel as though I'm getting pulled to the other individual. Was somebody forty when they passed?"

She nailed it. "Yes."

"Was this more like a freak accident? They're showing me it's not normal for something like this to happen to a family."

I breathed deeply, my fingers pressed against my lips.

"Did they walk across from somewhere? I get the feelin' a car was coming at them from the side, not from behind them—they could see it. I get the feeling that they passed, one, two, three, right? Yer mum went quick, then your dad with the heart attack, it's like boom, boom, boom. Yer mum and dad and the other person. I don't want you to get annoyed at this message, but the other person is saying 'I'm happy to go.'"

"Can I say something?"

"No. Don't say anything! It's funny how they're showing me, like a big jigsaw puzzle, chess pieces. I think I know who it is now, they're changing places, your dad moved here, and your mum moved over here. Is this yer mum and sister?"

I nodded.

"Is this about crossing the road? Because they're saying 'Fight for the cause' and putting their thumbs up. I don't know if there's gonna be a speed bump or crossing guard. Your mum is giving me goose-bumps. Look at them!"

Veronica had actual goosebumps on her arms! How could she fake that?

She put her fists together. "They're here, and then Dad, right here. They're like the Three Musketeers, if one goes, we're all going. It's like they have a pact. They're very strong together."

Though this was hard to accept, in that moment I realized it was for the best they went together.

"They're saying it's bizarre what happened. I don't know if you have anger for what happened. Your mum is saying all she wants for you now is a sense of peace. Oh! You're the one doing more to get the crosswalk?"

"Trying. Yes."

"Yer mum is flashing the feeling that something has to happen there."

"The councillor in that district said not enough people walk across the road, so she isn't able to do anything," I said.

"Yer mum is giving you the thumbs-up to go for it because of all the lives you could save. Even though something terrible has happened, you could do something wonderful. If it happens again, they'll probably say, 'Oh, we'll put one up now,' right?"

I must continue my efforts to fight for a crosswalk or traffic lights.

"Yer mum is saying you have to know they're so happy. She's saying not to stress too much, enjoy your life. Don't think about this all the time. Yer sister knows she was loved, there's a feeling of so much love."

I felt it.

"Yer mum is telling me to finish so we can chat. She's saying again how much she loves ya. And yer dad, ha, nothing's come out of him except holding the beer!"

We laughed again.

She spoke softly. "They're fading now . . . they're gone. Poof! Gone, all together. Quite honestly, I've never had a reading like this before. Normally people come behind each other, but your family were all beside each other."

That session was more therapeutic for me than seeing a grief therapist. I don't care if others think it's hooey. With so much truth revealed, I didn't see how it could be.

She handed me my CD copy of the reading, then I filled Veronica in on one more detail.

"Did you know Julie has Down syndrome? Maybe she was talking, but you couldn't make out what she was saying."

"Julie would no longer have Down syndrome on the other side. People lose their afflictions when they cross over."

Affliction: something that causes pain or suffering.

Julie hadn't lived a life of pain or suffering. According to Veronica's beliefs, the lame could walk, the blind could see, and my sister no longer had one extra chromosome. Julie had a "normal" brain in the afterlife? That bothered me. I took all the enlightenment of the reading with me and disregarded her comment about Julie. Julie was Julie, our special angel, because she had Down syndrome.

Chapter 23

Early September 2011, Don and I attended mass at the lake. We sat in our usual pew in the small heritage chapel, third row from the back on the left. I linked arms with Don and leaned into his shoulder. He placed his hand on my lap and lightly squeezed my thigh. I felt safe. Loved. Some parishioners glanced over at me with caring eyes. I acknowledged them with a soft smile.

Back at the house, Don brewed himself a coffee. I plunked an Earl Grey tea bag in a mug with a deer painted on it. I added a splash of skim milk and poured in hot water while dunking the tea bag. We spread peanut butter on whole wheat toast, grabbed the newspapers and took our breakfast to the screened-in porch that overlooks the shimmering lake. We read quietly for an hour or so.

After lunch, we drove two kilometres down the gravel road to Marvel Rapids Golf Course to hit a few balls at the driving range.

We laughed at our mulligans and cursed at balls that sailed too far left or right. Around four, back at the house, we grabbed a couple of drinks and went out for a tour around the lake in the pedal boat. On that glorious Sunday, not one person was on their dock or on the water. Once we reached the middle of the small lake, we stopped pedalling to savour the silence and the afternoon sun warming our bodies.

It was so warm that we lazed on the lounge chairs outside on our wraparound deck. Hidden behind a curtain of trees, we made love to the evocative music of Pink Floyd's "The Wall" playing over the outdoor speakers. We'd only had sex three times in nineteen months. I'd been too sad. But I wasn't sad on this day. Sated and lying naked on my back, I gazed up at the trees, the bright sun shining through the many shades of green leaves—chartreuse, evergreen, emerald and lime.

After our mutually satisfying romp, we took cocktails and a bowl of ripple chips to the dock. One drink led to two, as we talked and laughed for a couple of hours. Silly, witty, flirtatious, chatty me was back!

After dinner that evening, I curled up on the sofa in our bedroom to catch up on the latest episodes of *The Good Wife*, while Don watched football downstairs. Freddy snuggled up to me, Callie slept on the chair to my left. I was relaxed and feeling good until the lawyer, Will, gets hired for an organ transplant case.

I shivered. Suddenly I was no longer all right. I was not all right at all. I wanted to go downstairs to tell my husband, *I'm sorry, but your wife, she's not back yet. I tried to bring her back today, but your wife is not really back yet.*

But I couldn't do that to him. Don needed to relax before the start of another intense sixty- to seventy-hour workweek.

To release my tensions, I went to my writing chair and opened my laptop.

A few minutes later, Don came upstairs. "Whatcha doin' sitting in the dark?"

The only light was the glow from the computer screen.

"Writing."

"I'm going to bed to read," he said, as he plopped his empty Scotch glass on the bar-height counter.

He wasn't close enough to see my tear-stained face. I wanted to say, *Please, hold me.* I wanted to cry in his big strong arms. But I didn't. I didn't want to ruin the perfect day he'd had with the wife he used to know.

When I finished my entry, I wiped my face and headed to our room. Don was propped up on two pillows with a Tom Clancy book open on his barrel chest. I walked over and stood by the bed, looking down at him, wanting to share what had happened to me, but I couldn't.

He said teasingly, "What are you doing standing there like that? You're a crazy person. You are crazy."

With a tight-lipped smile, I said, "Yeah, I know."

I kissed him lightly on the lips and walked back to the living room to write some more. I could tell my computer anything.

THE COLOURFUL AUTUMN LEAVES of Ontario cottage country create one of the most beautiful settings in which to celebrate Canadian Thanksgiving. Don's kids had joined us at the lakehouse that weekend. On the holiday Monday, after we fed them a hearty breakfast of scrambled eggs, bacon and toast, they all left to go back to Toronto. Don and I were looking forward to relaxing on the dock with books, magazines and scripts.

Plans changed when he got an urgent call from the production office. There were problems on a location where they were to shoot the next day. They needed their big-gun producer to deal with it. I needed him too. He left before lunch.

But it *was* a weekend to acknowledge what we were grateful for in our lives. (I was.) Don had grown more supportive and understanding recently. Bananas and blueberries, which I ate almost daily, appeared magically in the kitchen. He cooked dinners on days I was too sad to do anything. He'd go to Blockbuster and rent rom-com movies, and watch them with me. He massaged my shoulders. His tone of voice had become gentler. He told me he loved me two or three times every day. I was indeed thankful for my husband.

It was a gorgeous sunny day, so to relieve my disappointment over his departure, I decided to kick-start the happy hormone, serotonin, by going for a walk.

For as long as I can remember, no matter what I was doing, I have listened to music. Doing chores, working out, driving, jogging, having sex with or without a partner. Music was my forever companion. I'd worked out with my portable cassette recorder in the '70s, walked with my yellow Discman in the '80s and my teeny iPod in the early 2000s. Today I strapped on my fanny pack, stuffed in some tissue (in case I had to pee in the woods), a whistle (in case I saw a bear) and my new larger-capacity green iPod. I put on sunscreen and a baseball cap and headed up the hill of our tree-lined driveway.

On my iPod, I clicked shuffle, then play. Peter Gabriel began singing "I Grieve" in my ear. With five hundred songs in storage, what were the freakin' odds of that song coming up?

As I strolled along the gravel road surrounded by the brilliantly hued forest, I thought of the time my parents and Julie had come to the lake for Thanksgiving. Treas's and Deb's families used to come too, before they had their own cottages. I missed the camaraderie of our big family Thanksgiving dinners.

When I returned from my hike, I thought of something to do to curb my loneliness. I'd make a collage of photos I'd never gotten around to putting into albums: Nance and Treas sunbathing, Carol with her kids on the dock, Cedar kayaking, Marley doing a silly pose on a raft, Jacob holding a tiny tree frog, Caitlin singing karaoke with Julie. Looking at their smiling faces, remembering those times, I didn't feel so sad.

Afterwards I shuffled down the leaf-covered path to the dock, drink and a bowl of chips in hand. Freddy skipped along ahead of me, rustling the leaves. Sitting and resting my head on the back of the chair, I admired the mirror image of the trees' orange, red and yellow leaves reflected in the still water.

While my siblings were eating Thanksgiving dinner and laughing with their children, their eldest sibling sat alone missing every one of them. But nevertheless, I felt good. Proud to be from such a big family.

As the sun shone through my acrylic tumbler, I raised it for a toast. I thanked my parents for my siblings, and said each of their names aloud.

A WEEK AFTER THE ACCIDENT, Don and my brother-in-law David had decided we should sue the driver's insurance company for loss of care and companionship, with the intention to help Dad financially if he needed a daily caregiver or had to move into assisted living. The process had barely begun when Dad died.

A few weeks after Dad's funeral, the lawyer informed us that, we, the children, could still sue if we could prove our case for "loss of care and companionship." Though it was Don's and Dave's idea, it was not *their* parents who died. A family member had to make decisions with the lawyer, so they handed the reins to me.

For the first year the process was straightforward, answering basic questions. All of the correspondence with the lawyer, Mr. Robertson, had been via email or telephone. In fall 2011, his secretary called to set up a meeting at his office to sign documents. It was time to get out of my yoga pants.

I figured if I dressed professionally, I'd feel more self-assured. I chose the charcoal grey suit I'd worn to Dad's funeral. The jacket still had the Gift of Life pin on the left peaked lapel. The once sexy, snug-fitting pencil skirt hung loosely on my grief-shrunken physique.

But wearing two-inch pumps, head held high, I walked confidently into the Bay Street law office and gave my name to the receptionist. She asked me to please take a seat on the leather sofa. There were magazines on the coffee table, but I didn't feel like browsing. My heart beat faster. Though I'd stepped into my professional look, that cool character apparently hadn't made it past the glass entry doors.

After a few minutes, Mr. Robertson, a tall, middle-aged, dark-haired man, entered the reception area. We shook hands. "It's nice to finally meet you," I said.

He led me down the hall to a meeting room. I sat on the opposite side of the boardroom table. He offered me a glass of water. I took a sip, drew a breath and sat up straight, ready for him to begin.

He surprised me by first saying, "It was thoughtful of you to send the driver a card letting her know it was an accident." Don had sent him an email suggesting he watch the *16×9* show in case new evidence was revealed.

Next Mr. Robertson explained that for the settlement to go through, the driver had to be interviewed. That was news to me. I was sure we'd been told that the elderly woman wouldn't have to be involved in the lawsuit, that the lawyers would consult with their clients and strictly deal with each other. She'd be eighty-seven years old soon and was probably still healing herself from the trauma of the accident. I didn't want to upset her further.

"The defence counsel is quite tough. He'll want to meet with each of your siblings individually."

My siblings wouldn't agree to being interviewed. And I didn't want them to have to go through that process.

I implored, "If it's possible to resolve this without having to question my siblings or the driver, that is my preference. I'm sure my family won't want to do it—can't do it."

He opened his mouth to speak, but I continued. "Do they have to? Most of them aren't interested in pursuing this at all. I'm doing it *for* them anyway."

He promised to see what he could do.

Next he said, "Did you see the photos of the car that hit them?"

"No."

I lowered my gaze to the table. He asked if I was all right, if it was okay to carry on. I told him he could throw anything at me. Nothing could hurt me more than I'd already been hurt.

"There were two distinct blood spatters, two patterns on the windshield of the car." Why was he telling me this? I thought we were going to talk about getting the settlement money.

He explained what happens when someone gets hit by a car. How the body jerks, folds in, and then the heaviest part, the head, hits the windshield. "Then the body bounces into the air and rolls onto the road."

I'd told him he could say anything, but I hadn't expected to hear that. I don't know what his purpose was in sharing that. He'd seemed so empathetic. Once he told me, I couldn't stop the vision of Mom's and Julie's heads smashing into the windshield. It made me want to throw up.

Julie and Mom had gashes on their temples. I hadn't seen the back of their heads. They probably had wounds on the back as well, one from hitting the windshield and one from hitting the pavement. As Mr. Robertson continued with more details, I tried desperately to maintain my composure. But I couldn't retain another word. I kept seeing a bloody windshield. With two distinct spatters.

In early 2012, I received a call from Mr. Robertson. He'd been able to dissuade the defence counsel from interviewing my siblings and the driver. They'd reached a settlement offer.

We did it, Dad!

IN MARCH 2012, my family was invited to a Trillium Gift of Life Donor tribute in Kingston.

Julie, as well as nineteen other donors, would be honoured. I still hadn't sent in Julie's quilt patch. This meant I could show my siblings what I'd painstakingly created before I handed it in to the Trillium representative.

Carol, Treas, Nance, Mike and my sisters-in-law Sharon and Barb attended the ceremony. While we waited for it to begin, I showed them Julie's patch. I didn't tell them it was made from the top she'd worn that night. Smiling, I pointed out the microphone stick-on and said, "She loved to sing."

A young man, the Trillium Gift of Life representative, stepped up to the podium and asked everyone to please be seated. As he said their names, photos of each of the deceased donors were displayed. Julie's warmth beamed from the big screen. She looked so alive and happy.

I looked around at the people in the room and wondered if the lung recipient lived in Kingston. If the young woman might even be in the room.

The tribute was held at the Harbour Restaurant, across the street from Dad's old hangout, the Ports. Following the ceremony, we went there for a drink. My family sipped their beers, talking, laughing, hiding their sadness from each other.

Nervously, I piped up. "Excuse me. I, um, have the cheques with me." The outcome of my two-year dealings over the civil suit.

No one responded.

I walked around the table and handed them each a cheque. Barely looking at me, each uttered a quiet "thanks" and took it from my hand. They had no idea what I'd been through emotionally. I'd hoped for acknowledgement that following through with the lawsuit, even though Dad had passed, was the right thing to do. Some or all of them hadn't wanted to pursue it. I followed through with it because I felt I should. If it was too late to help Dad, at least it gave each of them money for their grandchildren's postsecondary education.

They might have felt uncomfortable about the circumstances under which we were receiving the money, but "doing" was my way of dealing with grief. Dealing with the lawsuit. Trying to get a cross-walk installed on Days Road. Chairing fundraisers. Speaking out about testing for elderly drivers.

And writing about *it*. All of it.

Chapter 24

Two and a half years after the accident, I'd become a bit of a medium addict. In April, I booked another session. I didn't see psychic mediums for the mystique; they were my grief therapists. Medium sessions helped me recover from the extreme sadness and depression I was feeling. I still missed my parents and Julie more than ever, but hearing personal messages brightened my dark days.

My friend Ken told me he'd received personal messages from his uncle through a woman named Jaye. He swore she was the real deal. I'd seen two who seemed to be "real deals," but also a couple of quacks. One quack asked too many questions and gave dumb responses to my answers. "Has your mom passed?" Me, "Yes." Him, "She says she loves you." As if I didn't know that. "What do you do for a living?" I said, "I'm writing a couple of scripts." His brilliant forecast: "Well, I think one of them will be made into a movie." I felt like asking if he had five million to finance it.

That day, my front doorbell rang. I opened the heavy oak door to find an effervescent, quirky woman with a dimpled smile and a head of curly brown hair.

I led Jaye into our living room. The walls were painted a deep burgundy, which gave the room a cozy feel. My inner skepticism had me hide all personal photos before her arrival. I hadn't told her anything about myself. I hadn't emailed her, because I didn't want her to know my last name and Google me. I even dialled *67, so she wouldn't see my phone number when I called. I gave her my first name and address. That was it. To make sure she couldn't find out anything from my address, I Googled it. There was no mention of my husband or me. To the best of my knowledge, Jaye knew nothing about me except my first name.

She sat on the brown sofa beside the fireplace. She took a notepad and pen out of her bag and asked for a glass of juice. After handing it to her, I dragged an armchair in front of her, placed my mini-recorder on the coffee table and clicked it on.

Jaye began by telling me that she'd had a dream the night before. She spoke slowly and clearly, making it easier for my post-traumatic brain to absorb information.

"It looked as if you've come upon this car accident. At first there is an unsure feeling about getting involved, a little bit of fear of what's happened. Then it was, *I have to jump in, I have to organize, control the scene and do things to help.* Is this something close to what happened?"

"There's a connection to an accident, yes." I wasn't trying to take control, but I was trying to figure out what to do.

Jaye continued. "My second dream was of before the accident happened. I drew it, so let me show you what I've done."

She opened her notebook. Oh my gawd! She'd drawn an eye with thick black eyeliner, the liner extending well beyond the outside of the eye. "Does that look like the way your eyeliner actually came out? It's not regular eyeliner."

I couldn't believe what I was hearing.

"It came out in that particular way? Have you ever done your makeup that way?"

The night of Julie's party, I'd made up my eyes exactly like that— black vampire eyes. with the line extending out *in that particular way.*

I was so stunned that all I said was "Mm-hmm."

"Good. That's what we call, from the other side, a validating detail. I saw it so clearly, which is why your parents asked me to draw it and show you." My insides fluttered. "For validation, they mention names of people close to you. Do you know a Peter?"

"Yes." Peter is my brother-in-law, Nancy's husband. He doesn't believe in the afterlife. I wondered what he would think about a medium mentioning his name to me.

"There was a trip by plane shown to me."

"Yes." To New York with my mother and uncle, two weeks before she was killed.

"Something is hidden in the upstairs closet."

"I have a suit of Mom's with my dad's tie hanging on the same hanger in my closet. I hugged them before you got here."

Jaye said excitedly, "Oh, good! They're telling me there is a writer in the family. Are you the writer?"

"I guess so, yes."

Jaye scribbled randomly on her notepad while she spoke. "They're telling me that you often make other people nervous when they're meeting you for the first time, but that sometimes you get nervous too. There's an energy carried around you, like you're a bit of royalty. It's not a snobby thing, not with negativity, but like you were raised that way. Can you think of why that would be?"

"Nope."

"They're saying, 'Hold your head high, keep confident.' Do you know what I mean?"

I didn't know. Inside, I still felt like the girl from the big family who grew up in Kingston. Except that I liked to fly business class, and I didn't drink Baby Duck anymore.

"I've had a couple of references to bananas or banana bread."

Impressed, I said, "Banana bread." Mom always made banana bread when I visited. She'd keep a loaf in the freezer for me to take home too.

"That's all that came through before I sat down with you."

That was a helluva lot!

She continued in a more serious tone. "They want to connect with you. You need to hear from them. You want to hold onto them for dear life. They're showing you to me as two different people; there's the veneer you show to the world of who you are. You do a bit of an 'I don't want you to know I'm sad.' Even though friends are important to you, sometimes you hide your true feelings. People want to know you and be around you. You wear a natural suit of armour to keep people out, but under it, there's a reason. A holding-on-for-dear-life reason. Does that make sense to you?"

"Kinda."

She laughed. "Your dad's saying, 'It's like pulling teeth with you!' Your parents are laughing."

"Why won't Dad tell me my nickname? That's all I ever ask of him." As a test of their authenticity, I'd asked two other mediums this same question, but I did not receive an answer.

She leaned in closer. "The process is not like ordering at McDonald's. I know you want to know for sure if it's really happening, but you must try to let go of that. Who crossed their fingers?"

"My mom crossed her fingers to remember something." She'd walk around the house with her index and middle finger crossed until she did what she had to do. It seemed such a silly thing, but I do it too. Sometimes I forget what the heck I had them crossed for in the first place.

Jaye closed her eyes and scrawled circles in her notebook. When she opened them, she said, "Who plays basketball? They're saying something about the youngest?"

"Julie played Special Olympics basketball."

"Okay. Good. Julie says to say hello to Ruth for her."

Oh, my heart. Ruth Taite met Julie through Community Living Kingston. For several years, every Tuesday afternoon (unless I was in town) Ruth would take Julie shopping or to the pet store or for lunch. I only met Ruth Taite after Julie passed.

"You have a lot of interior strength. They're saying, you're a tough cookie. Has anyone ever called you a tough cookie?" she said, her eyes closed tight again.

Embarrassed, I said, "Yep."

Jaye laughed. "Good! Your mom is telling me of the strength and fortitude you have. That tough-cookie feel—you get that from her. She and you are strong but in a kind way."

"Thank you."

She closed her eyes. "Is there a thing with *Bewitched*? I keep getting Samantha."

Wow. "I have a niece named Samantha. My brother got her name from *Bewitched*."

"They're asking to move on to a serious issue. They're mentioning something about an accident. Has there been a recent accident?"

My tape chose that moment to run out of space. And I don't have a clue what she said after that. It doesn't matter. She didn't need to tell me about the accident. I knew those details all too well. She'd lifted my spirits with messages from my mother, and that was the purpose of our meeting. Jaye had confirmed that my parents and Julie were still in my life, whether I could see them or not.

After that enlightening session, I never, ever returned to my previous depth of sadness. Despite what would happen six months later.

Chapter 25

A few days before my thirteenth wedding anniversary, my cats and I were watching TV while Don was on set in Hamilton. Freddy was slumped across my body, and Callie, jealous and not too happy about it, was curled up at my feet. Callie had been my "baby" for four years before I adopted the quirky kitten.

When I got up, Freddy followed me downstairs. He meowed at the sliding glass door to the back deck. It was a pleasant fall evening, so I slid the door open to let him out. Then I went to the kitchen, put three scoops of vanilla ice cream in a bowl and went back upstairs.

An hour later, I came downstairs to put my bowl in the dishwasher. I turned on the outside light and called out for Freddy. He didn't come, so I watched an episode of *Mad Men*. When the show was over, I called him again. Usually he'd come running to me. He didn't.

In the warm months, Freddy occasionally stayed out late or even all night. I'd go downstairs during the night and find him sleeping on the deck furniture. I'd open the slider, he'd rush in, then run up the stairs ahead of me, criss-crossing back and forth, almost tripping me. Once I climbed back into bed, he'd jump up and flop against me. I'd wake to him sleeping, lying face-up like a Penthouse Pet, his fluffy white belly exposed.

At two in the morning, I woke up and went downstairs, opened the door and whistled. No sign of Freddy. I woke again at 5:30 a.m., whistled and called his name. Nothing. It was pouring rain. I felt apprehensive, but there'd been other times when Freddy hadn't shown up until sunrise. I'd joke with Don that Freddy was out picking up chicks at after-hour cat clubs. At 7:30 a.m., when he wasn't home, I started feeling sick.

I called my cat-loving friend Barbara, who said, "He'd let anyone pick him up. Someone probably has him and is waiting for the rain to stop."

I didn't believe her. "He's always here by morning."

"Remember at the lake? You got so upset, and he was sleeping in the closet the whole time."

I did, but that didn't help.

"You could put up posters in your neighbourhood."

I found an adorable photo of Freddy sitting on the deck at the lake. Don, eager to help me find my baby, elected to go to the office and print a dozen posters. The new thing to do was to post a notice on Facebook. I did that too.

When Don got back, we went out in the downpour, wearing rain slickers, carrying posters of Freddy in plastic bags. Don went one way, I went the other, taping the notices to poles in the few blocks around our house.

I was standing at the foot of my driveway sticking up a poster when friends from the lake pulled in. Jim and Sherry had come to celebrate our anniversary with us. I greeted them with a soggy hug, then we dashed in out of the rain. I didn't want to ruin their visit, so tried my best to hide how sick I felt.

While they were putting their luggage in the guest room, I excused myself to shower and change. I was dripping wet, towel on my head, when my cellphone rang.

"Hi. My name is Brian. I saw your poster."

I started shaking.

"I'm not sure if it was your cat, but I think it was. Last night around 9 p.m., I was walking my dog. As I approached my house, a woman asked if I had a towel or a blanket. There was a cat at the side of the road. I got a towel and held it open as she put the cat in my arms. She called Animal Services and had to leave, so I held him until they arrived. He was breathing when they took him away."

It had to be Freddy. My gut churned as the kind man kept talking.

"He was hit near the corner, below the stop sign. The car must have been speeding not to have seen him. I live at 69. Where are you?"

My head was floating. "Across the street."

"I'm not sure where they took your cat, but you can probably find out."

"Thank you so much, sir."

I put on my robe and, steadying myself on the railing, went downstairs to my office. I called Barbara again, explaining that our friends, whom she also knew, had driven from the lake to celebrate our anniversary with a dinner out. I needed to get ready.

"Can you please find out where he is?" I was afraid to make the calls myself.

As we were about to leave for the restaurant, Barbara called back. "I found him."

She didn't follow that with "He's going to be okay," so I knew he was gone.

"I'll call you when we get back. Thank you so much."

Somehow I made it through that dinner, and the minute we got home, I called Barbara. We both cried.

"I shouldn't have let him out," I said.

She tried to console me. "He always went out, Cath. It's not your fault."

Our unlucky thirteenth. "He was hit on a celebration weekend, just like Mom and Julie."

Fifteen minutes after I'd let him out, people had gathered near our driveway trying to save Freddy, while I was upstairs watching TV, eating ice cream, totally oblivious.

Barbara had brought Freddy to her home, so the next morning Don and I went to get him. She'd laid him in a cardboard box. To camouflage his injury, she had secured a black pirate patch over his eye. His legs were stretched out, as if running, frozen stiff.

I wanted to bury him at the lake, where he liked to chase mice and chipmunks. "We can put him in the freezer in the garage until we go up next week," I said to Don.

"Are you nuts?" he said, then insisted we make the 210-kilometre drive to Woodhaven right away.

Wearing work gloves and carrying a shovel, Don emerged from the workshop and headed to the forested area next to the driveway. I opened the tailgate of the truck and pulled out Freddy's "coffin." I put on gardening gloves and stroked the long fur over the length of his body. His beautiful coat was now flat, not fluffy. Through sloppy tears, I sang the silly song I used to sing to him: "*The greatest cat in the whole wide world, that's my Freddy! The cutest cat in the whole wide world, that's my Freddy . . .*"

Don yelled, "Okay, ready!"

I covered Freddy with a beige hand towel and placed him in the grave. Then I poured water in his cat food dish, put a black-eyed Susan in it and set it on the dirt. As we said our goodbyes, I looked at the flower floating in the bowl. I said something dippy about how much I loved him and that he was the best baby boy.

Don stood soaking wet, shovel in hand. "You were the dumbest cat ever, but cute."

My husband had used his entire day off to bury my "baby boy."

Don may not have understood how to be there for me during my first bout of grief, but he went above and beyond when I lost Freddy.

When we got home, I saw a man waxing his car in the driveway of house number 69. I grabbed a bottle of red wine and went to meet him. As I strolled up the sidewalk, I glanced down at the pavement and wondered where Freddy had lain. I looked to see if there were any signs of blood.

I took another step toward the man. He looked up at me, "Brian?" I said.

"Yes," he answered.

My defeated expression told him who I was.

I handed him the wine. "Thank you. For holding him."

Seeing the question in my eyes, he said, "He was hit right over there, where that new piece of dark pavement is."

Now, just as with Julie and Mom, I knew exactly where on the road my angel cat died. Pets grab your heartstrings and never let go. Freddy made me laugh every single day during the most traumatic time of my life. But I guess his work was done.

I was heartbroken over the loss of my "baby boy," but nothing could ever hurt as much as the day my mom and sister died. I would never stop missing him, but I was going to be just fine.

Chapter 26

Organizing fundraisers in Julie's memory became a passion of mine, and the process turned into an effective healing therapy. When I found out that Julie's forty-fourth birthday, in November 2013, fell on a Saturday, the planning began for another Special Olympics fundraiser. This time, in my hometown of Kingston. Most of Julie's friends attended H'art Centre, a non-profit school that provides people with disabilities opportunities to study and create work in the arts, so I decided to share the donations with them too.

Late morning on party day, Don and I went to the Overtime bar to set up tables, decorate the space with orange balloons, hang posters of Julie and lay out the auction items and bid sheets. The huge dark space had a stage for bands, a dance floor and pool tables at the back of the room.

The medium Bonita had told me "someone named Leslie" might assist with my philanthropic events. As it turned out, my niece Leslie, and her parents Dave and Barb, helped me. Besides selling tickets, they distributed flyers and obtained a few substantial auction items such as a bar fridge and a large area rug. My other siblings sold tickets too. My cousins Dale and Lyne donated Ottawa Senators hockey tickets. Don contributed movie memorabilia: *Resident Evil* posters, *Goon* DVDs, T-shirts and baseball caps.

Just after eight, the first guest arrived, a young woman with thick, curly brown hair. She approached me carrying a glass bud vase with a pink artificial rose in it.

"Hi. You're Julie's sister. I'm Amy, Julie's friend." Amy used to call Julie almost every day. She handed me the vase. "This is for Julie's grave."

I clutched the slender vase and gave her a hug.

Julie's basketball friends, Nathan, a red-headed, high-functioning young man with Down syndrome, and sensitive Coreena, arrived a few minutes later. I grabbed them soft drinks from the bartender. Excited to be at a bar, they said they couldn't wait for the music and dancing to begin.

By nine thirty about three hundred guests had arrived, including our cousins and classmates from Frontenac Secondary School. Pete, my brother-in-law, is a painter by day, and was then bass guitar player with the popular cover band the Rain Kings by night. They, along with another local band, The Monas, donated a precious Saturday-night gig for that fundraiser.

I'd spent weeks snapping digital pictures of Julie from old photo albums to use for the video presentation. I used Randy Travis's "Forever and Ever Amen," one of her favourite songs, as the score.

I'd created my own video tribute of our summer vacations together, as well, singing Eva Cassidy's "I Know You by Heart." I had called my friend Tony to record me. He's a skinny guy with a '70s moustache who wears a beret. He set up shop on my kitchen table. He slid the controls up and down on the soundboard while I struggled to maintain my composure, imagining I was singing my changed lyrics directly to Julie: "*You are my sister. You are an angel, lighting the lives of all that you touch . . .*" Even though recording sound and editing was what he did for a living, he didn't charge me a cent. *People don't know what to do, so they give you things.*

I needed to get up on stage to thank some people and say a few words. My family had told me they didn't want me to mention the accident, even though that was the reason we were there. It had taken place just around the corner from this bar. I didn't want to upset them, but this event was in honour of Julie on what would have been her forty-fourth birthday. I wanted her acknowledged, so I invited her friends on stage. Nathan, Coreena and Amy each spoke about loving and missing their friend. Coreena cried so hard she could barely speak. Don walked through the teary-eyed crowd selling 50/50 draw tickets. The winners, Patti and Bob Halliday, were so moved that they donated it all back.

My other intention for the special evening was to bring my family together for a happy event. A few tears were shed, but from across the crowded room I also heard the sound of their laughter.

And Julie's party raised over ten thousand dollars—10,001 dollars to be exact.

At the end of the night, when Don and I were packing up, the glass bud vase that Julie's friend had given me slipped through my fingers and smashed on the floor. Shattered at what I'd done, I collapsed, crying, and carefully picked up the broken pieces. *I'm so sorry, Amy.*

The next morning, I took Amy's plastic flower to the gravesite and told Julie all about her party.

A HIGH SCHOOL FRIEND, Bob Anderson, reached out to me for help in writing a script about the painter Tom Thomson, based on William T. Little's book *The Tom Thomson Mystery*. In my research, I stumbled on his grandniece, Tracy Thomson, also an artist. Intrigued, I perused her website and learned she lived in Toronto. Her expertise seemed to be paintings of dancers.

One in particular caught my attention and never let me go. The image is of a young girl in tights, her arms outstretched, her long hair flying behind her as she jumps up into a dark sky over what seems to be water. There are lights in the sky on either side of her that reflect in the shimmering blue abyss she's hovering above. The figure seemed to be faceless.

It could be Julie. It could be Dancer. I felt compelled to buy it and send it to Julie's lung recipient, but it was the summer of 2014 before I finally did so.

Because it was an original painting that would go through the postal service to wherever Dancer lived (which I assumed to be somewhere in Canada), I had to package it carefully. I had a roll of bubble wrap in my office, so I unravelled a few feet. As I held the painting, preparing to wrap it, I noticed Tracy Thomson's card taped to the back of the twelve-by-twelve-inch canvas. A naughty idea hit me. I opened my desk drawer and took out one of my business cards. As if someone might catch me in the act, I nervously wrote Dancer a quick note on the back.

If you want to meet me, I'd love to meet you.

My stomach did flip-flops over the possibility of my plan working. Carefully I pulled back the tape holding Tracy's card and slipped mine in behind it. The masking tape lost some of its stickiness after I removed it, but I hoped that it would stay intact until the Gift of Life personnel opened it up to check that none of my personal contact information had been enclosed. Once mailed, in order for my secret plan to work, for Dancer to find my contact information, the tape would have to fall off and release my card. I also wrote a letter to her asking how she was doing and saying I hoped she'd like the painting. I taped that to the outside of the parcel.

Then I wrote a short note to my contact at Gift of Life, explaining what was in the parcel and enclosing a photo of the painting, so he could see what it looked like, in the hopes they would not have to open the package at all. All part of my sneaky plan.

I had sent Dancer a gift once before, a Christmas ornament of Santa's reindeer called Dancer, so my liaison was not surprised that I wanted to send another present. I didn't want anyone to get in trouble, but my desire to meet the young girl with my sister's lungs far outweighed any scolding I might receive.

All I had to do was wait. It could take years, and I knew she might never find my card, or she might find it and choose not to contact me. But I prayed she would.

Chapter 27

On the fifth anniversary of the accident, I chose to be alone. After years of seeing mediums, therapists and counsellors, and organizing fundraisers, I finally felt more like myself. At last I was ready to go through the contents of the box.

On that dreary, rainy morning, I sat in my cottage chair at the lake with my Mac on my lap, checking Facebook and email messages. Callie slept on the chair in the corner window. I missed silly Freddy. If there, he would have had his nose in my lap, but now he was cavorting in heaven with Julie. I took a last bite of a piece of "Mom's" banana bread, which Nancy had made for me. It was so good that I cut another slice and made another cup of tea. My third cup, and it wasn't even nine.

I Googled my name to see if the accident article was still prominent on the first page of results. It was. First was the Internet Movie Data Base (IMDB) list of the films and TV shows I've worked on.

Next, a *Toronto Star* article about our home in the city. Third, "Accident Kills Two Women." I wanted that *Whig-Standard* article to slip to page three or four. To be buried deep in the archives.

My grief therapist had warned me that going through the box could "open a whole other door for me." Perhaps, but I had to do it. I can't explain why, except that I believed that touching their clothes would help lessen my sorrow over losing my sister and mother in such a horrific way.

The box was hidden in the back closet of our bedroom. To get at it, I had to move the yellow bin labelled "Bill's Winter Clothes." My dad's clothes weren't in there anymore, but I couldn't bear to rip off the piece of paper with Mom's handwriting on it. I'd filled it with items of theirs that I couldn't bring myself to donate or throw away. I hadn't looked in this bin since we sold our family home.

Pulling off the lid, I saw the remnants of Julie's orange top lying on Mom's forest green lounge robe. I'd stashed it in there after I made the patch. There was a sticky-page photo album in which Mom had kept an array of my black-and-white headshots. I was working in sales when I was "discovered" by a modelling agency while picking up my boss's ten-year-old daughter at a photography studio. Not tall enough to be a fashion model, I ended up being hired for catalogue modelling sessions for Woolworth, Zellers, Kmart and Eaton's department stores. My so-called big break was a one-liner on *The Wayne and Shuster Show*. Wearing a tight miniskirt, with a Farrah Fawcett flip hairstyle, I'd waved flirtatiously to Johnny Wayne. "Hi, Johnny!" My television acting debut—and finale.

On a piece of paper slipped into the album, Mom had listed fifteen films, the lead actors' names and details of the roles I had on each one, whether it was as an extra, actor, stand-in or assistant director.

For my parents' twenty-fifth wedding anniversary, in 1980, my siblings and I had all pitched in for their surprise gift. I arranged a trip for them to go to Las Vegas with their close friends George and Joan McCallum to see Tom Jones and Wayne Newton. My sentimental pack-rat Mom had kept a Ziploc baggie filled with mementoes: matches from Caesars Palace, and from Jubilation, Paul Anka's restaurant, a shower cap from the Dunes hotel, a button that said *Tom Jones, The Welsh Wizard*, and even a tiny bar of soap from Air Canada. I'd made the airline aware it was their twenty-fifth wedding anniversary, and as first-class passengers, they were gifted a bottle of champagne. Unfortunately, after having a few beers to calm his fear of flying, Dad accidentally left the unopened bottle for the stewardess.

I couldn't throw out any of the items, especially Julie's birthday top, which was no longer a top, so I put everything back in. My family could discard this memorabilia after I was gone.

Lonely, I tried to call Aunt Joan, but the line was dead. The telephone lines at the lake were underground, so we'd often lose service when it rained. Also, the cell service at that time was dreadful.

I went back to the closet and slid my summer dresses to the side. There it was. On the shelf. A regular cardboard box, closed up flap over flap.

I'd touched it occasionally as it lay hidden. Sometimes when the house was full of guests, my family even, I'd go to the closet, lay my hand lovingly on the box and say, "Love you, miss you" or "Hello there." I'd do that—to the box.

I lifted it out. It was heavier than I remembered. I carried it down the flagstone floor hall and plunked it on the coffee table in front of the fireplace. It was almost noon. I wasn't hungry but thought I should eat in case I didn't feel like eating after I opened it. Five years earlier, I hadn't been able to eat for three days. I opened a can of Campbell's tomato soup, poured it into a pot and added a can of skim milk. While that was heating up, I made a grilled cheese sandwich with the Kraft processed cheese slices I constantly told my husband to quit buying. I hadn't eaten that combo since I cycled home for lunch in grade school. I don't know why not. The plastic-wrapped cheese was gooey and delicious melted between buttered slices of pan-fried multi-grain bread.

I changed into Mom's yellow bowling T-shirt and slipped Dad's Amherstview Golf Course sweatshirt over top of it. Then I sat on the sofa and stared at the box. My breathing became rapid and shallow. Liquid strength was what I needed. It was 2:30 p.m. Too early for booze. As a stalling tactic, I took the "Bill's Winter Clothes" bin out to the library attached to the games room. There was more storage room there.

A pile of boxes and bags of photos and assorted mementoes from our old family home sat on the floor. I opened a bag and found a ripped slip of paper with *Nov. 7/8* written at the top.

It read:

KGH – Pt A/C's 613-548-2362. (Kingston General Hospital)
Julie – $45.00 Ambulance   Mom – $45.00 Ambulance
No Chg. OHIP Insurance will be billed

I was sure that was Nancy's handwriting. How long had she been at the accident site? How could she have been cogent enough to write? As difficult as it was for the rest of us, I can only imagine how devastating it would have been to see Mom and Julie lying on the road. To live with that horrific memory locked in your brain. Nancy was always late. Dad used to joke that she'd be late for her own funeral. If Nancy's family had arrived at the party on time that fateful night, she wouldn't have seen their lifeless bodies, but she wouldn't have been able to be there with our dad either. Anxiety kicked in as I imagined the trauma Nance would have faced that night.

I walked quickly back to the house and poured two fingers of vodka into a lowball glass, added water and ice cubes, and squeezed in a wedge of lime. I inserted *The Best of Terri Clark* in our CD player and pressed play, then took a big gulp of my drink. The alcohol eased into my bloodstream, almost immediately calming my rapid heartbeat. I pulled up the flaps, opening the box.

Lying on top was the envelope containing a thick stack of hospital records. That's why the box was so heavy. I'd forgotten I'd stashed them in there too.

In response to your request for medical records, we are forwarding reports on the following:

Julie – Complete Admission Nov. 7–8, 2009

Wanita – Emergency Report Nov. 7, 2009

William – No records as he did not expire in the hospital

The first section contained the records for patient number 625376. Mom.

Emergency contact was William Gourdier, spouse, but someone had handwritten *Nancy – daughter* and her phone number.

Somehow knowing I needed affection, Callie strolled over and rubbed her face on my leg. I lifted her onto the sofa. She nestled her head into my hip. I wished Don were with me. I picked up the phone to call him. The line was still dead. My cellphone didn't have service either. I took another sip of vodka.

It was after five when I realized I'd gone the whole day without putting face cream on. I'd become a certified esthetician at nineteen, so applying day cream was as automatic to me as brushing my teeth. I went to my bathroom and slathered on a moisture mask instead. Why not? No one was around to see me.

Reflected in the mirror were bathrobes hanging behind the door. My navy robe with the turquoise stars on it and, on a hook underneath it, Julie's child-sized turquoise robe with navy stars. A lovely coincidence that we had similar bathrobes. I hadn't been able to keep her robe tucked away in a box. She loved taking "hot steamy baths" in our big Jacuzzi tub, so our bathroom was a fitting place for it to stay. I'd often take my robe, wrap hers with mine and hug them tightly against my chest.

When I returned to the living room, Terri Clark was singing her version of "Smile." The lyrics spoke about a mom sending her little girl to her first day of school. I thought of Mom sending me off on my first day of school. Eventually, I had to wear a drab navy uniform. But not that first day. I wore a light blue, cap-sleeved dress with white lace trim on the hem and white bobby socks. I stood in our driveway behind our 1963 powder blue Pontiac station wagon holding my Disney Bus lunch pail and waved to the camera.

I smiled as teardrops dripped onto my sticky face mask. I grabbed a tissue and blew my nose, then continued reviewing Mom's records.

Time ambulance arrived: 18:30.
Pedestrian versus Car. No cardiac activity.

Illegible writing filled the pages. I'd paid eighty-eight bucks and couldn't read most of it.

Disposition. Home ___ Admit/transfer___ D.O.A.___
D.I.E <u>X</u>

Died in Emergency? Is that what D.I.E. means? If so, Mom was alive when she arrived at the hospital. Trauma time was 18:15, and 18:35 was the time her body was being transported. We got the call at 6:20 p.m. We arrived at the scene almost in time to hug Mom before she passed.

Trillium # 64232 – 2100

They'd contacted the Trillium Gift of Life representative? Had they removed Mom's corneas at nine that very night?

Two bystanders struck by car at unknown speed. Extensive damage to car windshield – poss. thrown 30–40 feet. CPR by bystander [Tina Carey]. Making agonal breaths [the last gasps of air before one dies], but no pulse felt. *That is weird. Breaths but no pulse?* Obvious hematoma to Rt forehead, bruising to LUQ [left upper quadrant] of abdomen. Bystander supplied blanket. *Randy's wife, Lorraine?*

Time of Death: 18:45. Diagnosis at Death – Multi trauma.

Scanning the report, I felt like a detective, but I don't know what I was looking for. The outcome would always be the same. Mom was gone.

The final page of Mom's report was the social worker's notes:

Julie and her mother, Wanita, were crossing Days Road on their way to Julie's fortieth birthday party when a car hit them. Wanita, seventy-nine, died at the scene, Julie was taken to ER. Police assessed it to be an accident and stated it is a badly lit area. Offered support and guidance. Family had to deal with the knowledge that Julie is brain dead and will not survive more than a couple of days. Due to the party, many family members were in town. Family was offered the family room. Bill, husband and father, was present at the accident, he avoided getting hurt b/c he was in the middle of them.

How could Dad have avoided getting hit? He'd said Julie's hand was ripped from his. He must have been one step ahead to be missed, which being a foot taller, he usually was.

Fifteen pages of notes to confirm Mom's death.

Thankfully the vodka had put most of my anxiety to sleep.

Page 16

Julie Gourdier

Paramedics arrived on the scene and Ms. Gourdier was in a decorticate position.

Decorticate: an abnormal posture in which a person is stiff, with bent arms, clenched fists and legs held out straight. The arms are bent in toward the body and the wrists and fingers are held tightly on the chest. This posturing is a sign of severe brain damage.

My heart ached as I envisioned innocent Julie in such a state.

By 7:40 p.m., my brain was exhausted. I'd have to continue in the morning.

Pitch-blackness surrounded me in the glassed-in great room. I'd been so engrossed I hadn't noticed the sun going down. The land-line phone was still out of service, and my cellphone wouldn't send texts.

I went back to the bathroom to remove my now dry and cracked face mask. I looked into my toiletries basket. Mom's Oil of Olay cleanser bottle was empty, but I wanted it. Lise, our cleaning lady, hadn't meant any harm, but she'd tossed it once before, and I'd retrieved it from the recycling bin. It may sound odd, but I liked to look at it.

Though I'd often felt lonely during the previous five years, that weekend, oddly, I was not. But I was in no mood to eat a proper dinner either. I prepared "calcium" and fruit—a big slice of blueberry pie topped with three scoops of vanilla ice cream. Eating from a wooden tray on my lap, I watched an episode of *Grey's Anatomy*, another one involving a brain-dead person. With the mixture of the relaxing effects of the booze and feeling the love of my parents, I felt okay though.

And I didn't even need any pills to put myself to sleep.

THE NEXT MORNING, I drank tea from my *Sisters* mug from Carol. On it are two girls hugging with *the bonds we have are everlasting* written inside the rim. Mug in hand, I sat on the sofa to read Julie's whopping 103-page report. These are a few of the notes:

She was intubated, good air entry bilaterally. No contusions or deformities of the chest. The abdomen was soft and non-tender. Pupils were non-reactive, given 30ml of 20% Mannitol. There was an abrasion on the right temple, her hair was soaked with blood. Patient was in a C-spine collar.

A long abrasion extended the length of the back. Alignment was normal. Patient was sedated and paralyzed with administered drugs.

Sedated? Did that mean she had been conscious earlier and could speak? Or did they drug her so she wouldn't feel pain? If she hadn't been paralyzed, could she have spoken to us?

CT scan of her body revealed three small fractures in her pelvis. CT scan of her head revealed her brain is extremely damaged.

Ms. Gourdier is an unfortunate 40-year-old female with Down's syndrome who was hit by a motor vehicle.

Once again, I wondered when they realized she had Down syndrome. Why had they even mentioned it? Why did it matter? Would they have said an "unfortunate female with diabetes" if she'd had that? One thing that's for certain, it was not unfortunate that she had Down syndrome.

The prognosis is poor. It was our pleasure being involved in the care of this patient.

Their "pleasure"? A nice but peculiar comment. Too bad they didn't get a chance to hear her giggle.

DONOR HEART Stats. Height – 4'10 and 1/2", weight
88 lbs.

Blood pressure was 103/57, close to normal. Organs unharmed.
Lungs clear. A whack of other readings all said, "Normal."
One note described her eyes as doll's eyes. Creepy.

Conclusion: Normal function.

Pages and pages of test results, organ reports in medical jargon I
didn't understand.

ICU Attending: I told the family she could not survive and
would likely die in the next few days. I met with three sisters
who expressed interest in organ donation.

I was not one of the three sisters. I'd gone to get my car, cats and
clothes, so I could stay in Kingston with Dad.

Midline incision from sternal notch to pubic bone. Kidney
retrieval. Crushed ice was placed on the kidneys. Bronchial
wash, left lung wash, right lung wash.

Prep, prep, prep for the removal of Julie's organs.
November 8 is stated as the date of her death on the funeral program and Julie's memory card. It's the date sandblasted into their

headstone. But Julie had been kept alive until the removal of her organs at 8:39 a.m. on November 9, 2009. Due to the time restraints on the life of her organs after she died, several surgeons worked simultaneously to remove her heart, lungs, kidneys and liver.

The heart was excised completely, placed into a sterile bag, then into cooler full of ice for transportation

Julie's heart was donated to a middle-aged woman. We received a letter a few months later informing us that she had died of "other complications." Though her family certainly would have treasured those extra months, it was upsetting to learn that Julie's healthy heart lived on for such a short time.

There are several variables involved with performing sustainable organ transplants—the most important being finding a blood and tissue match, followed by the size of the organ. Other variables can include the time and distance the organ might have to travel before reaching its recipient. The heart has to be transplanted within six hours, or it becomes an unviable organ. I also found out that Julie's lungs were tested for six hours before being transplanted.

My second cup of tea made me feel perky. I was finally ready to take their clothes out of the box.

On top was the clear plastic bag that held Dad's red and navy sweaters, the ones the paramedics had cut off him. Mom's sliced-up leather jacket was next. There were two brown paper bags sealed with red tape labelled "Police Seal—Do not break without authorization."

A stuck-on label said, "Evidence—Pair of black dress shoes—Seized." The seals of both bags had been cut open. Inside was a pair of black mules with white stitching. Mom's shoes. They looked brand new. Knowing Mom, she probably bought new shoes for the party. I put them on and walked down the hall. I wore them the rest of the day.

Next I pulled out a long, narrow, fuzzy red scarf. It had a dark, crusty stain on it. Mom's blood. I put it around my neck. I didn't want to wash away her blood, but I knew I would have to if I wanted to wear it in public and not have someone say, *You have something on your scarf.*

Folded neatly was a men's large, black windbreaker. It had a blood-stain on the white piping on the shoulder. Dad must have laid his jacket over one of them. Was it Julie's blood? Or Mom's?

I felt something in one of the pockets. I took it out, gasped and dropped it. My mother's lower dentures! They must have flown out of her mouth when she landed on the pavement. I wondered if Dad had the wherewithal to pick them up, or if the investigating officers had found them and placed them in the pocket. I'd been so disappointed with the doctor for taking out Mom's teeth, and her bottom dentures had been in Dad's jacket pocket the whole time. I put them back and zipped it up.

There was a small tin marked "Evidence." I shook it and something clanged inside. *Was it my mother's upper dentures?* I pulled back the seal and revealed the missing red stones from Mom's bracelet.

I found Julie's shoes, black loafers with a silver buckle. Size three. And her bra. The straps cut. Because of the way the sleeves were sliced, her red, lightweight hooded jacket looked more like Little Red Riding Hood's cape. The report had said she had an abrasion down her back, but there was no sign of trauma on her jacket. I pulled out a cut-up white blouse. It looked like a dirty rag. I held it up for a closer look. An eight-inch-long, two-inch-wide dried patch of blood on the inside clearly indicated her back laceration. She must have worn the orange top as a vest. Julie's black plastic headband was intact. I placed it on my head. Julie's pants were missing.

Mom's black socks were rolled up. Her black, red and white sparkly top was cut into pieces. I have a photo of her wearing that top on Christmas Eve 2008. Her bra had been snipped at the front between the cups. On the bottom of the box were Mom's black dress pants—in perfect condition.

That was it. Sheer curiosity must have pushed away my feelings of loss, because I managed to empty the box without shedding a tear or having a drink.

As I folded and returned their clothes to the box, I quietly sang "Somewhere over the rainbow . . ." Dad's windbreaker was unscathed except for the bloodstain on the shoulder. I should probably clean it and give it to charity. No. I liked the idea of Mom's dentures in Dad's pocket. They should remain there. I draped Dad's jacket over Mom's and Julie's clothes, now snug back in the box. It seemed the perfect place for it, laid protectively over their clothes.

I returned the box to its hiding place.

I didn't want to let go of them yet, so I went back out to the library to go through more memorabilia. I found a bag of cards and letters. In it, among other treasures, was a note I'd written at eight years old when Mom was in the hospital giving birth to baby number six, Teresa. *We miss and love you very much. We've been good and can't wait to see our new baby sister . . .*

I found a couple of dozen cards to our parents for their seventy-fifth birthday celebrations and fiftieth wedding anniversary, black-and-white photos from the '60s. One was from Halloween, of Mom and Dad in beatnik attire, wearing sunglasses and smoking with cigarette holders, Mom in black tights wearing a shift top barely covering her bottom. There were beach photos from our cottage days at Varty Lake, with my sisters and me wearing matching bathing suits that our mother had made, and another of all of us sitting on a couch, in order of our age, the girls in identical red dresses, the boys in white shirts, bow ties and grey flannel pants.

It had been emotionally draining to open the box all these years later, so looking at photos and memorabilia that brought back happier family memories was the perfect way to spend the rest of the anniversary weekend. If only my brothers and sisters had been with me. It would have been fitting to share the memories with them.

I glanced at my palm tree Margaritaville clock: 4:35 p.m. I wasn't anxious or sad, but it was time to get a drink.

I cooked a healthy dinner, a broiled chicken breast and steamed broccoli and carrots sprinkled with herbes de Provence. I placed my dinner and glass of wine on a wooden tray and carried it to my TV room.

As I sat on the sofa, tray on my lap, Callie hopped up and snuggled against my right hip.

I flipped through the PVR list of recordings looking for a movie, but I wasn't in the mood for any of them. There were three episodes of *Saving Hope*, a supernatural medical drama where the lead doctor sees dead people. Perfect. I clicked on one. The story featured the mother of a boy with Down syndrome who needed an organ transplant. There was no question I was guided by angels to select that particular show on November 8, the date my family said goodbye to our adorable youngest sister.

With a smile in my heart, I offered up a toast, to celebrate my parents' lives and everlasting love. "Mom, Dad, I love you. Thank you for our big, crazy and affectionate family."

Then I raised Julie's Tim Hortons wineglass. "Cheers to you, Jule. Your big sis loves you to pieces."

Afterword

In July 2018, I received a private message on Facebook:

Hi, Catherine, thanks to a little card taped to the back of a painting, I think you wanted me to reach out to you. I hope to hear back from you, Sincerely, Dancer.

Two months later, on a rainy day, I drove 450 kilometres to meet Dancer for lunch. I wore black pants and boots, a black and white floral top, accessorized with a coral scarf to add a splash of colour on this gloomy but significant day.

I arrived at the Italian restaurant just before noon. Except for the maître d', the intimate dining room was empty. I requested a table by the window. He poured me a glass of water. Though I was nervous, a warm feeling came over me as I watched a young woman scurry up the steps in the pouring rain.

When she entered the room, our eyes met. I stood up, clasping my hands tightly together, shyly smiling as she walked toward our table.

We had exchanged six letters over eight years, so I felt like I knew her. I asked if I could give her a hug.

"Of course," she said, smiling.

I held her slight body gently against mine. I thought, *Julie, I'm here honey, hugging you too.* I wanted to hold her tighter but did not want to harm my sister's lungs now living in this precious young woman's body.

She wore high-heeled boots, so I guessed her to be about five foot three. Dark glasses framed her gorgeous brown eyes, a rust-coloured pleated midi skirt met her boots halfway, and a printed scarf adorned her neck. The outfit complimented her wavy, almost-waist-length auburn hair. I was flattered that she had taken the time to dress so elegantly to meet me. Everything about her was graceful: her tone of voice, her long slender fingers, her refined manner of speaking.

After we sat down, I asked how she had found my business card.

"When I was unwrapping the package, your card fell into my lap."

My devious plan had worked seamlessly. So perfectly, I wondered if perhaps we'd had a little help.

Our pasta was delicious, but we didn't eat much. We were so excited to finally meet that we were too busy exchanging stories about our lives, the importance of signing up for organ donations and about how brazen I was to enclose my contact information with the painting. She told me how cool she and her mother thought I was to have had the nerve to do it. Her family had tried to find out who we were too. I hope to meet her mother someday.

I wanted more time with her, but she had to get to class. Her boyfriend came inside and took a photo of us, using my phone. We hugged again and promised to keep in touch.

Back in my car, the tears running down my cheeks mirrored the rain on the windshield. I spoke aloud. "My sweetie pie Jule, you have saved the life of a very special woman, and I got to hold her."

...

In Canada, approximately 250 people die each year waiting for an organ transplant. More than six thousand lives a year are lost in the United States. Please consider registering for organ donation.

Three hundred and thirty pedestrians were killed in Canada and 6,539 in the United States in 2018. I have not yet succeeded in getting a crosswalk/pedestrian crossway or traffic lights installed at the corner of Castell and Days Roads. It is my hope that this book will help launch some changes. Should you be interested in making the roads safer for pedestrians in your neighbourhood, please contact your local city councillor and local ministry of transportation office. If you believe your elderly parents or someone you love should no longer be driving, for their safety as well as that of others, please find the courage for a discussion about them giving up that privilege.

MANY PEOPLE THINK Special Olympics are games that occur every couple of years. That is not the case. Special Olympics, the world's largest organization for children and adults with intellectual challenges, provides year-round training and sports events to more than five million athletes in 176 countries around the world. Sports training helps the athletes develop social skills and gain more self-confidence. Eunice Kennedy Shriver founded Special Olympics in the United States in 1968, and Special Olympics Canada was initiated in 1969, the year my sister Julie was born.

On November 2, 2019, I held a fundraiser celebrating Julie's and Special Olympics' fiftieth birthdays. I feel honoured to be involved with her Special Olympics community and to date have held seven fundraisers in her memory.

The organization could not exist without the support of their donors and volunteers. Please consider bringing joy to a special athlete in your community by donating to your local chapter.

I BELIEVE IN PSYCHIC MEDIUMS. The good ones. And I will continue to book sessions when I need comfort or closure.

WHILE WRITING THIS MEMOIR, I thought of the elderly driver often. Every few months I would search her name online. I didn't want this book released until after she passed.

She died in December 2019 at age ninety-five. Sixteen years older than my mother. Predeceased by her husband, five siblings and two grandchildren. She has two surviving sisters, so like me, she also had seven siblings. I can't confirm where she was in the birth order, but given her age, I have a feeling she also may have been the eldest of eight. Her obituary reminded me of the daunting fact that I too might survive some of my siblings.

MOST OF MY FRIENDS are dealing with the decline of their parents' health—moving them into nursing homes, visiting parents who don't recognize them, or being caregivers to parents who can't walk, bathe or feed themselves. I have no idea what that would feel like. My parents did the jitterbug only one week before the accident that eventually claimed both of their lives.

It is hard to fathom that I attended two double funerals in one lifetime. But perhaps my cousin was right when she said Mom had to take Julie with her. And all those people who said, *Maybe it happened because you were all home* or *all together* were right too. I can't imagine having received such horrifying news and not being with my brothers and sisters.

This book started out as a self-help book to share my investigations into "alternative" healing therapies for grief. I later realized that for the effect of my loss to be more fully understood, I had to reveal everything that happened. I had to introduce the reader not only to my parents and Julie but to my whole family—because this tragedy happened to them too. My siblings will have their own recollections of the night of the accident and the weeks following. Still in shock, I began journalling four months afterwards. Some memories I recalled clearly, some were foggy and some occasions I couldn't remember at all.

The agony experienced after the sudden loss of loved ones can't be explained to others. Some days, I felt that I was in such an abyss of sorrow that I could never climb out. Being the eldest, I wanted to help ease the sadness my brothers and sisters were feeling, especially in the early stages when our pain was unimaginably raw. I soon concluded that there was nothing I could do to relieve their suffering. Grieving is an individual process. Each of us took our own meandering path toward healing. One of my paths wound up here.

With all my heart, I am deeply grateful for my brothers and sisters, in-law siblings and many nieces and nephews, my stepchildren, grandchildren and my husband. Don's kids and I are much closer now, and we are relishing the delight our grandsons have brought into our lives. Hopefully there will be a family reunion soon.

Even now, thoughts of Mom, Dad and Julie float in my head every single day. I still miss them so much.

Healing takes time. After five years of therapy and fundraising, I was finally rewarded when acceptance came and wrapped its arms around me. Sometimes, if you can find the strength to open your heart, you just may find some blessings on the other side of mourning.

I WROTE THE FOLLOWING POEM as a tribute to Julie on what would have been her forty-first birthday. It appeared in the *Kingston Whig-Standard* on the weekend of the first anniversary of the accident.

My Sweet Pie Angel

This week it was your birthday, threw a party just for two

Made two margaritas, one for me and one for you

The *Y & R* was playing as I set up a karaoke song

Was not the same without you to laugh and sing along

I loved to make you giggle, loved our summertime

Instead of God's new angel, I wish that you were mine

I now look up to heaven, Jule, please say hello

My sweet face Julie, I don't know why you had to go

With every breath I miss you, with every tear I shed

I wish you out of my dreams and in my arms instead.

You were my baby sibling, a friend too, once you'd grown

And although you were my sister, you're the only child I've
    known

Your feather touch and gentle kisses, a softness all your own

Thank you, Jule, for loving me, for sharing your warm heart

Life without your sparkle is so achingly hard

So, please say hello from Heaven, since you can't come home

Tell Mom and Dad I miss them, at least you're not alone

You're all in heaven, I know that to be true

And one day, Sweet Pie Angel, I know I'll be with you . . .

Your Big Sis

Cath xox

Me applying Julie's makeup on my wedding day, October 15, 1999. PHOTO COURTESY OF GAIL HARVEY

Acknowledgements

Writing this book was a definitive part of my healing process, but it was the encouragement from friends, healers and editors that reassured me that sharing my story could also help others struggling in the aftermath of lost loved ones.

I am blessed with a multitude of cherished friends. I would need a whole chapter to thank you all. Notably to this bunch, thank you for helping me even when you were not aware you were doing so: Nancy and Ron Aitken, Glenn Arnold, Suzan Ayscough, Chere Balani, Laurie Barker, Marlene Pereira Bird, Cheryl Boa, Ange Boudle, Susan Ettridge Clark, Wendy Clear, Lise Cole, Camille Dan, Sigrid Desoi, Tiana Eustis, Lee-Anne Fitzgerald, Margie Gourdier, Donna Herringer, Cathy Jennings, Fiona Koehler, Lesley Krueger, Yvonne Lip, Laura Love, Sandra Neubauer, Lise Post, Linda Raznick, Naomi Snieckus and Meg Walter.

To all my fellow Creative Nonfiction Collective Society writer pals, especially Cathy Cooper, Kirsten Fogg, Beth Kaplan, Gwen Lamont, Judy McFarlane, Nancy O'Rourke and Janet Wilson. Many thanks for boosting the confidence of this non-academic writer.

Cheers to my precious readers for your honest feedback: Mary Garofalo, Julia St. Louis, Norah Wakula and Georgina Yarhi. For your assistance, thank you, Maureen Garvie.

To my alternative healers, I offer my praise to each of you: Neuro-Modulation Technique practitioner Deborah Frenette; Reiki clairvoyant Bonita; spiritual medium Veronica Hart (Hart to Heart); and psychic intuitive Jaye McKenzie (Jade Intuitive).

My sincerest gratitude to my aunt Joan Gourdier and my uncle Mike Scullion, for their consistent love and faith in my endeavours.

My abundant thanks to these extraordinary women for their love, wisdom and unwavering support: Aileen Ahern, Shelley Brown, Christine Ellas, Karen Hannah, Alicia Keywan, Angie Mahoney, Barbara McCullam, Dina Morrone, Caryn Rea and Kirsty Reid.

Thank you to my early draft editor, Sandy Day, for reaffirming that my story was a powerful one. Jane Warren, thank you for your sensitivity with the substantive notes of my second draft. Diane Schoemperlen, thank you for your incisive suggestions and for agreeing to keep in some humour. To my line editor, Ellie Barton, thank for your delicate notes and microscopic attention to the details.

Allyson Latta, my copy editor, went above and beyond. Many thanks for your astute notes and for "virtually" holding my hand when I was feeling overwhelmed. (Coincidentally, when we were young, Allyson's family lived across the street from mine, in the house beside the church on Days Road, but we did not meet until 2015.)

I still pinch myself that HarperCollins offered to publish my book. Warm thanks to the kind-hearted Jim Gifford, for finding my writing worthy of publishing. Thank you to Iris Tupholme, for accepting me into the HarperCollins family. My deepest appreciation to the entire HarperCollins production and marketing teams, especially managing editorial director Noelle Zitzer—your tenderness did not go unnoticed. To my "leader," executive editor Janice Zawerbny, thank you for your sage advice and support, most notably when I became anxious about letting my family story go out into the world.

To the incomparable, tireless, firecracker of an agent, Michael Levine: you have become so much more than an agent to me. Thank you.

Much love to my husband, Don Carmody. You truly are my hero.

If my mom were here today, I'd gift her a copy of my book. But I'm sure that, just as she did when I tried to give her a DVD of *Some Things That Stay*, she would say, "I want to buy my own copy, honey. To show my support."

...

If you would like to view more photos, obtain donation links for Special Olympics or H'art Centre or find the contact details for my alternative healers, please visit my website at catherinegourdier.com.